Macroeconomics in
Small Island States

Macroeconomics in
Small Island States
The Dutch Caribbean Islands

Macklenan F. Hasham

authorHOUSE®

AuthorHouse™ LLC
1663 Liberty Drive
Bloomington, IN 47403
www.authorhouse.com
Phone: 1-800-839-8640

Published by AuthorHouse 07/23/2014

ISBN: 978-1-4969-0649-6 (sc)
ISBN: 978-1-4969-0648-9 (hc)
ISBN: 978-1-4969-0638-0 (e)

Library of Congress Control Number: 2014907787

This book is printed on acid-free paper.

The cover is designed by Clifton Hasham

Contents

Contents

Dedication

It is my wish to dedicate this book to Ena Dankmeijer Maduro. She has played an important role in the realization of the manuscript, arguing some of the points that, according to me, made the content different from other textbooks on economics. Miss Ena also encouraged me to make the publication available beyond college walls. We frequently exchange views about the economic situation and investment opportunities on our island as well as worldwide.

Miss Ena is active on the board of several local organizations and is the chairperson of the SAL (Mongui) Maduro Foundation that encompasses the museum and the library located at Rooi Catootje in Curaçao.

Thank you, Miss Ena.

Macklenan

Preface

ಸಾಂ

The study of economics helps to improve our understanding of the economic environment within which we live and work. As a field of study, economics is continuously in development, and many scholars concerned with the subject matter contribute with aspects that help us interpret the effects of economic activities and policies on the environment before and after they occur. This book is meant to encourage an understanding of how to appraise economic performance and seek improvement in economic growth from the perspective of small islands.

Islands vary from microsize like Saba and Saint Eustatius in the Dutch Caribbean, with a population of less than 5,000; to small like Guadeloupe in the French overseas departments with 300,000 to 500,000 in population; to relatively larger ones like Trinidad, Puerto Rico, and Jamaica, all with populations above a million. Haiti and the Dominican Republic, which make up the island of Hispaniola, each has more than 7 million inhabitants. Cuba has a population of approximately 11 million. The Dutch Caribbean consists of six separate island economies and has together a population of approximately 310,000.

Some islands are so small that it appears almost impossible for them to be economically feasible. Since 2010, three of these islands have become autonomous states within the

Dutch kingdom, and three are special municipalities of the Netherlands. Our theme is that regardless of the status an island has, it still needs to manage its internal economy to survive and thrive, notwithstanding its size and the scarcity of natural resources.

Consequently, in the process of economic thinking and analysis, one continuously has to question the usefulness or applicability of generalizations coming from advanced economies and found in common literature with respect to the actual experience of the policymaker in government or the business owner on a small island. This is an issue that becomes doubly difficult as small islands typically approach more advanced countries for financial assistance and contemplate measures for determining their financing needs from the perspective of the lender. Furthermore, the continuous flow of funds from foreign financial assistance destined for capital investments have in the case of the Dutch islands obviously not been sufficient to create the expected sustainable economic development, increased exports, and employment. Instead, it has created greater financial dependency.

Each island has to reinterpret the existing pattern of economic thinking and theory to find a fit for its own domestic economy. Sometimes this will lead to refinements of existing economic thought based on the special needs of the island. Sometimes this will require the introduction of new economic thought that better fits the conditions the island faces with regard to lack of resources and lack of an economic base to support needed domestic capital investments and financing.

We should not forget that these islands are themselves a product of concepts and practices like colonialism and mercantilism related to economic development of the parent countries. Nowadays, islands have to seek new ways to compete in production and trade with parent countries and the rest of the world. To facilitate this change in stance, ideas and concepts by Caribbean, Latin American, and other scholars are presented in several chapters in this book alongside economic thought developed earlier in Europe and North America.

This book consists of two parts. Part 1 (chapters 1 to 9) introduces basic principles of economic analysis, considering the economic environment, the issues of resources and supply and demand, the economic history of the Dutch islands, and the topics of debt and productivity—perennial issues in developing economies. Particular attention is given to reengineering the socioeconomic base to lower the dependency on foreign countries and to considering possibilities for development through healthy alignments with regional and global organizations.

Part 2 (chapters 10 to 16) is about growth, economic stability, and equilibrium. These chapters provide more insight with regard to macroeconomic behavior reflected by savings, consumption, investments, and their effects on the well-being of small island societies. Additionally, the chapters consider the influx of financial capital and its lack of impact on domestic interest rates, as well as the scant contribution of investment in foreign capital goods to the trickle-down multiplier effect. The chapters on employment and inflation are necessary additions for understanding other factors that influence the equilibrium between supply and demand. The last chapter discusses the need for insight into socioeconomic aspects that influence, to some extent, the pace of growth and the effectiveness of economic planning in an open economy.

The original focus of this book was on the Netherlands Antilles as a political union. But after the constitutional changes in 2010, the book now attempts to address the economic struggle of the six individual islands in the Dutch Caribbean. There is a certain bias toward the use of island-specific data from the Curaçao economic environment due to the traditional lack of access to sufficient data from other islands, a shortcoming that I hope to correct in the future. Still, the content, I hope, will serve as a background for the review of the individual islands' economic situation and enhance the understanding of how economic principles are to be interpreted in one's own insular situation.

Macklenan F. Hasham
June 2014

Acknowledgments

The idea for this publication originated when I started teaching macroeconomics in the faculty of engineering at the University of the Netherlands Antilles. The content is intended to provide readers with insight into general economic theory as well as an opportunity to understand and appreciate the economic environment where they are most likely to practice after graduating.

The approach is also inspired by conversations and discussions in the meetings and conferences among members of the Association of Caribbean Economists (ACE) in the several islands in the region. I am much indebted to the ACE family for their insights, research, and publications with regard to the region. The Dutch islands share the same common purpose and handicaps to development as most of the other islands in the Caribbean region. These circumstances are complicated by the fact that the Caribbean region consists of different language groups whose populations often live in relative close proximity but in almost completely separate worlds.

The Dutch Caribbean consists of such a scattering of islands with sometimes differentiating cultural patterns and language, with English and Dutch spoken predominantly on the three Dutch islands in the Eastern Caribbean and Papiamento (as well as Dutch, English, and Spanish) spoken in the three islands in the Southern Caribbean. On the island shared by Sint Maarten (Dutch and English) and Saint Martin (French and English), the corresponding languages prevail.

I am grateful to Peter Jordens for corrections and suggested changes to several chapters. I also thank Dennis Cijntje of the Antillean Development Bank and Runy Calmera of the Forum for Economists of the Antilles for their insightful comments on some of the chapters. Candice Henriquez and Kevin Kleist, economists at the Central Bank of Curacao and Sint Maarten gave interesting comments to the chapter on short-term effects of foreign purchases of capital goods on the domestic economy. Similarly, Mr. Dreischor of the Central Bureau of Statistics of Curaçao spared me the embarrassment of a faulty interpretation with regard to value-added in small islands. I could count on Mark Figueroa at the University of the West Indies, Mona, Jamaica, to provide helpful comments on subject matter I approached him on. A thanks also to Sander van der Holst of the Institute of Planning and Development, PLAN'D2 There are so many others who have helped in the process whose names do not appear here. But I still want to mention Natasha Snijders, Louella Blijden-Boelbaai, Tania Klooster, Nately A. de Jezus, Ronald Antersijn, and Angelo Crozier. I want to thank my family for allowing me to wander restlessly throughout the Caribbean.

Responsibility for omissions, wrong interpretations, or mistakes in this publication rests with me. If any are pointed out, I will do my utmost to correct them.

Macklenan

CHAPTER 1
THE ECONOMIC ENVIRONMENT

─────◈─────

This chapter introduces the reader to the importance of the study of economics as well as to some of the forces, events, and trends that influence economic growth and management. Some of the aspects influencing economic decision-making are purely external, such as the Lomé and Cotonou agreements and the formation of economic blocs in the immediate region and in Europe and North America, as well as the rapid pace of change in technology that brought an important increase in communication and international interaction via the Internet. But there is also a growing influence from within, as nongovernmental organizations (NGOs) participate more actively, influencing the political economy in areas ranging from gender issues to poverty to sustainable growth.

Introduction

The study of economics seeks to improve the way we identify and understand how resources are allocated or are to be allocated to achieve a level of development and growth that can help members of societies satisfy needs and wants over the course of time. This understanding allows individuals and organizations to better deal with the uncertainties in the economic environment and be proactive. If an organization has an idea where the economy is heading, it can take early steps to address issues that affect its well-being. A better knowledge of the economy allows for prioritization and identification of those areas that need immediate attention and action.

The economy of a small developing island can be as complex and complicated to deal with from the perspective of the domestic decision-maker as a large, more mature economy on the mainland. There are many dependencies, interdependencies, and interrelationships with other countries and with a variety of forces in the immediate environment that affect economic management.

This chapter looks at influential forces in the environment that affect economic decision-making. The study of economics answers the question of what makes a country progress or decline and how this relates to business activities or other forces that affect economic activity and vice versa. Some of the issues that generally would be considered in the study of economics include short—and long-term economic growth, fluctuations in economic activity, business cycles, recession, unemployment, inflation, government policies, and trading with other countries.

Analysis of the economic environment requires an understanding of how aspects of the natural environment and regional and global developments affect economics at home. Rapid advances in communication, medicine, and biotechnology bring an environment of constant flux, requiring economists to address the same issues time after time as they Influence the implementation of development strategies and sometimes place constraints on plans that were decided upon and funded in an earlier period. The selection of those elements in the environment that can have impact on the economy is by no means exhaustive, and other aspects may appear or be judged of more importance by others. One seeks answers by analyzing the national income accounting of a country and by evaluating government policy response taking into consideration how these forces affect economic behavior of the various actors in society.

Influential Forces in the Environment

The socioeconomic environment in the late part of the twentieth century and the beginning of the twenty-first is one of great technological breakthroughs and a gradual globalization that often is expressed as countries becoming mere villages in a smaller interconnected world.

Interconnections

There has been strong development toward more regional cooperation in economic blocs among countries with which the Dutch Caribbean has traditionally had trading ties. In Europe, the Netherlands has become integrated in the European regional economic and monetary union. In the Caribbean region, countries like Surinam, Jamaica, Barbados, and Trinidad and Tobago belong to the Caribbean Common Market (CARICOM). The islands close to Sint Maarten—like Grenada, Dominica,

Saint Kitts and Nevis, and Antigua and Barbuda—form an economic and monetary union as well.

Venezuela has joined the Mercosur customs union with Brazil, Argentina, Paraguay, and Uruguay. More toward the north, the Dominican Republic joined the Central America free trade area, and the United States formed the North American free trade area with Canada and Mexico. These regional agreements provide special benefits to the participating countries, such as easier access to a larger market for trade. Within a bloc, certain traditional nation-state sovereignty principles are set aside to allow bilateral/multilateral agreements to guide economic decision-making. The blocs that are organized as a common market generally have a common external tariff. Those countries that do not belong to the bloc face the bloc's entry requirements with regard to trade or personal traffic.

Overseas Countries and Territories

Many of the Caribbean islands are former colonies of or territories that are still dependencies of European nations. In 1957, with the Treaty of Rome, the countries that agreed to form the European Economic Community (EEC) also agreed to recognize and associate the non-European countries and territories (former colonies) with the EEC. From this followed several economic cooperation agreements between the EEC and the ACPs—the former colonies grouped together as African, Caribbean and Pacific countries that are now associated with Western Europe by means of agreements starting with the one in Yaoundé. The EEC established the European

4

Development Funds to assist these countries and territories in their development effort. The assistance continued after the unification of the EEC countries in the European Union (EU) and is reviewed every five years.

The Dutch Caribbean islands belong to a similar group to the ACP; they are called overseas countries and territories or OCT; in Dutch, this is translated to LGO (landen en gebieden overzee). The OCTs are constitutionally tied to a member state of the European Union. As of October 2010, the Netherlands OCTs consist of Saba, Saint Eustatius, and Bonaire, grouped together as special municipalities, and Curaçao, Aruba, and Sint Maarten as overseas autonomous territories. The United Kingdom has five OCTs in the Caribbean region and six other OCTs in the Atlantic and Pacific oceans. The Caribbean OCTs belonging to the UK are Anguilla, the Cayman Islands, Montserrat, Turks and Caicos, and the British Virgin Islands.

The French do not have OCTs in the Caribbean region. Instead, they have French territories that are integral parts of France and the European Union. The single act of the European Union includes common economic policies and free movement of individuals, goods, services, and capital. The same economic policies apply to these territories, which are referred to as départements d'outre-mer (DOM) or overseas departments (OD). The ODs in the Caribbean region are Martinique, Guadeloupe, and French Guiana. They are also referred to as ultraperipheral territories. The French section of Saint Martin belongs to this French DOM and falls under the prefecture of Guadeloupe.

Puerto Rico and the Virgin Islands have similar positions as the OCTs described above, but with respect to the United States. Puerto Rico is referred to as a commonwealth or associated state. (Independent islands and countries that were formerly British colonies and are still associated with the British Crown are referred to as Commonwealth countries.) The US Virgin Islands are overseas territories of the United States.

While the OCT arrangements are similar to ACP arrangements, OCT nationals, based on an association agreement (the one for the Netherlands Antilles was signed in 1964), can claim the advantages deriving from secondary legislation, just like the citizens of the EU member states. Additionally, there are trade arrangements providing free access to the EU market for products originating in the OCT under the generalized tariff preferences scheme (GSP) and free movement of workers. On the other hand, the OCTs, as laid out in the current conventions, can protect their labor market from being flooded with labor from the EU member state. Finally, the OCTs benefit from this cooperation where the EU member state can provide OCTs with financial and technical assistance.[1] New adjustments being deliberated on for the association agreement include a more reciprocal relationship between the EU and OCTs based on mutual interest, promotion of cooperation of OCTs with third parties, strengthening of OCT resilience and reduction of their vulnerability, and promotion of the EU's values, standards, and interests in the wider world via the OCTs.

Rules of origin

Notwithstanding the OCT arrangements and hypothetical free-trade conditions, the Dutch Caribbean islands met heavy resistance to trade in sugar and rice by several members of the EU, which led to the discontinuation of these privileges in the European markets in the late 1990s.[2] The resistance was partially because of the "rules of origin" clause included in the association agreement with the EEC to protect manufacturing in the EEC from imports of products that are not entirely produced in the ACP/OCTs. The ruling, which was put in place very early on, states that products exported to the EEC from the ACP or OCT are to have "40 to 45 percent" or more (dependent on the specific goods) in value-added in transformation of intermediate products from non-OCT territories or non-ACP countries. This ruling was found to be necessary, as the association agreement in principle allows the ACPs and OCT countries to benefit from internal (EEC free trade) tariff rules. In case of violation, the product will be taxed according to the common external tariff principle applied to non-EEC countries. The ruling was kept after the transition of the EEC into the EU.

Oil protocol

Another restrictive element in the association agreement between the Netherlands Antilles and the EEC regards an oil protocol that was introduced in the association agreement of 1964 especially to forestall a possible threat to the oil markets in the EEC member states. It was considered that the capacity of the oil refineries in Aruba and Curaçao together represented more than 40 percent of the total refinery capacity of the EEC in the 1950s and 1960s, and this could affect oil production in the member states if oil was freely exported there. The oil protocol specified the maximum exports to EEC member states from the Dutch Caribbean islands and the procedures to follow in case the maximum level of import was exceeded.

Lomé Convention

In 1975, the ex-colonies bundled as the ACP signed a new agreement with the EEC in Lomé, Togo, to promote the development of these territories. The old agreement dated from 1957 and was signed at Yaoundé, Cameroon.

The Lomé Convention was designed to promote the development of the seventy-seven ACP states by offering commercial stability based on contractual agreements and nonreciprocity. This was to be achieved by allowing these countries privileged commercial access for exports to the EU markets, commodity-export compensation, and financial aid. The ACP countries, on the other hand, could levy duties against imports from the EU. The Lomé agreement lasted from 1975 to 2000 and was replaced that year with the EU-ACP partnership agreement.

Cotonou Agreement

The new agreement of 2000, referred to as the Cotonou (Benin) Agreement, stresses a joint approach to combat poverty, to promote sustainable development, and to advance gradual integration into the World Trade Organization (WTO)system.

The nonreciprocal preferential trade agreements were phased out. This change has had severe implications for ACP countries, especially with regard to the export of agricultural products like sugar, bananas, and beef to the EU. The role of civil society and principles of participative development are central to this agreement.[3]

Global Organizations

There are several global organizations that have a notable role in economic and financial growth aspects within a country. The International Monetary Fund (IMF) and the International Bank for Reconstruction and Development (IBRD) provide financial support to independent nations, but support to the nonindependent islands consists mostly of economic analysis and intellectual assistance. The WTO is another global organization that is established with the purpose of promoting peace and free trade among nations. The WTO sets rules for trade and handles disputes regarding trade between nations. The WTO replaced the General Agreement on Tariffs and Trade (GATT), taking on broader responsibilities in 1995. The Dutch Caribbean islands are not listed as members of the WTO, although nonsovereign countries can be members. The Netherlands is a WTO member country.

Other organizations that seem to have a wide impact currently are the Organization for Economic Cooperation and Development (OECD) and the Financial Action Task Force (FATF). The OECD has assumed a role in fostering good governance in public service and in corporate activity around the globe. The Dutch islands have ratified the OECD's Convention on Mutual Administration Assistance in Tax Matters. As Vito Tanzi wrote in *Taxation in an Integration World*, this convention is important as "internationalization of economic activity introduces tax systems of foreign countries among the variables that influence the economic decision of the taxpayer of particular countries."[4] As a matter of fact, many European banks supported the growth of offshore low-tax activities in the Dutch Caribbean. These activities seemingly lowered the income-tax prospects in Europe, and consequently ECOFIN, the economic and financial affairs council of the EU, ruled to combat harmful tax competition. The ECOFIN rules designate activities in a foreign country with tax differentials favoring offshore companies over nationals as tax-haven activities and harmful to the country of origin.

The FATF was established in 1989 following the G-7 economic summit to set standards and promote effective implementation of general measures to combat money laundering, terrorist financing, and the flow of drug proceeds through financial institutions. This becomes more necessary as[5] deregulation and liberalization of domestic financial markets combined with advances in technology result in increasing cross-border trade. Bruce Zagaris and Scott B. MacDonald, in a 1992 article on money laundering and financial fraud, add that instantaneous transactions can be abused by those who intentionally seek to conceal the source of the earnings, which could be drug trafficking, arms smuggling, and terrorism, as well as credit-card fraud and insider trading.[6] The FATF has a regional head office in Trinidad and Tobago.

Natural Environment and Sustainability

Economic growth, generally the pursuit of every country, also brings side effects that in the long run can be counterproductive to an island's own economic pursuits. On one hand, physical structures are set up as part of development. But at the same time, they may become detrimental to development itself, as in the case of factories or other undertakings that pollute the natural environment. Firms that create pollution may be producing goods that are of great importance for the country's economy. The oil refineries in Curaçao and Aruba, for example, have served as a great generator of income for the islands for many decades but also as one of the worst polluters in as many years. The income-generation capacity and the provision of employment opportunities has been a reason for the government never to tackle this industry head-on, although it has had proven detrimental effects on the environment. The negative effects are with regard to health questions for the population living in the path of the pollutants, the buildings, and the vegetation, and even in the downgrading of areas pinpointed as proper for tourism development in the regions adjacent to the refineries.

There is a wide scale of issues that must be considered to achieve sustainability of the natural environment. The Nature and Environmental Policy Plan (NEPP) of 1990 for the Netherlands Antilles is a framework policy at the central-government level and instituted on the islands in their island regulations. There are a number of conventions that, notwithstanding the dissolution of the Netherlands Antilles, are still silently passed on to the former Netherlands Antilles islands. The NEPP framework states that the Dutch Caribbean is party to the Cartagena Convention that includes agreements to protect and develop the maritime environment of the wider Caribbean region, to combat oil spills, and to prevent, reduce, and control pollution of the marine environment by land-based sources and activities. The Dutch islands are also party to the 1988 convention to protect the ozone layer and the United Nations framework convention on climate change. There is a reef-management ordinance of 1976 prohibiting spear-fishing and breaking coral, and a sustainable-tourism policy of 1997 that regulates environmental permits and requires environmental impact analysis to insure adequate spatial development.

Conservation
In the process of carrying out economic activities, living and recreational space and natural beauty are affected, and natural resources like minerals, forests, and water are used up in the process. As Soumyen Sikdar observes in his 2002 book *Contemporary Issues in Globalization*, "the environment is used as the sink for all the waste products generated in the acts of production, distribution, and consumption."[7] There has been an obvious shift in the later part of the twentieth century throughout the world toward more attention to sustainable development. This entails more care being taken in the utilization of resources that can be depleted through use.

Sustainability[8] of the environment refers to the goal of insuring that descendants of the current generation can enjoy the environment as it is enjoyed now. In this concept, resources are considered as renewable or nonrenewable. Sustainable development, according to the World Commission on Environment and Development (the Brundtland Commission): "requires meeting the basic needs of all and extending to all the opportunity to satisfy their aspirations for a better life."[9] Conservation has become an important item for governments in economic management. There are suggestions to explicitly include the effect of national production on the environment in the national accounts[10] of the country. This is the so-called "green accounting," where the value of depletable resources and the effect of deforestation and destruction of natural beauty, together with pollution, are considered in the gross national product (GNP), creating an Index of Sustainable Economic Welfare (ISEW) as proposed by Herman E. Daly and John B. Cobb, Jr., in their book *For the Common Good.*

The ISEW is supposed to serve: "as an alternative or addition to the Gross Domestic Product, measuring human well-being."[11] When used, it includes value of household services, cost of pollution, depletion of nonrenewable resources, inequality of distribution, and public expenditures on health and education. This recent focus on sustainability influences a change in thinking about the benefits and weaknesses of the current growth paradigm and the way it is represented by the GDP. The GDP and the GNP are discussed in chapter 6.

The small size and lack of natural resources of many of the islands in the Caribbean region make the sustainability quest more acute. The fact that many of these islands are also continuously exposed to harsh climatic conditions and natural disasters, such as hurricanes and floods, puts the economies in an extra delicate balance with the environment.

Communication and Computer Technology

The Internet and the way it facilitates communication and dissemination of information for practically everyone in the world is another example of a major change that affects Caribbean economies. The current era, characterized by Internet communication, is one of rapid change, where change has become a constant factor. At the same time, the Internet provides a new stable source of storage and exchange of information that in the past was difficult to obtain freely. Information on all the existing treaties and regulations by global bodies are now readily available to everyone. This has opened up opportunities for an individual, a business firm, or a country to participate more fully in the global markets. The developments in communication and information technology are due to rapid advances in semiconductor equipment, in software development, and in hardware (personal computers and large computers). Thomas L. Friedman[12] comes to the conclusion that what gives the present globalization a "unique character is that now *individuals and groups* can collaborate and compete globally."

Globalization in the past was based first on countries globalizing and next on companies globalizing. Now it is the individual from all corners of the world who is empowered. Based on this, Friedman is of the opinion that the world is not only shrinking but it has become flat.

Changes in the workplace

The rapid advances in technology, especially in information processing, allow for greater interconnectedness among organizations globally. It is not surprising when an employee takes a funded pension plan based on the contribution system from one employer to the other. The trend in the workplace regards the demand for knowledge work beside skill work, a factor that requires people to continuously upgrade their knowledge to maintain their jobs. As employability of workers is based more and more on the worker's combination of skill and knowledge and not on the availability of lifelong jobs in a firm or industry, this change puts new demands on continuing education and training.

Political Environment

There have been a number of political changes within the Dutch Caribbean and in neighboring countries that have or will have a profound effect on the economic growth and development of specific islands. In the Caribbean region, there is a push toward a single market by the members of the CARICOM. Within the Dutch Caribbean, there is an opposite push toward multiple markets, with multiple currencies as end result. A referendum held in 2005 found that with the exception of one island—Saint Eustatius—the majority of voters preferred to procure a separate status with more or less autonomy within the Dutch kingdom in 2010. As it played out, the islands representing the smallest economies each became an extended municipality of the Netherlands, and the larger economies of Sint Maarten and Curaçao are autonomous states within the Dutch kingdom.

In Venezuela—located thirty to forty miles south of the Dutch Leeward Islands of Aruba, Bonaire, and Curaçao—the party in power at the time of this writing has opted for a more socialist type of government, with increasing involvement in private-sector enterprises, nationalizing firms in various sectors and rationing the amount of foreign exchange citizens could spend yearly. These actions affect the flow of tourism and the import of produce from that country to the nearby islands.

NGO and civil society

The policy-making role of government is being influenced by the growing importance of the Non-governmental organizations or NGOs. They have acquired a unique role among civil society in the determination of policies that affect the social and economic management of a country. Some NGOs are former government organizations or agencies that have been privatized and are entirely or partially funded by the government. Other NGOs are grass-roots organizations established with the special purpose of influencing policy and contributing to economic and social management.

The NGOs typically do not have a profit pursuit and are organized as legal foundations or associations. Examples of grassroots organizations are the NGO platforms and neighborhood organizations in various regions of the islands of the Dutch Caribbean. The NGOs collaborate on an interregional and international level to influence policy-making. The Caribbean Policy Development Centre (CPDC), for instance, operates as a coalition of regional networks. The activities of the CPDC, headquartered in Barbados, include examining, reporting on, and influencing local policies on the islands, from gender issues to issues relating to the WTO and the Free Trade Area of the Americas (FTAA) negotiations.

The NGOs are becoming important partners in economic management and social development. While they are typically nonprofit organizations, the activities by the *civil society* embrace both nonprofit and for-profit organizations. The activities undertaken cooperatively by government and civil society are considered private public partnerships. These could range from community projects to cooperation in policy-making with players in diverse sectors of the economy. Amigoe di Tera Curacao is one such NGOs especially concerned with protection of the natural environment and securing sustainable development.

Gender and Economy

The increased participation of females in the labor force is another social and cultural change that occurred in the second part of the twentieth century and has had a vast effect on the

17

economies of the island states. An example of the increased participation by females is shown in table 1.1 for Aruba.

Table 1.1: Participation rates of females in the labor force of Aruba

Participation rate of females in selected years and age groups				
Year	Ages	25-29	30-34	35-39
		%	%	%
1961		28.1	24.1	21.2
1991		76.9	74.2	68.9
2007		80.5	77.6	78.4
CBS Aruba: censusses: Labor force Participation rates by agegroup and sex B.a.1.03				

As table 1.1 shows, 77 to 80 percent of females in the age groups shown participated in the labor force in Aruba by 2007, as opposed to 21 to 28 percent in 1961. This change seems to be related to various factors. First, on the average, more females pursue secondary to higher education now than was the case in the years before 1960. Secondly, new economic sectors attracted females to participate; in Curaçao, this was primarily in the electronics industry, while in Aruba and Sint Maarten, the tourism industry and civil service provided new challenges for women. A third factor is that traditional industries that were predominantly manned by male workers, such as the petroleum industry, had in fact been downsizing since the late 1950s, with few alternatives for reallocation of many of the men who became unemployed.

The changes in participation rates occurred at the same time as changes in sociocultural aspects with regard to the position of females in society in general, including demands for equal treatment and equal wages in the job environment. Another aspect that relates to the growth in female participation in the workplace is the growing number of female heads of one-parent households. This growth in female participation in the workplace has been accompanied by increasing development of a consciousness among women of the active role they need to play in the improvement of their position in society and improvement of society in general.

The United Antillean Women (UMA) organization, the Steering Committee in Curaçao, and the Soroptimists Club and the Women Development Center (CEDEHM) in Aruba are examples of the many organizations that strive toward these ends in the Dutch islands. The UMA is also related to the Caribbean Association for Feminist Research and Action (CAFRA) and Developmental Alternatives with Women for a New Era (DAWN). The latter is a global network of organizations that is concerned with macroeconomic issues like globalization, sustainable livelihoods, and political economy.

Emergent Economies Share Global Market Dominance

Countries like Brazil, Mexico, Russia, India, China, Singapore, Indonesia, South Korea, and South Africa are gradually acquiring a more dominant role in the global market than in the past. There are other countries that show impressive GDP development of 7 percent or more on a yearly basis, like Chile and Columbia in South America, the Philippines and Singapore in East Asia, and Nigeria in Africa. There are a growing number of emergent economies whose GDP and GDP per capita are rising to that extent that by 2030 or 2050 they will have matched or surpassed those statistics for the industrialized developed countries in Europe and North America.

This development changes the economic (industrial and commercial) panorama away from the traditional focus and provides new opportunities for exporting and economic cooperation for the small islands in the Caribbean Sea. These developments also promise a different flow of development financing, from the usual route from Europe and North America to the South. The five countries referred to as BRICS—Brazil, Russia, India, China and South Africa, the five large emergent economies that have become players in the international markets because of their dominance in either manufacturing, services, raw material supplies, or a combination of these—are founding a development bank to bail out members in case of a financial crisis and also supply development money to poor countries. This shift undoubtedly enhances the chances of trading of goods and services for the islands. With the increasing wealth among the populations in these emergent economies, exports based on the relatively expensive production cost of the Dutch islands will become more competitive in the world markets.

Dominant Thoughts in the Pursuit of Domestic Goals

Amidst these turbulences and changing patterns, there are certain aspects of macroeconomic importance that seem to dominate in the search for economic growth in the Dutch islands. These aspects are frequently mentioned by governments as expressions of macroeconomic strategic goals. They are seen as influential factors to achieve and/or maintain a sustainable standard of living.

The economic perspectives include the following aspects:

1. The need for basic industries in domestic economic activities
2. Foreign financial assistance and financial dependency
3. A bridge function in a changing competitive environment
4. Each island to determine its own welfare

Domestic Economic Activities

General well-being and increased standard of living of the Dutch Caribbean societies in the twentieth century has been largely determined by developments in three economic sectors and the long-term international financial assistance relationship with Europe. These three sectors contributed relatively more than other sectors to exports, to government revenue, to GDP, and to employment. They are petroleum refining, the finance sector (with offshore finance activities), and the tourism-related sector that includes retail trade and hospitality.

The international offshore finance sector and the refinery sector are dependent on external decision-making. The tourism sector is managed domestically. All three leading sectors are vulnerable to the economic situation in countries where demand for the products and services originate. With the understanding of the conditions leading to volatility in the sectors, the islands are forced to constantly refocus on finding new leading sectors that can fill in the gaps produced by downturns in a leading sector. In this way, further advances in the level of material well-being obtained in society by contributions to economic growth by past leading sectors can be shifted to other growth industries. The major challenge is maintenance of national income and employment, with a goal of positive net exports—that is, higher exports than imports—playing an important role.

Chapters 6, 7, 11, 12, and 13 explain the macroeconomic concepts utilized to interpret the economic performance of a country. Additionally, chapters 2, 9, and 16 provide some insight as to constraining or stimulating factors to achieve equilibrating growth.

Foreign Financial Assistance

The Treaty of Rome in 1957 and the subsequent agreements at Yaoundé in 1963, Lomé in 1975, and Cotonou in 2000 brought a new positioning by the Netherlands and the EU in general regarding financial support, technical assistance, and training for the Dutch Caribbean possessions. The financial support in the various decades from 1960 on has become a virtual substitute for expansion of or addition to basic industries, providing a dependable source of revenue, savings, and employment. As a result, the stream of financial support became, together with the output from the basic industries, the source of relative well-being for the islands.

The stream of funds coming from the donor country has not always strengthened the industrial capacity of the island, as the donor often assumes the role of both donor and recipient, which requires buying of technical assistance and equipment and material in the donor country.[13] However, the foreign funds that are a valuable input for the build-up of the physical economic infrastructure and the social infrastructure became an important mitigating factor to help maintain the value of the local currency in lieu of local production and exports.

Dependency

The continuous flow of foreign funds allows consecutive governments to continue an expansionary economic policy, with additional increased borrowings on the local market with the intention that the utilization of the funds will enhance the capability of the country to generate sufficient output and exports to obtain the necessary income to service the local and foreign debt. The consequences of continued increases in the national debt are treated in chapter 8.

Table 1.2 provides an overview of the designation of international financial assistance by development objectives.

Table 1.2: Distribution of foreign financial assistance by sector

Curacao, Bonaire, St Maarten, St Eustatius, Saba Combined Foreign assistance expenditures 1998-2005							
Sectors :	1998	1999	2000	2001	2002	2003	2004	2005
Public Utilities	0.001	0.003	0	0	0	0	0	0.004
Airports	0.084	0.069	0.005	0.055	0.05	0.121	0.029	0.001
Harbors	0.035	0.053	0.046	0.02	0.003	0.046	0.037	0.038
Road and bridges	0.037	0.005	0.033	0.059	0.087	0.198	0.091	0.052
Education	0.287	0.205	0.143	0.152	0.166	0.281	0.449	0.338
Health	0.267	0.145	0.065	0.025	0.111	0.004	0.029	0
Housing	0.13	0.133	0.109	0.056	0.074	0.008	0.003	0
Tourism	0.024	0.027	0.016	0.014	0.223	0.089	0.044	0.118
Agriculture, animal husbandry and fishery	0	0	0	0	0	0	0	0.003
Trade, Industry	0.051	0.004	0.002	0.001	0.031	0.008	0.01	0.013
and other services								
Various	0.084	0.357	0.582	0.617	0.254	0.246	0.305	0.433
TOTAL Fls xxx.xxx	96.6	93.3	82.8	76.2	57.8	50.5	38.3	78.8

The totals, as shown at the bottom of the table in millions of florins, are an important input for investments, maintenance of spending power, and economic stability, and as a factor in the balance of payment. Without other means of producing similar cash flow, it is understandable that the yearly stream of funds becomes an important instrument for economic management by the government.

Bridge Function in a Changing Competitive Environment

A recurrent economic thought is to generate a more durable base for domestic economic activities through a facilitating role to stimulate commercial activities between Europe, alternatively the BRICS, and countries in the Caribbean and South and Central

America. As opposed to the way things were done during the colonial and mercantilist period, the islands have an internal knowledge and know-how base as a legacy of the system of education and the centuries of exposure to international trade through trading companies and harbor services, the intermediary role in petroleum refinery and export, and the international financial intermediation with offshore firms.

The EPA dimension

The growing number of multilateral agreements by independent neighboring countries in the Caribbean region, North America, Central and South America, as well as in Europe and the Far East, is upsetting, perhaps temporarily, the hope for global free trade. The pursuit of a facilitating role, functioning as a bridge between Europe and the region, is being influenced by this rapid growth in economic blocs.

The competitive environment for the Dutch islands is changing even more with the introduction of economic partnership agreements (EPA). These agreements are intended to improve and centralize negotiations and involvement by the EU member countries in development funding and provision of expertise to ACP countries. With this new approach, many barriers to free movement of goods, services, and investments between EU and the ACP members are gradually reduced or eliminated. The Caribbean EPA is referred to as CARIFORUM and was established to serve as an economic partnership representing the ACP countries in the region in negotiations with the EU. The EPA established by the CARICOM and the Dominican Republic became operational in 2007. With this new trend, the ACP members who are part of the EPA agreement receive several trade advantages with Europe that were previously accorded only to OCTs.

Each Island for Itself

With the political restructuring after the Netherlands Antilles ceased to exist, the Dutch Caribbean islands continued as four economic and political entities, each separately pursuing improvement in the well-being of its respective society. The islands, due to distance and/or political and economic independence from each other, separately face the persistent prospect of an internal economic debacle as described in chapter 9 due to an expensive infrastructure and expensive civil service whose maintenance could hardly be financed from the local earnings and savings. The small domestic market and expected limited savings dictate a constant search for external capital to finance projects that generate exports and support the maintenance of the current infrastructure. These circumstances of smallness also require that the islands develop export-led economic growth strategies in order to produce foreign exchange to cover the import expenditures necessary to maintain a standard of living.

The next chapter introduces the reader to broad economic concepts that provide a basis to economic analysis, like national goals, government policy analysis, resources, and the effects of open economies on development. It also introduces thoughts on economics by Caribbean scholars. Chapters 3 and 4 throw light on the economic history of the islands from the period of mercantilism to the present.

Appendix 1

This appendix is intended to provide context for the reader regarding the economy of the Dutch islands Aruba and Curaçao, the latter as part of the Netherlands Antilles, and the effect of volatility in basic sectors. The data used is from published sources and concerns the period 1960 to 1998.

From the 1920s to the early 1960s, the two Dutch islands Aruba and Curaçao had a boost in economic activity that centered on the petroleum-refining industry. The population in the Netherlands Antilles in 1920, including Aruba, stood at about 63,000. By 1960, the population of the six islands comprising the Netherlands Antilles was 189,000. Exports per head were roughly 68 USD per annum in 1920 and rose to 1,742 USD by the year 1960. The only other island in the region with a comparable export per head in this same period was Barbados with approximately 80 USD in 1920 and 1,242 USD in 1960. The Barbados population in 1920 was at 198,000 and grew to approximately 231,000 by 1960.[14]

After 1960, as reported elsewhere in this writing, the petroleum industry began automating and rationalizing production processes, which led to a decrease in demand for labor. Growth in contribution from this sector to national income after 1960 became relatively flat, as can be inferred from the growth in per capita

GDP shown in tables 1.3 and 1.4. The GDP, explained in chapter 6 of this book, is one of the major indicators of how the economy is doing. Growth in the GDP in a year indicates growth in economic performance. This growth is typically adjusted for inflation.

The Netherlands Antilles data illustrates the economic growth for the combination of the five islands of the Dutch Caribbean forming a political and economic union at the time. The revenues contributing to the GDP, one performance measure used to gauge the health of the economy, are apportioned in such a way that more toward 1998 revenues of Curaçao make up approximately 70 percent of the total, Bonaire 5 percent, and the Windward Islands as a group 25 percent. The table illustrates that while there was a relatively fast growth in population, the GDP per capita after 1960 did not show a similar pattern. This masks the contribution by oil-refining activities for the period.

Table 1.3 Exports and GDP per capita Neth. Antilles

Population and GDP growth	Neth Antilles Population Growth	NA Export $ per head	NA GDP $ per head
1960	135000	847	11,495
1970	159000	552	10,805
1980	174000	7,331	10,262
1990	189500	9,446	10,767
1998	212520	5,924	11,698
Effect of dwindling exports on NA economy			

References: *Integration and Trade* 15, Volume 5 (September-December 2001); Inter-American Development Bank; Integration and Regional Program Department; Institute for the Integration of Latin America and the Caribbean

The other set of data concerns exports per capita. It is visible that exports per head decreased in the time that oil refining was the sole basic industry in the 1960s and 1970s but rose rapidly with increased activities in the tourism and offshore-finance sectors in the 1970s and beyond. Exports per head increased because of growth in the tourism sector (for a great part in the Windward Islands) and activities in the international finance sector (for a great part in Curaçao) after 1970. Furthermore, Curaçao also stimulated economic activities in the period after 1960 in manufacturing industries and free-zone services in an effort to create a modestly diversified economy given the receding contribution from oil-refining activities. The data allows the student of economics to make certain simple deductions about economic growth. Insofar as the data is right, the GDP for the nation grew by 60 percent between 1960 and 1998. (Aggregate GDP is per capita GDP times the number of people in the country.) Population for the period grew by 57.4 percent. However, per capita GDP remained stagnant.

Aruba

The result of redirecting the focus is apparent in the economy of Aruba. Although Aruba suffered similar downturns in terms of petroleum refining as was the case with Curaçao, table 1.4 illustrates a different picture in the last decades. Since the 1980s, the focus has gone toward tourism as the one basic industry. After Aruba gained an autonomous status in 1986, the same year that Exxon withdrew from refining, the main focus of the government and private sector went to boosting the tourism sector.

Table 1.4: Exports per head and per capita GDP, Aruba

Population and GDP growth	Aruba Population Growth	Aua Export $ per head	Aua GDP $ per head
1960	54000	555	9,484
1970	56874	1,268	9,968
1980	59711	2,906	9,868
1990	65939	8,591	15,558
1998	93424	26,834	16,186
Aruba growth in exports in the 1990's			

References: *Integration and Trade* 15, Vol. 5 (September-December 2001); Inter-American Development Bank; Integration and Regional Program Department; Institute for the Integration of Latin America and the Caribbean.

The data for Aruba has been segregated from that of the Netherlands Antilles as of 1960. A rough estimate is that GDP increased by close to 200 percent (actually 196 percent) in the years after 1960, with concomitant growth after 1980 mostly in industries supporting tourism, accompanied by a fast rise (73 percent for the period) in total population. Export appears to have increased by 4,400 percent, or 44 times the 1960 export.

The data above illustrate rather briefly the macroeconomic accomplishments of the two countries after 1960 up to 1998, and even more briefly what basic sectors contributed the most. With the changed political configuration of the Dutch Caribbean, each island more than before is responsible for GDP (per capita) growth to satisfy the needs of a growing population.

1   Charlotte Bretherton and John Vogler, *The European Union as a Global Actor* (Routledge, 1999).

2   The World Bank, *Netherlands Antilles: Elements of a Strategy for Economic Recovery and Sustainable Growth* (World Bank, Latin America and the Caribbean Region, 2001).

3   Olufemi Babarinde and Gerrit Faber, *The European Union and the Developing Countries: The Coutonou Agreement* (Martinus Nijhoff, 2005).

4   Vito Tanzi, *Taxation in an Integrating World* (Washington, DC: Brookings Institution Press, 1995).

5   Kern Alexander, Rahul Dhumale, and John Eatwell. *Global Governance of Financial Systems: The International Regulation of Systemic Risks* (New York: Oxford University Press, 2006).

6   Bruce Zagaris and Scott B. MacDonald, "Money Laundering, Financial Fraud, and Technology: The Perils of an Instantaneous Economy," *The George Washington Journal of International Law and Economics* (January 1992).

7   Soumyen Sikdar, *Contemporary Issues in Globalization: An Introduction to Theory and Policy in India* (Oxford University Press, 2002), 13.

8   Eban S. Goodstein, *Economics and the Environment* (Prentice Hall, 1995).

9   Brundtland Commission, "Toward Sustainable Development," in *Our Common Future* (Norton, 1987). Excerpted by Stephen Wheeler and Timothy Beatly in *The Sustainable Urban Development Reader* (Routledge, 2004).

10   Herman E. Daly and John B. Cobb, Jr., *For the Common Good: Redirecting the Economy Toward Community, the Environment, and a Sustainable Future* (Beacon Press, 1989).

11   Stephen Wheeler and Timothy Beatley, eds., *The Sustainable Urban Development Reader* (Routledge, 2004). Discussion of Herman Daly's 1973 publication "Toward a Steady-State Economy."

[12]   Thomas L. Friedman, *The World Is Flat: A Brief History of the Twenty-First Century* (Farrar, Straus and Giroux, 2005). Friedman is also the author of *The Lexus and the Olive Tree*, published in 1998.

[13]   See Henri-Bernard Solignac-Lecomte's article "Effectiveness of Developing Country Participation in ACP-EU Negotiation," working paper, Overseas Development Institute, London, 2001

[14]   Data from Victor Bulmer-Thomas, "The Wider Caribbean in the Twentieth Century: A Long-Run Development Perspective," *Integration and Trade* 15, Volume 5 (September-December 2001), eds. Richard L. Bernal et al. Published by the Institute for the Integration of Latin America and the Caribbean.

CHAPTER 2
APPROACHES TO ECONOMIC ANALYSIS

~•~

This chapter introduces thoughts and principles on which to build economic decision-making and analysis. First is the major goal and central problem in economics—that is, economic growth and how resources can be allocated to obtain economic performance. Governments play an important role in the allocation of resources at the microeconomic level, and this has repercussions at the macroeconomic level. As a result, it becomes more and more necessary to be able to analyze the consequences of these decisions. Readings by George Beckford and W. Arthur Lewis provide additional understanding of the possibilities and deterrents to economic growth and a chance to become acquainted with economic thinking in the Caribbean region.

Introduction

To attend to an island country's needs, it is very important to know how the economy works. This includes knowing what takes the country forward as well as those aspects that can thwart efforts based on generally prescribed economic theory. The analysis of the economic situation of a country is a way to get an impression of how the goals and expectations of individual consumers, the government, and business and nonbusiness organizations are being met. Macroeconomics generally makes a distinction between these three groups, mainly to gauge how their actions affect the performance of the economy. In the Keynesian framework, which we will discuss in chapters 6, 11, 12, and 13, the outcome of the actions of these groups is presented as aggregates of consumption, private investment, government spending, and net export. The activities of these three groups in the process of producing and procuring goods and services and trading with other nations form the underpinnings for the macroeconomy.

To analyze the economy, we look first at the goals and the limiting factors in the pursuit of them, and then turn to the concept of a positive and normative approach in economic decisions that affect the lives of most or all of the citizens of a country. An example is decisions regarding introduction of a minimum wage, general pension, or health-insurance scheme, or a decision to introduce structural changes with the intention of redirecting the income generation of government revenue through indirect taxes and increase the flexibility of the labor market. Any of these decisions will have repercussions on the existing economic order in society.

For islands with limited land area and natural resources and a relatively small population, success will depend to a great extent on the development of local human capital and the proper utilization of foreign expertise and physical capital. For this reason, we must pay particular attention to human capital as an important extension of labor as a resource.

Two aspects related to the pursuit of economic goals are openness to and integration with the rest of the world (colored by the relationship between the islands and the past colonial powers) and motivators and constraints to development. The arguments for both aspects are pointed out in the readings at the end of this chapter.

Major Goal and Central Problem

The major goal with regard to the economy of the Caribbean islands is the achievement of an adequate and sustainable standard of living for the populations. An adequate standard of living can be described as a state in which all members of society have an equitable income that can provide for at least minimum needs above a subsistence level. This minimum varies from island country to island country and will depend on the capacity of the country to obtain sufficient income from economic activities. It also depends on the way total income is redistributed throughout the country. Income produced as a nation—the national income—should in principle be of sufficient magnitude to make health-care, adequate housing, education, (social) security, and leisure affordable to all if it is properly distributed.

Small, Developing Islands

Very small islands, especially those sometimes defined as microterritories, often do not have the means to produce enough savings relative to the size of the population to warrant the provision of education and healthcare and investment in infrastructure—at least, not at the level that is required by the population to obtain a higher standard of living. Furthermore, what can be procured with individual savings can be easily upset by external circumstances, such as drastic changes in the price level of goods and services. As an example, the increase in purchases and construction of dwellings by foreigners on a very small island in a short period of time can have as a direct effect the bidding up of prices to such a level as to put adequate housing out of the reach of the locals.

On the other hand, the establishment of one new basic industry can catapult economic growth in such a way that an island in addition to capital and raw material needs to import labor in order to cope with the increased production requirements.

As economies progress, domestic populations tend to constantly desire more and better goods and services, as well as an acceptable quality with regard to these goods and services. Cars are a good example. On each island, the number (and make) of cars has been increasing gradually. But motorized transportation is not the only attribute sought. Comfort and safety also play a role. As a result, for a gradually increasing number of inhabitants, a car has to have certain features, such as automatic transmission, air-conditioning, airbags, and a CD/DVD player to be considered acceptable.

Similar behavior is visible in the education and health sectors, which gradually require import of advanced education services through scholarships and loans to study abroad, and sending out sick people for more specialized medical service in designated countries. There is conclusively a variety of wants and needs that the population tries to satisfy, and if this represents the standard of living desired, there is a general pursuit in this direction.

Chapters 9, 10, and 11 look in more detail at the many problems and opportunities faced by small islands. The major problem for now remains the allocation of new and available resources to the benefit of the population, balancing the unlimited and competing wants in society and still achieving the goal of quality of life for all involved, despite shortcomings with respect to market and resources.

Solutions to the problem will be contingent on the responsible but effective utilization of existing resources to develop economic activities that are sustainable in the island context and produce economic growth. This requires special attention to the development of the domestic human capital and enhancing the entrepreneurial capability. It also requires that where there is conflict with regard to the use of resources or market failures, the government can step in to correct and direct.

Positive and Normative Approaches to Analysis

Although most economic activities occur without any intervention from the government, modern societies gradually allow more and more support from government with regard to direction and pace of growth. The intervention by government is generally through policies that affect the entire population. The decisions are generally made from a *normative* or a *positive* perspective. The normative approach highlights the social benefits that the policy provides. Although the positive approach also highlights the social benefits, the policy is stated in a way that allows analysis of the effectiveness of the policy. It is more descriptive in nature and deals with the economic consequences of policy.

Policy decisions can affect a variety of resources and resource utilization. The way the policy is worded and the subsequent actions can make an assessment of the effectiveness of the policy more or less difficult. As an example, the debate on the construction of a general hospital financed by the government can be worded in a normative way:

> The current hospital is in a deplorable condition. For that reason, the government should finance the construction of a new hospital.

or in a positive way:

> The cost of running the current hospital is rising every day. The construction of a new hospital will allow introduction of additional patient services and more efficient operations. Fewer patients will need to be sent abroad for additional care. For that reason, the government should finance the construction of the hospital.

While both statements ultimately result in the same decision, one is more normative and one is more positive or descriptive in approach. The latter approach makes sense given that the government will be spending people's resources—in this case, tax revenues—and it also makes sense to measure the results of this spending, as the money can be used for alternative purposes. It is easy to see how the second statement provides an opportunity to do pre- and post-construction analysis.

Ceteris Paribus

It could be useful to carry out the evaluation of specific aspects of resource use by holding other variables constant while one variable or its effects is being studied. This is a condition found in scientific studies. In economics, it is referred to by its Latin name: *ceteris paribus*. One resorts to this condition in order to obtain an insight as to the workings of the economy. The examination is facilitated by studying the use or disuse of the resources available and how this affects society as a whole.

For example, the introduction of a general health-insurance scheme that allows everybody on an island to participate will affect existing private-sector firms within the chain of health-insurance services. The effects can be with regard to the loss in investments and employment positions in the private sector. Under such circumstances, a policy in this direction will be successful if the trade-off involves maintenance of jobs and maintenance or increase in the general wealth of the nation, both in the short run and the long run. Thus, the effect of the loss in investments is tested while holding everything else, including employment, constant.

Resources

The resources that are generally the subject of examination include land, capital, labor, and entrepreneurship. They are utilized as factors of production. The application of these factors generally determines economic performance and growth. Economics is about how a society deals with the issue of varied and unlimited wants versus the actual available resources.

Land and Natural Resources

The Caribbean islands, except for a few, are typically very small, and land is often the major (political) economic factor. Most of the islands in the Eastern Caribbean focus on agriculture—growing bananas, nutmeg, sugarcane, coffee, tobacco, and so forth as export products. Land and labor are the primary resources used. The island seeks to get an income from the application of the available resources.

Income from exploitation of land and natural resources is generally referred to as *rent*. The rental income from land and property can vary depending on supply-and-demand conditions. Each island in principle wants to obtain a source of income from available resources, as is the case with Dubai and some other emirates in the Middle East, where the revenues from petroleum production allow relative wealth for the population.

A resource is generally exploited in conjunction with another resource. The beaches of Sint Maarten and Aruba are natural resources that have influenced the building of large hotels and attracted numerous workers from abroad. The protected deep waters of Schottegat Bay in Curaçao are a natural resource for bunkering and are exploited through large capital investments that allow ship repair and shipping services.

Existing land and water is used to extract minerals, produce agricultural products, or build structures for institutional purposes or individual reasons. Aruba, Curaçao, Bonaire, and Sint Maarten desalinate sea water, a natural resource, for consumption purposes. Electricity is generated in that process. On the other islands, cisterns are predominantly used as rain catchments for business and home water consumption.

Physical Capital

Physical capital includes hotel buildings and furnishings, rain catchments, dry-docks, refineries, utility plants, harbor-mooring facilities, and all other structures and equipment used in production and service processes. School buildings, government offices, hospitals, clinics, and recreation parks are also physical capital. There is generally an inclination to leave out homes (houses and apartments) in the calculation of national income and only include apartments used for tourist-accommodation purposes. However, where property rights allow owners of a property to sell homes for gain, these structures are additions to capital in the context mentioned above.

Financial Capital

Personal or borrowed funds are used to finance the construction or purchase of real or physical capital. The personal and/ or borrowed funds are referred to as *financial capital*. This represents the real capital, or the tools, equipment, plant, and machinery used in a production process. The utilization of real capital in a business process should result in gains that could be used to pay back the principal to lenders and pay on top of this interest to lenders and a dividend (a share of the net gains) to owners. It is the financial value of the physical capital minus its depreciation that is generally used in the valuation of the wealth of the nation.

Labor

Labor include efforts by people to utilize land and water for productive purposes—to extract minerals, invent and make machines, utilize the machines, and provide services to tourists or to society in general. Labor is the resource provided by humans. Labor is used in a production process to produce goods or services. The income from labor is referred to as *wages*. Those providing labor receive and spend (at least part of) their income on consumer goods. Part of the income is generally taxed by the government to provide, together with tax revenues from firms, a basis for transfers to those who cannot work and have no income.

Human Capital and Entrepreneurship

The effective use of the resources in a country for production and/or service is contingent on the ability of the population to exploit the resources properly. The existence of an educated workforce and entrepreneurial attitude tend to enhance the opportunities for sustained adequate deployment of resources. Labor has a distinctive characteristic in that it comes from a resource pool of humans who are employed in a production process and/or act as creators of a production process.

The term *human capital* can be construed to include all those providing labor and forming an educated workforce that is versatile enough to participate in creating business and utilizing modern technology. This theme was elaborated on by Xabier Gorostiaga in a 1993 article "Education, Human Development and Competitiveness,"[1] in which he stressed the need for a concerted effort involving universities and research centers to work on the development of human capital fostering professional capability on the regional and national level.[2]

The human-capital concept encompasses the entrepreneurial ability to conceive, develop, engage in, and manage projects and processes that produce goods and services benefiting society. Entrepreneurs play a major role in the process of expanding the production capabilities of a country and helping it reach its economic potential. In certain countries, entrepreneurship is weak, probably due to uncertainty regarding risk/return conditions or because of insufficient know-how. This is generally illustrated by a low level of domestic innovation.

In some cases, governments, in order to achieve a fast pace of economic growth, may take on the entrepreneurial function, with as an extreme a command economy where the state plans, owns, and is involved in the production process. In countries where entrepreneurship is prevalent, the economy generally develops as a market-oriented economy displaying a greater degree of innovation in creating production processes.

Lack of entrepreneurship can happen as a result of certain factors indigenous to the island economy. There could be structural features that impede the widespread growth of a local entrepreneurial class. One is a gap between research and application. Although individuals and institutions in a country carry out research concerning problems and bottlenecks hindering development, the country will remain dependent on external support and innovation if there is a gap between research, training, and application.

Lack of innovation can also be blamed on impossible entry requirements for new entrepreneurs to the market by settled business. Or, as Harvey Leibenstein argued:" settled entrepreneurs may spend their time on nontrading activities to ensure a greater monopolistic position, or engage in trading activities that secure them a greater monopolistic position. Alternatively, they may engage in speculative trading or in activities that use up net savings in enterprises that add little social value."[3] Even if there are entrepreneurs with entrepreneurial ability and energy, if they do not seize on the opportunities to engage in activities that lead to growth, their contribution to economic growth remain minimal.

The arguments above could be a reason that, notwithstanding a similar education system and a generally higher per capita income, the islands in the Caribbean that share a common colonial past with islands in East Asia do not show a similar economic development pattern as that of the NICs of East Asia. As related by Ralph M. Henry East Asian countries like Singapore, Mauritius, Hong Kong, and Sri Lanka have been able to achieve faster economic development than their Caribbean counterparts and have established themselves as world level competitors.[4] The answer, some argue, may be in improving the vocational orientation of secondary education, where one learns to *use* knowledge instead of *store* knowledge.

Basic Industries

Another important thought related to the exploitation of local and imported resources is the presence of leading sectors that drive general economic performance. Basic industries act a bit like anchor stores in a shopping center. They contribute directly or indirectly to growth in the national income and employment, and they can be instrumental in generating economic activity in several adjacent sectors. The function of a basic sector with respect to economic growth is illustrated in the Sir W. Arthur Lewis reading at the end of this chapter. Basic industries are referred to in that way as they contribute more than other sectors to the earnings of the nation. Generally, basic industries provide at least 30 percent of the national income and/or employment.

Openness and Sustainable Growth

Resource availability and use is impacted by the amount of economic (trading) and financial integration a country has with the rest of the world. The lack of resources makes small islands vulnerable to external forces, which affect the ability of theisland government and/or the central bank to be effective with measures to curb imports and stabilize the economy in times of recession and expansion. The openness, when based on a narrow integration between the home country and the rest of the world, as is the case with the plantation system, will affect the pursuit of economic growth and proper distribution of income.

George Beckford proposes that in order to assure the rate of growth of output, the islands will have to gain full control over their resources and the whole environment in which they live. His thoughts are shown in the second reading at the end of this chapter. The plantation system as described by Beckford can be seen to represent any foreign ownership of large-scale local business activity for foreign gain with foreign control over the production process and the utilization of resources. The problem lies in the fact that although the per capita income increases with these activities, there is little or no change in its distribution. This thinking brings up questions regarding the balance between resource use and sustainable economic growth reflected by growth in employment, as well as regarding the dependency condition that is created through the influx of international funds needed to create an economic infrastructure, which is hardly repayable from the domestic revenue sources.

The readings at the end of this chapter, which are shortened versions of the original text, are especially included for readers from the non-English-speaking territories in the region so they can become acquainted with the writings of Sir W. Arthur Lewis and George Beckford and assess how their thoughts apply to the economic growth and development issues of the reader's own island or country. Lewis's writings are predominantly from the 1940s to the 1970s, while Beckford's ideas were developed from the 1960s to the 1990s, the period when the English-speaking Caribbean was striving toward independence.

Lewis pinpoints in his writings factors that constrain or stimulate growth, leaving it up to the country to analyze the existing conditions and do long-range planning. Beckford urges increasing self-reliance to establish a society that embodies quality of life. For him, quality of life includes material goods but also equity, dignity, and independence. For this to work there has to be regional support among the islands. The work of these two authors can be used as underpinnings for continuing efforts toward the development of small economies in the Caribbean region.

Reading 1

Sir W. Arthur Lewis

The Theory of Economic Growth Development Planning: The Essentials of Economic Policy

Sir W. Arthur Lewis, from Saint Lucia, West Indies, received a Nobel Memorial Prize in Economics in 1979. This was primarily based on his contributions in an article in 1954 ("Economic Development with Unlimited Supply of Labor") with regard to the dual-sector model of development and a terms-of-trade model between developing and developed nations. The dual-sector model portrays a traditional agricultural sector and a modern industrialized sector. The modern sector attracts workers from the rural areas, offering a higher quality of life. This generates more profits and savings, also due to the fact that the wages of those coming from the rural areas remain lower. As a result, investments increase and the income generated by a sector trickles down throughout the economy. The terms-of-trade model refers to the description of the situation where two groups of countries both produce foods and other products and trade the products that are not produced in common. The terms of trade in such situations are determined by the relative labor productivity, especially in the agricultural sector. This synopsis presents a bit of his ideas from two of his publications: *Theory of Economic Growth*[5] and *Development Planning: The Essentials of Economic Policy.*[6]

Determinants of growth

In his book *Theory of Economic Growth,* published in 1955, Lewis refers to the fact that macroeconomics of developing economies require that certain conditions have to be present in order for sustainable economic growth and development to occur. A number of factors act as growth determinants, like rewards, economic freedom, institutional change, growth of knowledge, application of new ideas, savings, investments, population, output, public sector, trade and specialization, and power and politics. Some motivate and some constrain growth.

Motivators of growth

The agents of growth are proper training; development of know-how and skills in ways that they promote entrepreneurship; and fiscal and financial incentives. This improves the exploitation and management of existing locally developed or imported techniques. Other motivators of growth would be rewards and recognition, economic freedom, investments, specialization, growth of knowledge, and application of new ideas.

The development of an economic infrastructure through, for example, construction of roads, schools, airports, and harbors, is important in laying a foundation for development and growth. Similarly, an educated and healthy workforce is fundamental for growth. The lack of adequate intercountry transportation and intracountry transportation facilities can also constrain development. These factors in themselves are not primary agents of growth. They are basic, though, to supporting development efforts.

Constraints to growth

In his book *Development Planning: The Essentials of Economic Policy*, Lewis comments about the constraints to growth, stating that the fundamental constraints in developing countries are lack of natural resources and skilled manpower, the physical capacity of the capital-goods industries, and finance.[7] In planning economic development, it is necessary to pinpoint the new resources or techniques whose exploitation is going to carry the economy upward. Using Lewis's example, growth will depend on increased productivity in the most basic industry of the country. For most developing countries, this is (was) agriculture. However, he says, the prospects do not seem to point to high rates of growth in this sector. In money terms, he says, services tend to grow faster than national income and productivity increases faster in commodities. If average growth rates can be estimated for the various basic economic sectors in a country, it is possible to determine the rate of growth for the whole country. The growth can be estimated based on historical data and expectations from returns on investments in those sectors.

In table 2.1, the expected growth in national income is 4.7 percent. This is estimated using the previous year's proportion of GDP for a sector times the expected rate of growth. Adding up the absolute increases for the sectors provides a weighted average for the country. This is estimated using the previous year's proportion of GDP for a sector times the expected rate of growth, and adding up the absolute increases for the sectors provides a weighted average for the country.

The following example from Lewis illustrates growth rate averages for the three sectors.

Table 2.1: Growth characteristics

From A. Lewis

GDP Year 0 Proportions	Proportion GDP	Average Growth rate	Absolute Increase
Agricultur	50	3	1.5
Manufactu	15	10	1.5
Services	35	4.9	1.7
	100		4.7

Determination of desired growth rate
From: W. A. Lewis, *Development Planning: The Essentials of Economic Policy*

Lewis uses the concept of Incremental Capital Output Ratio (ICOR) developed by R.F. Harrod in the Essay in Dynamic Theory[8], and E. Domar in a journal articleCapital Expansion, Rate of Growth and Employment[9] to determine what the savings percentage for the country needs to be in order to be able to obtain the expected investments and growth for the country.

ICOR is a measure of the incremental capital investment needed to generate an extra unit of output. The model suggests that the rate of growth in an economy depends on the level of savings and on the productivity of investments. Investments stimulate aggregate demand and add to the capacity of the economy to produce goods and services. To obtain economic growth, the level of investments in fixed capital and human capital needs to be expanded. For example, with an ICOR of 3 and growth rates expected at 4.7, savings (that can be turned into investments) must be close to 15 percent (3×4.7) of national income.

According to Lewis, it is very difficult to get a country that was previously saving and investing at 4 to 5 percent of its national income or less to convert itself into an economy where voluntary saving is running at about 12 to 15 percent of national income.

Even if it were possible to obtain the needed savings, to achieve the expected growth the sectors have to be able to increase productivity, have the capacity to expand production to meet increased demand, make capital investments, and recruit sufficient skilled manpower. Not meeting these requirements can pose a constraint to overall growth.

Lewis remarks that manpower can impose constraints on the rate of growth with regards to skilled labor and administrative capacity. For instance, one may be able to build schools and hospitals but not to man them with teachers and nurses. Generally, the requirement for those with intermediate skills like nurses, teachers, secretaries, and technicians is large and the cost of importing them is high.

With regard to capital formation, Lewis writes that there is less of a constraint if the economy is an open one, as savings can be converted into foreign exchange to import machinery.

He admits that the imported machinery can become more expensive in real terms and that it would pay to produce more machinery at home. But, he says, small countries that do not have the natural resources will find it profitable to start with consumer goods and to move into capital goods via repair services only as the home market expands and accumulates services. Another constraint regarding the rate of growth is money. There is a need for large expenditures on growth in public services, such as research and surveys, road maintenance, agricultural extension, education, and public health.

Reading 2

George L. Beckford

Persistent Poverty: Underdevelopment in Plantation Economies of the Third World

Different from that of Sir W. Arthur Lewis, George Beckford's writings on economic progress of developing countries focus on the islands and countries in the Caribbean region. His vision, as observed by Kari Levitt, is one of an independent, sovereign, and self-reliant Caribbean nation based on a common culture of English-, Spanish-, French-, and Dutch-speaking peoples.[10]

Beckford was born in Jamaica and studied agricultural economics and international economics in Canada and the United States respectively. He observes in *Persistent Poverty*,[11] written in 1972, that the Third World, although vast in area and rich in resources, does not know to provide adequate levels of living for its people. The Third World comprises the countries of Latin America, Caribbean, Africa, and Asia that show malnutrition, disease, poor housing, deficiencies in sanitation and medical services, very low income levels, and little or no education. This is in contrast to the countries of the North Atlantic that stretch from Canada and the United States on one side to Russia on the other.

Beckford makes the conjecture that in most underdeveloped countries, the distribution of income among the population is very unequal; an increase in per capita income may not change, and may even worsen, these inequalities. All Third World countries are, in one way or another, colonies of the North Atlantic, which means that the underdeveloped economies are controlled in important ways by the North Atlantic nations. The Third World countries, consequently, need to improve their patterns of income distribution. In order to assure the rate of growth of output, they will have to gain full control over their resources and the whole environment in which they live. Increased output, he says, can be secured by increasing the quantity of inputs or factors of production; by improving the quality of these inputs; by introducing superior techniques that raise the productivity of existing inputs; or by any combinations of these.

However, there are certain preconditions for development to take place. Among these, the most important, it would seem, are a highly motivated population willing and able to make the sacrifices involved and appropriate institutional arrangements that provide the necessary incentives and rewards for effort.

Beckford mentions numerous obstacles to development as emanating from the plantation system itself and the way it influences the social and political structure. For purposes of brevity only, just a few of the obstacles are listed below, with the hope that this does not distort too much from the meaning that Beckford had in mind with the list of obstacles.

Some obstacles are plantation-system-related, like the fracturing of supply and demand, inequality in the distribution of wealth and income, and foreign ownership of producing units that drains the supply of investible funds from the income stream. This system leads to resource-use distortions that prevent the flexible deployment of resource services to high-income-producing activities.

Other obstacles are related to social and political aspects coming from a weak community structure and loose family organization that prevent the emergence of viable local and regional units of administration and control, thereby making it difficult to raise local taxes and execute local development projects. A rigid social structure also inhibits factor mobility while there is a strong correlation between race and class that creates a caste system and generates social tension and instability. A general absence of social responsibility results in poorly developed educational systems. Additionally, the strong central government administration with a generally undemocratic political structure discourages effective popular participation in the development process. These obstacles to development can be recognized as such within every country, at varying intensity.

For Beckford, a process of transformation is needed to ensure a benefit to everyone in plantation society. This transformation will not come without sacrifice. It must involve radical change in the institutional structure—particularly economic, social, and political arrangements. The plantation system, he says, creates persistent underdevelopment, as it denies the majority of the people of plantation society a real stake in the country. There is a legacy of dependence because the locus of decision-making concerning fundamental economic issues resides outside of the plantation society. Furthermore, the majority of the people are not sufficiently motivated toward the development effort because of the first two considerations.

The entry of plantations in previously uncultivated areas is of great importance to the economy, as it helps with the creation of social and overhead capital like roads, electricity, schools, railways, ports, telecommunication, water supplies, and hospitals. A second obvious development impact is, of course, the expansion of production and income resulting directly from plantation activity. A third comes from contributions to technology in underdeveloped countries. A fourth derives from the demonstration effect of plantation production on the output and income of peasant producers. A fifth immediate development impact comes from the multiplier effect. This follows the increase in investments, output, and incomes.

Beckford also notes the apparent limitations in a plantation system with foreign ownership and imports of foreign capital goods. Foreign ownership, he says, results in a diminution of the surplus, which becomes available for reinvestment in plantation economy because a part of this is paid out as interest and dividends to investors outside the economy. Payments for capital goods, which are imported (like factories, machinery and equipment, and building materials), do not form part of the investment benefits accruing to plantation economy in terms of multiplier effect but rather give rise to increased incomes in the countries from which the goods are imported.

---

[1]   Xabier Gorostiaga, "Education, Human Development, and Competitiveness," in *Roads to Competitiveness: Human Development with Export Growth*, ed. M. F. Hasham (1995, 1997).

[2]

[3]   Leibenstein, Harvey; Economic Backwardness and Economic Growth; Wiley; 1957.

[4]   Henry, Ralph M; Accessing the Embodied Capital for Caribbean Development; in Roads to Competitiveness, Human Development with Export Growth; the Caribbean Challenge; Editor M.F. Hasham; Association of Caribbean Economists; University of the Netherlands Antilles, 1997.

[5]   W. Arthur Lewis; The theory of Economic Growth; George Allen and Unwin Ltd. Publishers; 1955 London.

[6]   Add publishing information for book here.] Other publications by Sir Arthur Lewis include *Principles of Economic Planning* (1949), *Economic Survey 1918-1939* (1949), and *Overhead Costs* (1949).

[7]   Lewis, W. Arthur, Development Planning; the Essentials of Economic Policy; pp 153; George Allen and Unwin Ltd. Publisher; 1966 Other publications by Sir Arthur Lewis include *Principles of Economic Planning* (1949), *Economic Survey 1918-1939* (1949), and *Overhead Costs* (1949).

[8]   R.F. Harrod, An Essay in Dynamic Theory; Economic Journal 49, pp 14-33 March 1939

[9]   E. Domar, Capital Expansio Rate of Growth and Employment; pp 137-147 Econometrica, 1946.

[10]   Levitt, Kari; The George Beckford Papers; Canoe Press; Unversity of the West Indies; 2000

[11]   Beckford, George L.; Persistent Poverty; Underdevelopment in plantation economies of the Third World; Oxford University Press 1972; Maroon Publishing House, Morant Bay, Jamaica; 1988.

CHAPTER 3
ECONOMIC HISTORY OF THE
DUTCH CARIBBEAN

~~~•~~~

This chapter is intended to introduce some historical events that have importance in the economic development of the Dutch islands in the Caribbean starting from the 1630s, when the Dutch West Indian Company invaded and took the islands from the Spanish, up to the 1970s, when the Aruba population voted for Aruba to gain a separate status in the Dutch kingdom. Further historical moments are outlined in the next chapter.

Introduction

The economic history of the Dutch Caribbean islands helps us understand why the islands are where they are today and how the past can affect future development processes. William Demas of the Caribbean Development Bank once said that, "Before the Caribbean man endeavors to create the new Caribbean society, first he must know, understand, and come to terms with the history of the Caribbean. We cannot create a new society unless we know who we are, and we cannot know who we are unless we know where we come from."[1]

And to quote Rex Nettleford, "an appreciation of the collective heritage, particularly in pluralistic societies, helps to foster the self-confidence, resourcefulness, and unity so essential to self-reliant and self-sustaining growth."[2]

This chapter attempts to throw light on certain salient features of the economy from the time the islands became a possession of the Netherlands to the end of the 1970s.

The Netherlands Antilles consisted until recently of the islands Aruba, Curaçao, Bonaire, Sint Maarten, Saba, and Saint Eustatius, and was an autonomous part of the Netherlands realm. The seat of the central government was in Willemstad, Curaçao. The cabinet of ministers, the parliament, and the governor operated from this island. In 1986, Aruba left the Netherlands Antilles and gained a separate autonomous status in the kingdom of the Netherlands. In 2005, the remaining islands, in cooperation with the Netherlands, opted to seek a different political structure, with Sint Maarten and Curaçao continuing as autonomous islands in the kingdom and Saint Eustatius, Saba, and Bonaire obtaining a special status with direct links to the government of the Netherlands, in some respect an extra-periphery status. The complete breakup of the Netherlands Antilles into separate parts was completed by October 2010.

The Netherlands Antilles as an autonomous country in the kingdom of the Netherlands existed from 1954 to 2010. Before 1954, the Netherlands tried to keep control of the Caribbean possessions by establishing one point of control out of Curaçao. Before 1845, there were two points of control, Saint Eustatius and Curaçao reporting for, respectively, the Windward Islands and the Leeward Islands to the governor of Surinam. Even earlier, the islands were mere individual possessions of the Crown, run by the West India Company (WIC).

Colonization

The economic history of the Dutch Caribbean dates back to 1631 when Sint Maarten was first colonized by the WIC. The WIC did settle other islands like Tobago, Saint Croix, Anegada, and Tortuga for a while but lost these within a short time. The WIC also had settlements in Brazil, Guyana (Essequibo, Demerara, and Berbice), and North America but eventually lost these to other European countries.

The WIC was chartered in 1621 and obtained similar conditions and privileges from the authorities in that part of Holland (the name Holland and the Netherlands are used interchangeably throughout this writing) that was not under Spanish control at the time as those given to the East India Company in the South Asian Ocean. These privileges included the following[3]:

- twenty-one years of monopoly in the Caribbean Sea, for navigation and trade on the coast of Africa between the Tropic of Cancer and the Cape of Good Hope, and on the American coast between Newfoundland and the Straits of Magellan

- power to wage wars, negotiate peace, and establish treaties and alliances
- power to construct factories, colonies, or fortified bases in the conquered territories
- liberty to assign governors and deploy troops on land and sea
- the privilege to mint coins
- the exercise of judicial and legislative power in all the areas of its operations

The WIC had as an additional goal to attack and take the Spanish Fleet that brought back resources to the "Metropolis" to fight the war against the Dutch territories. Several Dutch provinces were at the time under Spanish rule, and they fought an eighty-year war against the Spanish that lasted until 1648, when a peace treaty was signed at Munster, Westphalia.

The island of Curaçao and the five other islands became official possessions of the Dutch sovereign government in 1648 but remained in the hands of the WIC. It is not until 1792 that the WIC actually allowed the islands to be incorporated by the States-General of Holland.[4]

This occurred during the term of the second or "new" Dutch West India Company that was established in 1674 and lasted until 1791. The first Dutch West India Company went bankrupt. The new WIC still seems to have "disembarked 13,500 slaves in Curaçao."[5] Of course, they were not the sole slave traders. There were also Portuguese and French slavers that disembarked slaves in Willemstad. Many of the blacks were "exported" to the mainland or other Caribbean Islands.

Sint Maarten

Sint Maarten was settled by the WIC in 1631, which took it from the Spanish just like it would do later on with regard to Curaçao. The aim was to gain control over the salt lakes on the island and export the salt to Europe. The Dutch appear to have discovered the island and its natural salt pond around the late 1620s but only moved in years later.[6]

By this time, Sint Maarten was also seen to be located at a perfect spot to carry out a "bridge" function between Pernambuco (Brazil) and the Netherlands. The Spanish recaptured the island in 1633, but after a time, the Spanish left the island and in 1648 it became partitioned into a French and Dutch section. Earlier, in 1644, Peter Stuyvesant, who was now managing the WIC out of Curaçao, tried to retake it. It was on this occasion that he was shot by the Spaniards in his right leg, causing him to lose the leg.

The first inhabitants of the island of Sint Maarten were Arawak and Caribs. The Caribs called the island "Soualigia," or Land of Salt. The island is about thirty-five square miles, of which twenty-one are French and fourteen Dutch. During the Spanish period, the Caribs remaining on the island were deported to, for instance, Dominica. When the Spanish troops withdrew in 1648, the Dutch and the French signed the treaty of Concordia, which allowed the French to occupy the northern part of the island and the Dutch the south side.

Sint Maarten was a major salt exporter up to the middle of the twentieth century. In the seventeenth century, Sint Maarten also cultivated and exported tobacco and indigo, used to make a blue dye. In the eighteenth century, the focus turned from tobacco to sugarcane and cotton. The population grew significantly with the importation of African slaves to work on the plantations in this period. Since 1970, Sint Maarten has been experiencing fast growth in tourism, which generates spillover activities in other sectors. Nowadays, the island has a separate status as an autonomous state in the Dutch kingdom.

Panoramic view of Sint Maarten:
Courtesy of Hubert Panthoflet; Original by TKA Architects, Almere.

Saint Eustatius

The Dutch colonized Saint Eustatius in 1632 to better position themselves to win the trade of the "leeward islands."[7] As related by Dr. J. Hartog[8], the island was called Estatia around 1523. The Spanish seem to have renamed it to Saint Eustatius. There is no indication from the readings that the Spanish settled on the island earlier.

The French, the English, and the Dutch (Zeelanders) did occupy the island though. The Dutch built the Fort Oranje after 1636. The size of the island is twenty-one square kilometers. Saint Eustatius's first known crop was tobacco. Later on, the people on the island turned to planting cotton and coffee. During this period, commerce from Saint Eustatius was at its peak. By 1740, these crops were replaced by sugarcane. This did not take off, though, as expected. However, Saint Eustatius became a central commercial port in the eastern Caribbean for the sugar trade and the slave trade, and served as an important stop for ships traveling from Europe or between Brazil and North America.

According to information from the writings of Dr. J. Hartog[9], the island changed (colonial) hands at least twenty-two times during the period 1636 to 1816, being alternatively Dutch, English, French, Spanish, and then again a Dutch possession. Like Curaçao, the island was run by the WIC whenever it was under Dutch rule. Saint Eustatius became the base from which other islands could be colonized.

The commander of Fort Oranje raised the Dutch flag in 1776 as a salute to the Andrew Doria, an American ship. This was at the time of the American war of independence against Britain. For the British, this was a further sign that the Netherlands and Saint Eustatius not only acknowledged the flag of rebelling

America, a country that was at war with England, but also were helping the enemy obtain food and munitions. During the following years, the British would frequently stop Dutch ships after they left the island to check for arms that could be transferred to American ships at sea. In 1780, the British declared war against the Netherlands.

A year later in 1781, the British under Captain Rodney attacked Saint Eustatius with a large fleet and raided, looted, and ransacked the island, destroying the lower town completely as well as Dutch ships still in the harbor or sailing away from the island. Saba was also occupied by the British troops a day later. The invasion did not last long. Halfway through that year, the French invaded Saint Eustatius and held it up to 1984, when it was returned to the Netherlands through the Peace Treaty of Paris. However, Saint Eustatius never regained its previous economic prowess, since many of the merchants had left in the interim and settled in nearby Saint Thomas. The activities around an international oil terminal are the major source of income for the population and government. A small offshore medical school brings a bit of economic diversity. Nowadays, Saint Eustatius has a status of special municipality in the Dutch kingdom. The official currency is the US dollar.

Lower Town. Statia, never recovered its old glory after the
English destroyed it for saluting the Andrea Doria during the
British-American War. The Quill volcano in the back.
Courtesy of Gerold Goossen Ascon N.V.

Saba

Saba was colonized by settlers out of Saint Eustatius in
1640. Saba also became a Dutch possession under the WIC.
According to *History of Saba* by Dr. J. Hartog[10], Saba is the name
most frequently recorded for the island even before the Dutch
settled it in 1640. The Carib Indians seem to have called it
Amonhana, a word for which the meaning is not known. From
the artifacts found there, the first inhabitants of the islands
must have been Caribs. Although Saba is very small at thirteen
square kilometers, it is mountainous, with flat land a scarce
resource. The economic importance of Saba was and is the rich
fishing grounds of the Saba Bank.

Saba the Picture Book Island of the Dutch Caribbean
Courtesy of Melisa and Juni Juana

The Dominican priest Jean Baptiste Labat reported shoemaking as the main business of Saba in 1701. Interestingly, another author, M.D. Teenstra [11], reports that according to Governor Canz'laar, there were neither shoemakers nor tailors on Saba by 1829. After changing flags about eight times since the first Dutch settlement, the island became permanently Dutch in 1816. In the first half of the eighteenth century, Saba cultivated and exported sugarcane and cotton and manufactured cotton hammocks and stockings. However, after a short time of prosperity, agricultural gains decreased and as the economy did not show signs of improving, various residents emigrated to the United States around 1870. Such large migration occurred again between 1927 and 1950 when, as was the case for Saint Eustatius and Sint Maarten, many Saba residents migrated to Curaçao and Aruba to work in the refineries.

Nowadays on Saba, a medical school caters to mainly foreign students. This institution greatly influences economic growth, which in turn has lured many foreigners to the island, almost doubling the number of people living there. Saba has been a special municipality of the Netherlands since October of 2010. The official currency is the US dollar.

The Leeward Islands

Dutch supervision of Curaçao, Aruba, and Bonaire dates back to the years 1634 to 1636, when the WIC settled in Curaçao and Aruba. In fact, Johan van Walbeeck and Pierre Legrand, managers of the company, together with a certain Jan Otzen, took the island of Curaçao from the Spanish for the WIC, built fortresses, instituted a government, minted their own coins, and carried out multiple business activities—clandestine and otherwise—from these locations.

Bonaire

Bonaire is located to the northeast of Curaçao, and its economy has generally been very interdependent with that island. With its 288 square kilometers, Bonaire is the second largest island of the Dutch Caribbean. It was first discovered by the Spanish in 1499 and referred to by Juan de la Cosa as *Isla de Palo Brasil* because of the abundance of dyewood. Later, it was learned that the Indians called the island *Bojnaj*, which name seems to have been adjusted to Bonaire. In another publication, the island was also referred to as Buon Ayres.[12]

As with Curaçao and Aruba, the native population of Bonaire was Arawak (Caiquetios). The Spanish deported most of them to Hispaniola in 1513 to work in copper mines. By 1527, the island had a small contingent of Caiquetios again who came primarily from the continent.

The Dutch had been off and on in Bonaire previously; however, Bonaire was not occupied by the Dutch WIC until 1636. In 1639, an economic development plan was developed for Bonaire with stock-breeding for meat (especially salted goat meat, *yorki*) at the base. The other major industries were salt-making and the lumber trade. Bonaire exported the watapana (or divi-divi) to as far as Germany.

The British also ruled Bonaire from time to time, and from 1810 to 1816 leased out the island—including three hundred slaves—to an American. The Dutch afterward used Bonaire as a government plantation. Because of the difficulties in agriculture and the low demand for salt, the Dutch government saw itself compelled to sell the island (crown-lands) and its salt ponds by 1867. It was sold to two families, Neuman and Helmundt. Those living on the island had to work for them and buy at their stores. As was the case with Curaçao and Aruba, many inhabitants emigrated to Venezuela, Cuba, and Puerto Rico in the early part of the twentieth century. After the establishment of the refineries in Curaçao and Aruba, thousands of Bonaireans settled on those two islands. By October 2010, Bonaire took on the status of special municipality of the Netherlands. As with Saba and Saint Eustatius, the US dollar is official tender.

Salt hills in background. Salt is one of the more important exports of Bonaire
Courtesy of Evy Martis van der Wall Arneman

Aruba

As Dr. Hartog[13] wrote, the 193-square-kilometer island of Aruba was first visited by the Spaniards in and around 1500. The first colonization of Aruba (along with Curaçao and Bonaire) was carried out by the Spaniards in 1527. The native Indian population was fairly small. Aruba also seems to have had other names, *Oruba* among them[14].

The Spanish imported horses, goats, sheep, dogs, and donkeys to Aruba. Cattle were bred for export of hides to places that had tanneries. Occupying Aruba and Bonaire in 1636 was a strategic move to make it impossible for the Spaniards to mount an attack on Curaçao from those two islands.

As part of the strategy, the WIC focused in the development plan of 1639 on agriculture for Curaçao, cattle breeding for Aruba, and cattle breeding, maize cultivation, and salt mining essentially in Bonaire. This was all on behalf of Curaçao, which was being used as a harbor from which the Dutch could attack Spanish ships. Aruba exported horses and cattle. The Venezuelan revolutionary Francisco de Miranda spent a brief period in Aruba in 1806.

Gold was found in 1824 in Rooi Fluit and Rooi Daimari on the north coast and later on at Tibushi in the western part of the Island. Machinery was imported for crushing and melting, with Bushiribana and Balashi as center of the activities. This activity lasted until 1916, with the outbreak of World War I. Later attempts at gold mining seemed unprofitable.

Aruba also exported phosphate for a while between 1879 and 1914. Other export products that thrived for a while were divi-divi pods for tannin and carmine processed from the cochineal insect for coloring. Aloe is, since the 1840s, an important export produce as raw material for foreign manufactures, but since the 1970s it has become the raw material for cosmetic products manufactured on the island. A savings and loan bank was established in 1866.

As was the case with Bonaire and Curaçao, many Arubans also had to seek employment in the region, in places like Venezuela, Colombia, and Cuba (toward the end of the nineteenth century and early twentieth century) where opportunities were more plentiful. The establishment of the oil refineries in the 1920s and 1930s acted as a trampoline to a quick economic boom that attracted a vast number of foreigners to settle adjacent to the domestic population that was then predominantly of Amerindian origin. From the 1960s on, the hospitality business has started taking form, and this sector has become to date the most important contributor to the gross domestic product (GDP).

Aruba gained a separate status as an autonomous state in the Dutch kingdom on January 1986. A governor represents the kingdom. The currency is the Aruban florin.

Tram transporting shoppers and tourists in main street of Oranjestad, Aruba
Courtesy of Earon Matthew

Curaçao

Curaçao is located north of Venezuela. Perhaps the most outstanding historical feature for the 444-square-kilometers island was its harbor facilities. Ships sailing in the region stopped there for bunkering and transshipment of merchandise leading to a relatively active commercial sector involved in import and export. The Dutch after 1636 deported the majority of the Indians (and Spanish) who were living on Curaçao to the South American mainland. Since then, the people who came to inhabit Curaçao were of predominantly African and European origin.

Linda Rupert writes about Curaçao[15]:

The major economic activity on the island for the Spanish when they controlled Curaçao was one of raising cattle and other livestock for the hide which was shipped back to Europe. In fact the Spanish, just as the Dutch later, thought the island was a convenient base from which to operate in the rest of the region. At this time, Curaçao's deep water harbor offered a comparative advantage as it is located outside the hurricane belt, and is located on the sheltered south coast. This relative advantage was especially true for the temporary depot of African captives, who are sold in the Spanish colonies. Because of these functions other related functions evolved where Curaçao became a trading center for agricultural products from the region and manufactures from Europe.

Rupert states that Curaçao was declared a free port in 1675, and trade through Curaçao, at 10 to 15 million guilders, was half of the total Dutch Atlantic trade by the end of the eighteenth century. The trade toward Europe in this period included tobacco, cacao, hides, coffee, indigo, precious metals, and dyewood. The ships returned from Europe with manufactures and enslaved Africans. The ship traffic between Curaçao and the mainland of South America was particularly important, as these countries were dependent on foreign suppliers.

The island of Curaçao and especially its merchant class, as was the case in Saint Eustatius, played an important role in the economics of the region as a depot for a vibrant slave trade. Trading slaves from Curaçao to the region was often more profitable than bringing the Africans in for plantation purposes, due to the arid conditions of the island. Nowadays the majority of the population of most of the islands in the Caribbean region is of African descent. This ethnic group, which came in as slaves, became the ruling elite later on in most of the islands in the region.

Curaçao appears to maintain a very important intermediary position among countries of the world, next to bunkering for provisions. For instance, during the war between the United States and France from 1797 to 1799, several businesses were relocated from Baltimore in the Unites States to Curaçao. In the Latin American war of independence from Spain from 1816 to 1822, much of the arms and ammunition were supplied through Curaçao. The oil refinery and related activities that started in the early part of the twentieth century further emphasized this supporting position among countries and led to a reasonably diversified domestic economy with comparatively even distribution of income and employment in the financial sector, the manufacturing sector, the retail/wholesale sector, and the hospitality sector.

Ferry transporting passengers between Punda and
Otrobanda across the Schottegat Bay in Curacao
Courtesy of Clifton Hasham

Monetary affairs

In Curaçao, a central bank was instituted in 1828 as the Bank of Curaçao. The bank was involved in credit and bill brokering in the beginning but gradually assumed total responsibility for money matters in the Dutch islands. This was not achieved swiftly, as the Dutch government tried to maintain control over monetary matters. An example is that the Dutch introduced the silver standard in 1847 and the gold standard in 1881 through the Curaçaosche Bank, but these standards did not necessarily function because of the scarcity of coins.

The bank's business evolved gradually to the point where it published aggregate economic reports summing up the island data at its disposal to show the country's economic picture. Most of the information found in these publications refers to the aggregate for the Dutch islands belonging to the Dutch Caribbean. Nowadays, the central bank has monetary jurisdiction over the Antillean florin, which is still in circulation in Sint Maarten and Curaçao. The central bank is lately referred to as SBSC, the Central Bank of Curaçao and Sint Maarten.

Administration

Around 1845, the Leeward and Windward Islands were grouped together and administered out of Willemstad, Curaçao. This put an end to a period of much uncertainty where the islands were being administered out of Surinam, with Curaçao and Saint Eustatius being alternatively subadministrations for the Dutch Leeward Islands and the Dutch Windward Islands. A colonial council was instituted in about 1833 as a follow-up to the administrative council of 1815.

Early 20th Century

The economies of the several islands were so depressed in the late nineteenth century and the early years of the twentieth century that a substantial number of people migrated from these islands to, for instance, Cuba, Puerto Rico, and the

Dominican Republic to assist in agricultural production, especially related to sugarcane. There was much fluctuation in economic activities, and as they do now, the islands turned to the Netherlands for help with finances. The entry of the petroleum industry in the Leeward Islands created a great economic boost that persisted despite the depression of late 1920s and the Second World War. Aruba and Curaçao became industrial centers while the other Dutch Caribbean islands became mere economic peripheries leaning on the centers. The population of the Dutch Caribbean in 1900 was approximately 50,000 in all; by 1930, it had grown to about 76,000.

The Beginnings of the Oil-Refining Industry

The arrival of the Shell Oil Company, locally known as Curaçaosche Petroleum Industrie Maatschappij (CPIM) or Curaçaosche Petroleum Maatschappij (CPM) in 1914 marked a moment of huge turnaround in the economy of Curaçao and the rest of the islands. Not only did this activity attract thousands of workers from the rural areas of Curaçao, it also increased labor mobility throughout the region, with import of workers from the other Dutch islands and Surinam, from most of the Eastern Caribbean islands, and even from as far away as Madeira.

Shell Oil became the largest employer of the island of Curaçao and apparently had at one time about 12,000 workers directly involved in the refinery process and another 10,000 indirectly involved through satellite companies providing service to the refinery. An additional direct impact occurred in the construction sector, with the building of plants and residences for expatriate workers.

On Aruba, Lago Oil and Transport Co. Ltd. established a refinery in the midtwenties. This refinery was acquired by Standard Oil of New Jersey in 1932. The common name for Standard Oil was first Esso and changed later to Exxon.

In 1928, Shell also established a refinery in Aruba with the name of Eagle oil refinery. This refinery was closed in 1953. The activities of the Lago Oil and Transport Co. and the Eagle oil refinery, as was the case for the Curaçao refinery, had far-reaching consequences for Aruba and the Caribbean region as a whole as many immigrants from the surrounding islands and South America flocked to the island for employment. Exxon, like Shell in Curaçao, grew to become one of the largest oil refineries in the Western Hemisphere refining the heavy crude oil from the Maracaibo Lake of Venezuela.

Industry and Finance

Although the format of ownership was closely akin to that of the plantation model as referred to by George Beckford[16], Curaçao and Aruba have become partially industrialized islands with a so-called "dual economy," with productivity and labor income in the petroleum and related sectors considerably higher than in the other more traditional economic sectors on the islands. The economic activities of the time influenced the fast growth of various finance and trading houses. Three of the names that were known back in the 1910s and 1920s and are still around are the Maduro and Curiel's Bank, the Curaçaosche Hypotheek Bank, and the Postal Savings Bank that started in 1904. Maduro and Curiel's Bank is the result of a merger between Correa and Maduro's Bank with Morris and Curiel Bank.

Organized Labor

In this period, the islands, especially Curaçao, saw the development of organized labor activities. There was a wildcat strike in 1913 by dockworkers, but it was only in 1922 that the first organized labor-union action was felt. This was organized by the (Harbor) Dock Workers Union. The several labor unions that were established between 1922 and 1945 were predominantly supported by the Roman Catholic clergy. The labor unions that came into existence after 1945 were more independent from the Church and employers. Examples are the Petroleum Workers Union and the Democratic Workers Union in Curaçao. The development in labor unions had as an important side effect the introduction of labor legislation like the Shop Closing Act of 1932 and the Sickness Insurance Act of 1936.

1940-1959

Several events in the early 1940s marked a route toward more autonomous internal government. The world war increased the demand for petroleum products, and the geographic position of the refineries in Aruba and Curaçao was handy to supply the American and allied troops. This led to strong economic growth. The stronger economy made the establishment of the local florin as an independent official currency possible. Furthermore, with the introduction of general suffrage, where all men and women 21 years or older could vote, the existing appointed colonial council could now be replaced by a government based on the outcome of general elections. Parties were formed on each island to compete for the opportunity to govern the country or the island. The forties and fifties were filled with new developments on the constitutional front.

In the following sections, a closer view is given to the introduction of a local currency, the statute and island regulations, and the first efforts of the government to deal with an economic meltdown.

Finance and Labor

By 1940, the Curaçaosche Bank had become officially responsible for monetary supervision and the maintenance of the value of the Curaçao guilder. The strong economy that occurred with the oil-refining activities, international commercial activities, and allied manufacturing activities seemed to have been instrumental in forcing the establishment of a domestic currency, the Curaçao florin. The continuous disappearance of coins from the system led to the replacement of the coins with paper money issued locally, sometimes by finance houses, and compelled the central bank to restrict the international exchange, or convertibility, of the local currency. Although the Dutch authorities tried often to keep the Curaçao guilder integrated with the Dutch currency, it was to no avail.

Ultimately, and also because of the Second World War, the Curaçao florin, also referred to as the guilder, became officially independent from the Dutch currency in 1942 and was fixed to the US dollar at the rate of Fls 1.89 to $1 in 1947. This fixed exchange rate prevailed up to 1973, when it was revalued as the Netherlands Antilles guilder at ANG 1.79 to $1.

On the labor front the government[17] abolished the limitations on labor-union activities in the law and introduced an ordinance that allowed collective labor agreements in 1958.

Autonomy

The implementation of the charter of the kingdom served to establish each territory as an equal partner. The territories were the Netherlands, Surinam, and the Netherlands Antilles. The Netherlands Antilles consisted of the six islands referred to as Leeward and Windward Islands. In the 1950s, each island territory obtained a status within the Netherlands Antilles, with responsibility for its own financial matters. The island regulations followed subsequent to the acceptance of the constitution of the Netherlands Antilles.

Constitution
The Netherlands Antilles constitution regulated the political cooperation among the islands. There were central and island governments. The constitution delineated the autonomous position of the country of the Netherlands Antilles within the Dutch kingdom. The negotiations with the Dutch

government to establish a new political order started for the Netherlands Antilles in 1951 and for Surinam in 1950; both were concluded in December 1954. The principle was that each country would administer its internal affairs autonomously, while each country committed autonomously to the administration of common interests and mutual assistance. Certain external affairs remained a uniform kingdom matter, needing uniform constitutional provisions. Examples were independence and defense of the kingdom, foreign relations, and nationality.

The publication of the Island Regulations in 1955 occurs as a supplement to the Netherlands Antilles constitution (referred to generally as the Statutes) and gave the islands special provisions. The constitution, which regulated the autonomy of the country and the islands, had certain articles that directly affected decisions about national revenue and expenditures and consequently economic management and development. For instance, monetary loans in the name and to the debit of the Netherlands Antilles could only be contracted on the strength of a federal ordinance. Contracting or guaranteeing a monetary loan outside of the kingdom in the name or to the debit of the Netherlands Antilles required an agreement with the government of the kingdom. Consequently, it became easier to turn to the Netherlands directly for funds.

According to this constitution, the government had to care for education, and teaching at least at the primary and secondary level would be free. Education was to be paid for from public funds. This had immediate consequences for the revenue production by the government and how it was to spend the revenue.

Taxes and government revenue

A major provision from the constitution—actually, this was found in the island regulations—that had repercussions on economic growth was the way tax levies would accrue to the central government. For instance, 45 percent of the proceeds of import, export, and transit duties—as well as sales and excise taxes collected in a particular island territory—would accrue to that island territory, and 35 percent of the proceeds of the principal amounts of the income tax and profit taxes would accrue to the central government. A few of the islands—Bonaire, Saint Eustatius, and Saba—could only scantily contribute to the system, as their internal economies were too small to produce meaningful tax revenues.

Another issue was that interisland commerce between the Windward and the Leeward Islands was somewhat restricted by the fact that import duties were levied in the Leeward Islands on goods originating from the Windward Islands. The constitution and island regulations remained in effect from 1954 to 2010.

With the presence of the oil refineries, the Leeward Islands of Aruba and Curaçao experienced more economic activity than the other Dutch islands. The population of Aruba in 1960 was about 54,000 and the rest of the Dutch Caribbean islands had 135,000 people. A third of the population of the two islands and of other Dutch islands left the countryside to work in the refineries. As a result, agriculture and fishery activities deteriorated on all the islands.

Housing

One of the first activities by the young governments in Curaçao and Aruba, aware of the housing scarcity due to the demand for labor by the refineries, was the large-scale building of public housing in several areas of the islands and parceling land for lease-holdings. The government additionally established a *bouwkredietbank* to finance construction and ownership to meet the demand for housing.

But toward the second half of the 1950s, the oil-refining companies in the two islands started to automate the refining processes to stay competitive. In Curaçao, the CPIM conducted layoffs between 1957 and 1964 that brought the headcount down to 4,000 employees from the 12,000 in the earlier period. Many of the foreign workers returned to their specific islands. Many of those who remained, including Curaçao natives, were unemployed.

1960-1979

The economic model for the Dutch Caribbean islands started changing from a predominantly private-sector-led economy to one with much government intervention in the 1960s and the 1970s. But the dispersion of the internal economy over a set of islands rather far from each other created a difficult situation for a central government to manage, and much was left to the islands to determine their economic future.

The major frustration in the 1960s was brought on by a forgotten phenomenon: unemployment. If in the decades earlier there was a case of importation of workers, now there was a sudden growth in unemployment despite the "relocation" of many workers to their home countries. The unemployment situation, with the loss of almost 8,000 petroleum jobs in Curaçao, made for one of the worst economic downturns for the island since the early part of the century. In Aruba, a similar process took place because of automation in the refinery and various immigrant workers returned to their respective islands.

Early Responses

The quick fall in employment brought about several responses. Families responded first by allowing close kin to move into the parental home, which produced many households of multiple families. Several members of an extended family came to live together in the same household, with one or very few wage-earners. Some relief came when Dutch firms like Bronswerk NV and BATA NV invited Dutch nationals in the Antilles to seek a position with the firms in the Netherlands. This led to one of the first flows of migration of workers toward the Netherlands.

Economic planning
The governments created long-term and short-term development plans, the first being for ten years. The plans

stressed the improvement of the economic infrastructure and a renewed focus on education, especially technical education, as a support to industrial development. These were to be important cornerstones for the development foreseen. The department for "well-being" of the central government was soon changed to the Department of Development Cooperation, which intermediates to enhance more active participation by the other Dutch Caribbean islands in the processes to obtain international-assistance funds for infrastructural development.

Tax holidays
The government also responded to the recessionary trend, trying to boost economic activity by inviting foreign companies to establish manufacturing firms. To this end, a tax-holiday legislation was introduced allowing foreign firms investing on the islands a ten-year holiday from tax on profits. The tax-holiday system was patterned after the "industrialization by invitation" example used in Puerto Rico in the previous decade. The tax holiday worked to attract foreign companies like Rockwell and Texas Instruments to the island of Curaçao. However, there were obstructions in the trade agreement through the clause of origin that made access to the European market difficult from the Dutch possessions. So the assembly plants were quickly closed and the companies moved away.

Other motives cited for the early departure of these companies were the presence of and demands by a strong labor-union organization on the island of Curaçao and high wages. These might well have been reasons for not considering other export markets for the products that they assembled on the island.

The companies provided much-needed jobs at this time of high unemployment, and a large number of females were drawn into the workforce and received training in the electronics-assembly industry. After these companies left, the labor force grew considerably with a higher participation rate of female workers.

Additional focus

External financing, also as a result of the Treaty of Rome decisions, occurred primarily through the Netherlands Development Assistance Funds and European Development Assistance Funds. The Netherlands for quite a while provided a portion of the funds as a nonrepayable grant and a portion as a soft loan, meaning that the loan is given at a low interest rate, generally 3 to 4 percent. These funds were used to improve the economic infrastructure to support infrastructure activities in the manufacturing sector, the financial sector, and the utilities. The external financing since 1990 is in the form of grants.

Social and Growth Legislation

The 1960s was also typified by the first set of social legislation. The government introduced the AOV—general old-age insurance—in 1960; the AWW or the general widow-and-orphan insurance in 1964; and the Cessantia Laws in 1965. The Cessantia funds were created to compensate employees who were laid off without due cause.

Next to social legislation and the focus on the industrial sector, the government also gave attention to factors that stimulate growth. This included efforts in the area of banking, private/ public endeavors to enhance financial offshore activities through tax treaties, and taking a position in the market economy by acquiring companies in the private sector. The government stepped in with industry protection to boost import substitution and exports, and it also became active in the tourism sector by picking up market failures, which could later be sold off.

Government banking

In the early 1960s, the government made efforts to correct the economic situation by establishing a *volkskredietbank* to achieve goals that could not be achieved with the *bouwkredietbank*, now defunct. It was also in this decade that the GIRO, now GIRO Bank Curaçao NV, was started as a deposit bank for the government and government employees.

Tax treaties

In the sixties, some new opportunities were visible in the international-finance sector, and the central government enacted laws to facilitate the development of this sector and close double-taxation treaties with the United States and, through the Netherlands, subsequently with a number of other countries. This permitted much growth in the international-finance sector, especially offshore finance activities. The sector grew quickly and spontaneously and consisted of different types of offshore companies, like investment holding companies, finance companies, patent holding companies, real-estate companies, mutual funds, offshore trading, offshore banking, and captive insurance.

Turning Point

Notwithstanding the efforts to stimulate growth and development and the introduction of social legislation that has had a permanent impact, the 1960s closed with the scars of a series of riots on May 30, 1969. These mishaps were seemingly a result of the socioeconomic situation in Curaçao and culminated in the burning of several edifices in Willemstad, the capital city of the island and the center of government for the Netherlands Antilles. The upheaval started with an action by workers at one company, Wescar in Curaçao, and grew into a popular uprising. It soon became clear that there were many latent social issues in society that need to be tackled. The result of this uprising is often identified as a pivotal point in the political and economic history of Curaçao.

Government enterprises

The tax revenues from the financial offshore activities and the access to plentiful development funds made for a financially stronger government. There was substantial growth in the number of personnel in the government apparatus. Additionally, the Curaçao government nationalized the water distribution firm (OGEM, a Dutch concern) and took over the ailing Curaçao dry dock and the Antillean Television Corporation.

Tourism

The 1970s left an important mark on the tourism industry in the various islands. Aruba and Sint Maarten developed in this period a mostly leisure-oriented tourism. These islands saw a fast growth in the number of stayovers, particularly from the United States, and experienced a substantial expansion in new hotels and related tourism facilities. In Curaçao, tourism growth did not take on the proportions of the other islands, forcing the island government to set up the Curaçao Holding Company to run the affairs of the hotels under guarantee. All in all, with tourism burgeoning, the Antilles as a whole became a relevant travel alternative to well-known destination like Puerto Rico, the Virgin Islands, Barbados, the Bahamas, and Jamaica without cannibalizing each other's market.

Infant industry protection
The manufacturing industry constantly plays a role in economic thinking, and in the 70s a round of protection measures was introduced to stimulate local manufacturing. The manufacturing sector was often represented by just one company, and these were established most often on the island of Curaçao, which was the reason for friction with some of the other islands as the protective measures often led to higher domestic prices, while the islands did not all benefit the same way.

Territorial waters
In 1978, the Netherlands and the Netherlands Antilles government signed a treaty with respect to the demarcation of the territorial limits with Venezuela. With the treaty, Venezuelan ships were permitted to navigate and airplanes to fly over locations designated by the treaty in the Antillean territory.

Changing political arena
If the 1960s closed with the riots in Willemstad, the 1970s ended with Aruba's decision to secede from the Netherlands

Antilles and double-digit inflation. In 1977, 83 percent of voters in Aruba showed preference in a referendum for a separate status for Aruba outside the Antillean constellation. A few years earlier, Surinam, which is located in the northeast of the South America continent, became an independent country and did not form part of the Dutch kingdom from then on.

Oil, inflation, and indexation
Another event that required much attention around the world was the establishment and activities of OPEC, the Organization of Oil Exporting Countries. OPEC was an instrumental player in raising the price of crude oil from around $2 per barrel gradually to $20 and then to $30. This had as an effect enormous cost-push inflation, so that toward the end of the seventies all the islands were experiencing double-digit inflation. The government responded to this challenge by introducing wage adjustments based on the consumer price index for civil servants to help maintain purchasing power. Several companies in the private sector followed suit.

Shell and Exxon lost the concessions they'd had with Venezuela in the 1970s. This had repercussions on the Curaçao and Aruba refineries, since neither the quantity nor the price of the oil imported from Venezuela was guaranteed. The new situation demanded that the refineries negotiate short-term contracts with the state-owned petroleum companies in Venezuela.

Syndicates
Aside from the fact that some labor unions were involved in the turmoil described earlier that led to riots in 1969,

in the following decades the labor unions took on a major responsibility in educating their members, created union syndicates, and became affiliated with several international labor organizations like the Central Latino Americana de Trabajadores (CLAT), Organización Regional Interamericana de Trabajadores (ORIT), and the Caribbean Congress of Labor.

---

[1] Dr. William Demas was an advisor to Dr. Eric Williams, the prime minister of Trinidad and Tobago. He also served as the secretary general of the Caribbean Common Market (CARICOM) and president of the Caribbean Development Bank. This quote is taken from a speech by Mr. George F. Tyson, Jr., of the Island Resources Foundation on the "Inclusion of Historical Resources in the Development Process," given at a 1983 workshop in St. Kitts on the "Uses of Historical Resources in Eastern Caribbean Island Development."

[2] Ralston Milton "Rex" Nettleford authored several publications, including *Rastafari* and *Mirror, Mirror: Identity, Race, and Protest in Jamaica* (1970) and *Caribbean Cultural Identity: The Case of Jamaica in Cultural Dynamics* (1978). Rex was a professor at the University of the West Indies in Jamaica. This quote is taken from the speech mentioned in the note above.

[3] Cardot, Carlos, Felice; *Curazao Hispanico: Antagonismo Flamenco-Espanol*; *1973; Caracas: Fuentes para la historia colonial de Venezuela*; 1st edition.

[4] Ibid 3

[5] Cornelis, Ch. Goslinga, *Curacao as a slave-trading center during the war of the Spanish succession(1702-1714)*; IN: Nieuwe West-Indische gids; No. ½; 52ste jaargang; Novemebr 1977; Publishers: Stichting Nieuwe Westindische Gids, Utrecht.

[6]   Jean Glasscock; Sint Maarten, *the making of an Island*; Windsor Press, 1985

[7]   Robert Greenwood, *Sketchmark of the Caribbean*; MacMillan Education Ltd. 1991

[8]   Dr. J. Hartog; *Geschiedenis van St. Eustatius*; Publishers: De Wit Stores N.V. 1976, Aruba

[9]   Ibid 4

[10] Dr. J. Hartog; *History of Saba*; Van Guilder N.V. Publishers; 1975

[11] M.D. Teenstra; *De Nederlandsch West-Indische Eilanden, Curacao; In derzelver Tegenwoordigen Toestand*; Tweede Stuk; C.G. Sulpke; Amsterdam 1837 pp 308

[12] M.D. Teenstra; De nederlandsch West-Indische Eilanden; C.G. Sulpke, 1837.

[13] Dr. J. Hartog; Aruba zoals het was, Zoals het werd van de tijd der Indianen tot op heden. Publ. De Wit; 2de druk 1952.

[14] M.D. Teenstra; *De Nederlandsche West-Indische Eilanden*; C. G. Sulpke, publishers, 1837 p.196

[15] Linda M. Rupert; *Contraband Trade and the shaping of Colonial Societies in Curacao and Tierra Firme*; Presentation to American Historic Society; November 2006

[16] Beckford, George; *Persistent Poverty; Underdevelopment in plantation economics of the Third World*; Maroon Publishing House, 1972; Jamaica

[17] Dr. Rene Romer; Labor Unions; West-Indische Gids; 1981

CHAPTER 4
RECENT HISTORY OF THE
DUTCH CARIBBEAN

This chapter continues the historical overview with events that took place from 1980 to the present and were instrumental in taking the economy to where it is today. As stated in the last chapter, an improved understanding of history helps foster new insights as to how to contribute to and shape the future of one's home country. The insight will help some in developing detailed research with regard to topics that seem to need deeper evaluation.

1980s

At the beginning of the 1980s, the islands had to cope with a high inflation rate that was primarily the result of price increases in the petroleum sector. The decade of the eighties was marked by events that produced yet another major economic downturn in Curaçao and gave little opportunity to correct the unemployment situation that had its roots in the 1960s. The decade also saw Aruba's separation from the Antilles, difficulties in the international financial sector, and the closing of the Shell Oil refinery in Curaçao. Among the few high points of the 1980s was the disappearance of the inflation threat.

Inflation

The high rate of inflation in the late 1970s brought what has been called *stagflation* to many countries. Stagflation indicates economic stagnation, with high unemployment along with inflation. This trend was curbed significantly in the United States in the 1980s during the administration of President Ronald Reagan. The governors of the US Federal Reserve, under the leadership of Paul Volcker and later Alan Greenspan, came up with a strategy to target inflation by controlling money supply. When it was clear that controlling reserves without controlling interest rates brought about recession, the Federal Reserve decided to also target interest rates. This had a lowering effect on interest rates, and subsequently the inflation rate in the Netherlands Antilles too came down from the double-digit figures of the previous decade to less than 4 percent. This is perhaps an indication of a large degree of integration of the island economy with that of the United States.

To wit, in neighboring Venezuela, inflation was above 20 percent persistently during the 1980s. The Venezuelan government devalued the bolivar each year during the period 1983, 1984, and 1985, allowing it to float in the exchange market. The general price level in Curaçao and the rest of the Dutch Caribbean was not directly influenced by the inflationary situation in Venezuela, but because Venezuelan tourists could not afford sufficient US dollars to travel and purchase in the stores in Curaçao and Aruba, this had a direct effect on the Punda and Otrobanda (the twin cities making up Willemstad) stores in Curaçao and on Playa, the popular name for Oranjestad, in

Aruba. Several stores gradually moved away from the centers to service the growing suburban population in Curaçao and Aruba.

Growth and Demise of the International Financial Sector

From the 1960s to the mid-1980s, the Netherlands Antilles operated as an international financial center with a low tax rate of 2.9 percent on interest and profits for those companies registered as "offshore." The tax income from this sector was significant. It contributed 25 to 45 percent of the total tax receipt in the period from 1980 to 1983. According to the brochure "Parlement-onderneming kontakt" of May 30, 1984, the income from currency exchange (*deviezen inkomsten*) also impacted the economy positively, as illustrated in table 4.1.

Table 4.1

Income from offshore activities In millions FLS/ANG			
Year	1980	1981	1982	1983
Offshore profit tax	100	137	220	292
Currency exchange income	141	179	184	221
Total income	241	316	404	513

Source: Adapted from *Thesis* by Melinda Whyte
(De Offshore Sector op Curaçao, 1985)

During those years, the offshore sector in Curaçao employed about 1,300 individuals. This meant additional payroll tax and other employment-related contributions for the government.

The offshore sector, as Nicholas J. Braham (1992)[1] observes, is a unique industry driven by market forces in such a way that government intervention can be avoided. Interestingly, with the Netherlands Antilles, it was the tax structure and the tax regulations that made this industry a success. The tax treaty between the Netherlands Antilles and the United States was instrumental in the development of the Netherlands Antilles Eurobond[2] finance companies. Utilizing this treaty, US corporations were able to borrow funds outside the US at a cheaper rate until the 1984 Tax Reform Act put an end to this. The financial sector consists basically of two different kinds of activities:[3] those of trust companies managing offshore companies and those of offshore bankers doing financial transactions like lending, pre- and post-export financing, import financing, and money-market deals. The treaties, especially with the UK and the US, were of interest for international fiscal planning with regard to real-estate companies, royalty companies, building and finance companies, and shipping companies.

The requirements for success as a financial center include an accommodating tax base that entices a company to establish a subsidiary or division in the country, and tax treaties that would help businesses and individuals who operate through an offshore company to avoid double taxation and at the same time take advantage of the lower taxes. The double-taxation treaty would be especially important for companies and individuals who come from a country with a citizenship—or residency-based taxation system. Countries using the residency basis levy taxes on residents' domestic and foreign source income, while those with a citizenship basis allow taxes to be levied worldwide based on citizenship. The Antillean islands levy taxes on a territorial basis. Territorial income tax is paid only on income sources from within the country.

To complement the low taxes and double taxation treaty, the country with the financial center needs to display a degree of sophistication. The country's competitive strength as a financial center is enhanced through the degree of professionalism and sophistication present. Details of the package that is offered to companies abroad include the following:

- political and economic stability
- attitude of the country to lower taxes for business
- other taxes and fees
- prospects for continued freedom from taxation
- tax treaties
- exchange controls
- ability to conduct substantial business activities
- convenient cost of incorporation
- liberal corporation laws
- up-to-date transportation and communication
- banking and professional facilities

Evidently the growth in income shown in the table as income from offshore activities was a direct result of the fit of this sector with the needs of the firms registered on the islands. These supply-side factors reflect indices of competitiveness that are determinant for attracting foreign direct investments and guaranteeing potential exports.[4]

By 1985, the US government unilaterally revoked the double-taxation treaty with the Netherlands Antilles. This was as a reaction to the loss of important tax income due to the growing tendency of domestic companies to use tax havens. Across the ocean, the Netherlands, notwithstanding the fact that it had a territorial base for taxation, revised its tax system to introduce a "tax arrangement for the kingdom" in 1984 with a residence-based withholding tax on corporations and individuals who were residents of the Netherlands to stop possible abuse and tax avoidance by locals. Dutch companies registered in the Netherlands Antilles as an offshore paid a 5 to 7 percent withholding tax on income generated at the source.

By the end of the decade and after the introduction of the euro as common currency in 1992, new directives by the Economic and Financial Affairs Council of the European Union (ECOFIN) set major restrictions on the use of offshore centers that act as tax havens. These restrictions and the revocation of the tax treaty made, according to the World Bank, the share of the government revenue of the Netherlands Antilles accounted for by the offshore sector drop from 60 percent in 1986 to below 20 percent in 1999; related contributions to foreign exchange fell from 27 to 14 percent of gross domestic product (GDP) during this period.

Petroleum-Refining Sector

The uncertainties in the petroleum industry at the beginning of the decade due to the posturing of PDVSA in Venezuela vis-à-vis foreign companies and the active role of OPEC as a new player globally led Exxon and Shell to react with strategic moves, closing the refineries on the two islands in 1985. This affected thousands of families. In Curaçao, about 2,000 families were immediately affected, and another 5,000 working in related industries and supplying sectors were indirectly affected. The Aruba story is similar. The closing of the refinery in Aruba ended up with 1,300 people working directly with the refinery losing their jobs as well as an estimated 6,000 to 7,000 people who were indirectly employed with the company through contractors.

This led to major societal dysfunction and disruption on the two islands. The loss in foreign exchange and tax revenue caused a drastic fall of about 25 percent in the GDP for Aruba. The World Bank estimated in 2001 that the accumulated effects of these problems, which contributed to a lasting recession, as an equivalent of at least 20 percent of GDP for the Netherlands Antilles. According to the World Bank: "the country of the Netherlands Antilles was able to maintain its fixed exchange rate without sudden internal economic disruptions thanks to the cushioning effect of additional financial aid from the Netherlands, spontaneous emigration, a drop in international reserves, an increase in domestic debt and arrears, and reduced outlay for the maintenance of public assets."[5]

Aruba Status Aparte

Aruba's secession from the Netherlands Antilles in 1985, withholding its portion of the tax revenue in the budget and taking its share in central-bank reserves, affected the economy of the islands remaining in the Netherlands Antilles. Aruba gained total control over its economy, which required building new institutions to run the government, introduce a new currency, staff its own central bank, and deal with the closing of the refinery that left many people without an income. The Aruba government introduced the islands' own monetary system and an Aruban florin pegged to the US dollar at AFL 1.79 to $1. Aruba from here on has determined its own monetary policies. The Aruba central bank supervises the sound development of the banking and credit system, issues bank notes on behalf of the government, acts as a banker for the government, and functions as central exchange bank.

The new nation-state of Aruba adopted all of the social legislation that was in place in the Netherlands Antilles before its departure and recuperated the economy from the recession fairly quickly by giving tourism a major emphasis. In this process, much attention was given to language development and culture appreciation. The west/northwest section of the island had become almost completely dedicated to tourism. The Aruba government decided to lease the refinery plant years later to Coastal, an independent oil company.

Slowly the political economy of Aruba becomes less intertwined with that of Curaçao and the other islands. To support the tourism-centered economy, the Aruba government acted as guarantor for the financing of an increasing number of hotel rooms to attract luxury tourism and for deregulating air traffic. Article 1.20 of the Aruba constitution states that "education may be freely given . . . and may be freely received, and that private primary education that satisfies the conditions laid down by Land Ordinance shall be financed from public funds according to the same standards as public education."[6]

Solidarity fund

With the departure of Aruba from the Netherlands Antilles political union in 1985, the three "countries" (Netherlands, Aruba, and the Netherlands Antilles) negotiated and agreed to a solidarity fund, with the Antillean[7] government contributing 45 percent, Aruba 25 percent, the Netherlands 20 percent, and Sint Maarten 10 percent. The purpose was to alleviate budgetary problems in the smaller economies of Saba, Saint Eustatius, and Bonaire.

Industry Protection

In the period from 1984-1986, the central government of the Netherlands Antilles introduced stiffer industry-protection measures with the goal of achieving more import-substitution and import-competing activities as well as activities to boost outright exporting. As the economic situation became more dire, the government of the Netherlands Antilles introduced protective measures to boost local manufacturing and production for import substitution and outright exporting.

This approach was abandoned in the early 1990s, allowing, as Hellen Chirino-Roosberg reported in 1992, "protected companies to waive their protection rights acquired under the 1986 protection scheme, which was focused mainly on import-substitution, in exchange for export incentive protection under the 1991 scheme."[8]

The Windward Islands

In the Windward Islands, there was a rather fast growth in the tourist industry. The growth was stimulated by foreign investment in hotels and an accompanying increase in air transportation. This development attracted a great number of foreign workers to especially Sint Maarten, and between 1980 and 2000 the population grew by 60 percent. The 1980s and 1990s were also characterized by the growing efforts by Saba and Saint Eustatius in the Eastern Caribbean, focusing on niche markets. Saba, for instance, for a while exported a service catering to the Dutch driving-permit market, and later focused on the offshore medical-school market.

In the specific case of Saba, the island's population grew by 60 to 70 percent with the introduction of the medical-education institute. Such economic activity obviously had spin-offs to other commercial activities and made the island less dependent on solidarity-fund injections. Saint Eustatius also established offshore medical-training facilities, creating a degree of diversification in the economy with expansion in the oil-terminal activities.

1990s

Results of a referendum held in 1993 showed that the peoples of the Dutch Leeward Islands and the Windward Islands wanted to remain in the Netherlands Antilles political union. This was especially important since the central government was financed by the tax revenues from the participating Islands, and Curacao which contributed close to 75 percent to the union was facing a loss of offshore income and sharply reduced income from tourism from the southern mainland and reduced income with the changeover from SHELL to PDVSA. The islands decided to introduce an indirect tax, the Algemene Besteding Belasting (ABB), in Bonaire and Curaçao and a turnover tax in Sint Maarten, but two major hurricanes in 1995 and 1999 had a devastating effect on the economy of Sint Maarten and the two other Windward Islands, Saba and Saint Eustatius, adding pressure on the already fragile economy of the political union.

Halt in Economic Growth

The 1990s showed, more than any period before, a halt in the economic growth of the Leeward Netherlands Antilles. The crisis was so severe that the government of Curaçao—and as a result, the central government—not receiving sufficient revenue, could often not comply with its liabilities and had to instate a costly early-retirement and layoff program. This had a direct effect on many firms supplying the government and took the country into a deep recession, with unemployment rising out of proportion to more than 17 percent of the labor force. Many emigrated to the Netherlands, and it is estimated that the Curaçao population shrunk from approximately 150,000 in 1990 to about 130,000 by the end of the decade. The population in Bonaire seems to have declined from 15,000 in the midnineties to about 10,000 by the end of the decade. Sint Maarten, by contrast, experienced continued growth, with both legal and undocumented immigrants more than doubling the number of people on the island.

Restructuring

The International Monetary Fund (IMF) found that inadequate policy adjustments were the underlying cause of the weakening economy in the Leeward Islands. Because of fiscal imbalances, most of the financial resources available to the economy were being absorbed and left little room for investment in education and infrastructure.[9] The conclusion was that the old base of the economy had eroded and a restructuring of the economy was necessary. This was evidenced by the decline in employment in the oil sector in Curaçao and the reduced tax earnings from the offshore sector.

The restructuring, a medium-term effort, was to be based mostly on a supply-side economics premise, which involved the following:

- changing the emphasis of revenue collection from direct toward indirect (turnover) taxes
- increasing flexibility in the labor conditions
- privatization of government owned utilities

- strengthening of the business environment in the financial sector
- renewed focus on export

The turnover tax in the Windward Islands and the revenue tax in the Leeward Islands were adjusted to help the government regain some of the income it had lost. Furthermore, a new tax, the AVBZ (Algemene Voorziening Bijzondere Ziekten), provided for funds to cover cost of chronic illnesses. Social-net provisions were introduced with the establishment of Reda Sosial to help alleviate poverty.

On the business front, a new fiscal regime (NFR) was introduced to sustain the international financial sector, and the Netherlands adjusted the Kingdom Tax Arrangement (BRK) that required holding companies from the Netherlands registered in the Netherlands Antilles to retain a withholding tax of 8.3 percent, which would in due time be transferred to the Antilles.

In this decade, the labor unions also forced some form of restructuring, demanding and obtaining elimination of the discrepancy in salary between males and females in the civil service and an increase in the salaries of civil servants by 14 percent based on loss of purchasing power due to inflationary trends that had not been compensated over a period of time.

Sovereign Debt

The Netherlands Antilles government was not able to solve the economic problems characterized by increasing unemployment and rising poverty by utilizing continuous issues of debt obligations to maintain aggregate spending. The new millennium started out with requests to the Dutch government for help. The combined debt of the Netherlands Antilles government to the public and to the Netherlands grew to approximately 80 percent of GDP. The Curaçao economy had deteriorated to the extent that it could not provide the needed support to the central government and the several islands as provided for by the statute. The Aruba situation was different, as at the end of the 1990s Aruba had a debt position of 34 percent of GDP and a growing economy.

The New Millennium

In the year 2000, Sint Maarten held a referendum to secede from the Netherlands Antilles. The outcome further threatened to weaken the income base for the central government. The government prepared several major reports in an effort to obtain financial support from the Netherlands to restructure the finances of the Netherlands Antilles. However, the sovereign debt of the Netherlands Antilles and Curaçao was close to 90 percent of GDP by 2003, and interest charges amounted to around 30 percent of the tax revenue since 2002. There was, additionally, fear of major capital flight and destabilization of the Antillean currency that would take the country into a deep recession. Instead of a financial rescue, the Netherlands and the Netherlands Antilles decided through referenda and round-table conferences on a complete restructuring of the Netherlands Antilles.

The outcome was that on October 10, 2010, Curaçao and Sint Maarten became autonomous countries in the Dutch realm, and Saba, Bonaire, and Saint Eustatius continued as a special municipality of the Netherlands. The islands of Sint Maarten and Curaçao, like Aruba, would not have to share their tax income with the other islands anymore. In the first five years, budget oversight was taken care of by a financial supervisory committee instituted by the Netherlands. An adjusted constitution was accepted by the governments of the various islands.

Reading

Understanding the Whole

The following is part of a keynote speech delivered by Dr A. F. Yandie Paula on the occasion of a prayer breakfast of the Asosashon di Industrialistanan Antiyano (ASINA) on Curaçao Day, July 26, 1987. Translation and publication sponsored by Maduro and Curiel's Bank.

The outlook of Curaçao's economy was none too bright at the end of the nineteenth century and during the early twentieth century. The island was poverty-stricken, and it remained in very poor circumstances, worsened by the world economic depression of the thirties. [Things began to brighten up only after the establishment of the oil refinery in 1915.]

News concerning the sad condition of life in Curaçao was widespread. The deplorable economic situation was known not only in the Netherlands but even in East India, where some Dutch subjects decided to organize a collection in 1912 on behalf of Curaçao. A moderate amount of money was also received from Dutch subjects living in La Guaira to aid the needy inhabitants. As there was no apparent way out of the difficulty, the local authorities encouraged emigration to Santo Domingo (Dominican Republic), Colombia, and Venezuela. Curaçao laborers also emigrated to Surinam during the beginning of the twentieth century to work in the construction of a railway.

Of far greater importance, as far as the duration of emigration and the number of laborers were concerned, was the emigration to Cuba during the years 1917-1937. But even that did not have the positive effect which everyone hoped for. The majority of laborers who left for Cuba could hardly provide for themselves or for their families, who they left behind in distressed circumstances. . . . Another negative aspect of the migration to Cuba was the neglect of agriculture in Curaçao, as the majority of laborers who abandoned the island were fieldworkers, even though Curaçao never had any worthwhile agrarian importance to the region.

The history of the economic development of Curaçao in the last century is in fact, the history of that [the Shell] refinery. The Shell expanded at a rapid rate and soon occupied a considerable area around the natural harbor of Curaçao. The establishment and consequent activities of this economic oasis not only raised the importance of industrial life, but its influence was so all-embracing that it afforded new life and vigor to the existing commercial enterprises. Unemployment ceased to exist, because the refinery and other commercial concerns could afford to employ more manpower. The less profitable enterprises, such as fishing and moderate farming, were all abandoned in favor of the better-paid jobs in the industrial and commercial world. Graduates had no trouble whatsoever finding jobs in the industrial and commercial world. As Curaçao, or for that matter the Netherlands Antilles, was not able to supply the number of laborers required by the oil industry, thousands of laborers were recruited in the British colonies of the West Indies, in Madeira, in Surinam, and in Venezuela. A considerable number of "Europeans," mainly Dutch, were employed by the company and as a rule occupied supervisory positions . . . The city of Willemstad slowly and surely developed into a center where a large variety of luxury items could be purchased. In fact, the island became renowned as a shopping center, especially among the North American tourists . . . The decline of Curaçao's economy began in the [nineteen] sixties. During that decade, the refinery began to lay off people as a consequence of automation.

Chronology

1527	The Spanish settle the ABC Islands.
1631	Dutch West India Company settles on Sint Maarten.
1634	ABC Island transferred from Spain to the Netherlands' West India Company.

1636	Dutch build Fort Oranje on Saint Eustatius.
1640	Dutch settle Saba.
1648	Treaty of Concordia Sint Maarten signed between the French and the Dutch.
1790	The SSS (Windward) Islands are under constant Dutch rule.
1791	Dutch States-General assumes direct political control over Surinam and the Dutch Caribbean (from WIC).
1795	Slave revolt in Curaçao
1806	Francisco de Miranda occupies Aruba.
1824	Gold found at Rooi Fluit on Aruba.
1828	Curaçao central bank is established.
1840	Aruba concentrates on aloe production.
1862-1863	Slavery is abolished in the Dutch Caribbean.
1865	Popular representation is made law.
1915	Oil Refinery Curaçao is established.
1922-1937	The islands change from colonies to territories.
1925	Oil Refinery Aruba is established.
1942-1948	Constitution is revised toward complete self-reliance and freedom to conduct internal affairs. Administrative councils and general suffrage are instituted.
1947	The Antillean florin is fixed to the US dollar.
1951-1954	A new constitutional order brings an autonomy charter. Surinam and Netherlands Antilles administer internal control autonomously. Three countries make a commitment on the basis of equality to administration of their common interest and to mutual assistance.

1957	Treaty of Rome establishes ACPs, OCTs, and EDF.
1958	Multiannual plans for development assistance begin.
1960	Old-age insurance (AOV) is introduced.
1963	Protocol and double-taxation treaty with the United States is signed.
1964	General provision for widows and orphans is introduced
1965	Cessantia regulation is introduced.
1969	Riots shake Willemstad.
1977	83 percent vote pro on Status Aparte Aruba.
1983	The island of Aruba reaches agreement with Netherlands and the Netherlands Antilles for a separate status.
1984-1986	Manufacturing industry protection rounds established.
1984	Venezuela devalues the bolivar.
1985	Shell and Lago close.
1985	The United States revokes double-taxation treaty.
1986	In an adjustment to constitutional order, Aruba obtains separate status.
1986	Aruba central bank and currency are established.
1992	Review is conducted of Netherlands Antilles development aid policy.

1992	In the European Union, Netherlands is now member of a single economy and currency area.
1993	Referendums are taken to determine constitutional makeup of the five islands of the Netherlands Antilles.
1995/1998	Devastating hurricanes hit Sint Maarten, Saba, and Saint Eustatius.
1997	IMF institutes comprehensive medium-term financial and economic adjustment and reform plan.
1999	Euro replaces EU member state currencies.
2000	Sint Maarten holds referendum to obtain separate status.
2002	Alternatieve MedeFinanciering Organisatie (ANFO) offers incentives to NGO movement throughout the Dutch Caribbean.
2002	The Dutch Foundation oversees channeling process of Dutch financial aid. USONA is established as operational office.
2005	Saba, Saint Eustatius, Bonaire, and Curaçao hold constitutional referendum for change in status in the Dutch kingdom.
2010	A new constitutional order is instituted, involving a break-up of the Netherlands Antilles into three separate jurisdictions: Sint Maarten, Curaçao, and the special municipalities of the Netherlands: Bonaire, Saba, and Saint Eustatius.

1   Nicholas J. Braham, "Cooperative Laissez Faire" in *Free Enterprise in Curacao*, eds. M.F. Hasham and D. Dare (Curacao Chamber of Commerce and the University of the Netherlamds Antilles, 1992).

2   *Eurobond* refers to transactions in bonds issued in Eurodollars. *Eurodollar* is a term that came from transactions based on surplus currency available outside of the original jurisdiction. It started with the huge amount of US dollars that were present in European banks since the period of reconstruction after World War II and which could not be returned to the United States without causing undue inflation. Later, the term was applied to all transactions that took place with foreign currency available outside the original jurisdiction.

3   Henk Schutte, "Offshore, Free Enterprise, and the Role of Government," in *Free Enterprise in Curaçao*, eds. M. F. Hasham and D. Dare (Curaçao Chamber of Commerce and the University of the Netherlands Antilles, 1992).

4   See, for instance, Ganeshan Wignaraja's *Competitiveness Strategy in Developing Countries: A Manual for Policy Analysis* (Routledge, 2000). Focus of competitiveness is from a macroeconomic perspective. The book essentially looks at manufacturing export competitiveness indices. There is no real difference with what was required for the offshore business.

5   The World Bank. Latin America and the Caribbean Region; Netherlands Antilles; Elements of a Strategy for Economic Recovery and Sustainable Growth. April 2001;

6   Ger F. van der Tang, *Draft Constitution of Aruba*, established by island regulation of August 9, 1985; unofficial translation in *Constitutions of Dependencies and Special Sovereignties*, eds. Albert Blausteing and Eric Blaustein (Ocean Publications).

7   *Antillean* refers to Netherlands Antilles.

[8]   Hellen Chirino-Roosberg, "Market Protection, the Constitution and the Courts," in *Free Enterprise in Curaçao,* eds. M. F. Hasham and D. Dare (Curaçao Chamber of Commerce and Industry and the University of the Netherlands Antilles, 1992). The objectives for market protection included increase in employment, increase in level of prosperity, creation of know-how, promotion of healthy financing methods, saving foreign currency as a result of the import substitution policy, avoidance of dumping of foreign inferior goods, avoidance of products subsidized by foreign countries, and avoidance of total dependence on oil-refining. These goals were hardly met.

CHAPTER 5
MICROECONOMIC FOUNDATION

~⌒•⌒~

Economic models evolve as a way to describe and deal with issues in the economy that affect economic well-being. The models describe interrelationships as those between supply, demand, prices, and resource availability. This chapter highlights the behavioral characteristics in an economy from a microeconomic standpoint and as a foundation for macroeconomic analysis.

Introduction

The economic performance of a country is appraised by the perspective of aggregate results and what influences the results. The results are generally influenced by factors of a microeconomic nature. *Microeconomics* addresses the problems related to supply and demand, price-setting, market-efficiency issues, the behavior of the firm, competitive environment of firms, and consumer behavior. Microeconomics also looks at such aspects as factors of production and labor-market equilibrium. The behaviors in society, from a helicopter perspective, center around some simple but basic questions: what to produce, how, and for whom. In the aggregate, the answers to these questions determine success or failure with regard to economic growth.

The Choice of an Economic Model

Scarcity or alternatively abundance of resources or of factors of production—be it land, labor, capital, or entrepreneurship or a combination of these—play a role in the obtainment of a domestic standard of living level for countries. The objective of a country to upgrade the standard of living of society requires answers on how to tap the available resources, how to increase the productive capacity, and how to organize the distribution of production.

Although an answer can come as a result of pure external circumstances, as in the case of the West India Company (WIC) activities or the oil-refinery location in the West Indies through decisions made abroad, sooner or later inhabitants of a country find it necessary to answer questions like the following:

- What goods should be produced—tourism services, oil services, alcoholic beverages, economic-zone services, intermediate products, agriculture? Should a small island have a more diversified economy with many producing sectors?
- How will these goods be produced? Should it be through the government or through privately owned businesses? What technology level? A question relating to the first and the second point is whether certain protections or incentives should be given to any one sector.

118

- For whom will the goods be produced? Is all production for the people of the country? Who gets what and how much? Will production be mainly for export? Does everyone get an equitable share?

While the questions are answered individually by private citizens or firms, there is generally a tendency toward an economic system that prescribes a mode of behavior for the country with regard to the degree of private and public involvement. In the Dutch Caribbean, the first economic development plan by the government in the 1960s suggested the construction of technical schools to support developments in manufacturing. The various reports by the World Bank, the United Nations Development Programme (UNDP), and the International Monetary Fund (IMF) enhanced the focus on the development of certain sectors to promote growth.

Similarly, the industry protection measures in favor of import substitution instituted in the 1970s and 1980s signaled the direction that the government was promoting. Successive governments have cooperated with the private sector in the development of legislation to benefit growth in the industry. Recall that in the eighteenth and nineteenth centuries, the WIC made development plans for Aruba and Bonaire.

Economic Systems

Economic systems tend to develop gradually, and countries acquire a model that is suitable for existing aspirations. Most economies started as barter economies where goods and services were exchanged for other goods and services. This was referred to as a *traditional* economic system. There are times when more developed countries fall back on a barter system when there are market failures. It has happened, for instance, that Surinam offered to pay an existing debt to the Antillean Airline (ALM) in the 1980s with lumber. Of course, in this countertrade deal, ALM itself had to look for buyers to cancel the Surinam debt.

As countries moved away from the barter system and the economies became more complex, a debate arose as to whether these questions regarding what to produce, how, and for whom were to be answered with or without government involvement. The economic system that is shaped according to the laissez-faire free-enterprise system is known as a *pure capitalist system*. In this system, the market is completely free and without any government intervention. On the other extreme is the *centrally planned economy*. In this model, only the government decides what is to be produced. What is most prevalent in the world today is a *mixed economic system*, with a bit of government intervention in a free enterprise environment.

Free enterprise in Curaçao

Kenneth Abraham comments that the concept of free enterprise in the simplest meaning of the word is that the individual in the economic system has the freedom to start whichever economic activity he or she desires. "Free enterprise," he continues, "also entails that, once an enterprise is established, the entrepreneur can in principle determine the nature and size of his/her production by him/herself. A market mechanism creates order in the economic activities, and in principle, production of goods and services takes place in companies owned by private individuals. Everyone is basically free to develop an activity. On the other hand a number of vital production enterprises are the property of the State like the Utilities, the Telecommunication Services, and the Dry Dock Company."[1]

Market

The market mechanism mentioned by Abraham refers to the interaction between what is supplied and what is purchased that happens through a market that is formed by the buyers and the sellers of a good or service. The markets could be highly organized or less organized and even sporadic, where the buying and selling only occurs once in a while. Markets could be highly competitive, with many sellers and many buyers. In this case, the suppliers and demanders have individually very little impact on the price in the market.

Markets could be, in principle, perfectly competitive when the goods offered for sale are identical and the buyers and the sellers are too many to influence the price. In certain economic sectors of the Dutch Caribbean, such as retail trade, some areas of the financial services, and personal services, near-perfect competition seems to exist, with many buyers and sellers and the easy possibility of entry for new firms. The automobile retail sector, for instance, shows a high level of competitiveness, with a number of car dealers making cars of all makes available to the buying public. Individuals are also free to import used cars from abroad. Generally, under these conditions, none of the firms has a direct influence on the market and the price of the products. The freedom given to firms and/or the government in the market often leads to structures that can have great influence on the economy and can lead to an environment where certain aspects of economic activities are determined or at least heavily influenced by firms in the marketplace.

Markets can also be noncompetitive. With monopolies, where one firm supplies the market, that firm dictates what is produced and sold as well as the price. Such a structure can exist in a free-market system or in a mixed economy, while in a command economy it is generally the standard. There are several such monopolies in the Islands. Some are owned by the government and some are privately owned.

Mixed Economy

The mixed-economy system can develop with more leaning toward the free-enterprise system, with moderate government intervention. The public sector takes responsibility in those areas where the government considers that the private sector falls short.

In most countries, street lighting, police and military protection, and infrastructure development (like streets, highways, drainage, and sewerage) are provided centrally. These are public goods and can generally not be left to the initiative of individual investors. In addition, governments play an increasing role in the provision of goods and services that were provided at one time by organizations outside the public sector. Government has an increasing involvement in health care, formal education, housing development, water, and electricity production. These goods and services are referred to as *merit goods*, as they are important in the social and economic development of the country.

When companies representing an industry of great importance to the economy are failing and there is limited local capability to finance the continuation of an otherwise viable industry, governments in the Dutch Caribbean islands tend to fill the gap by taking over the failing company. This has been the case in the water and electricity distribution industry, the refinery industry, the dry-dock metallurgy industry, the air and sea transport industry, and the telecommunication industry, including television broadcasting. The intervention by the public sector is said to be due to market failures. These industries generally consist of just one firm (monopolies) or very few firms (oligopolies) and could in principle be privatized in due course.

Command Economies

With centrally planned economies, the government decides on what to produce, how to produce, and for whom to produce. There are two visible trends. One is where the country has embraced principles of Communism, instituting a central command regarding political economic issues, with examples like the People's Republic of China, the Soviet Union, and Cuba.

Nowadays, this approach, which is considered totalitarian, is slowly being relaxed toward a more pragmatic approach allowing more freedom of enterprise in selected areas.

There is also a trend in the opposite direction nowadays, with countries that previously adhered to a free-market system displaying tendencies to give government a stronger role in the planning and execution of economic activities by introducing socialist principles. This seems to be the case in several Latin American states, such as Ecuador, Venezuela, and Bolivia.

Scarcity in Resources

Notwithstanding the presence of free enterprise, scarcity occurs when the goods and services demanded are not available or supplied. Scarcity can be structural or incidental. It is structural when the resource that is used as a factor of production is not available and cannot be obtained in the short term. Land and potable water are not abundant on the Windward and Leeward Islands. Desalinated water using common procedures is expensive and, as an example, makes large-scale agricultural production uncompetitive vis-à-vis imports if applied in this sector.

It is incidental when scarcity, as related to the product, results from a decision by domestic suppliers to reduce the availability of certain products in the market because of a conflict, for instance with the government. Or local suppliers may not have the needed contact, communication, and ways of transporting goods produced abroad to provide for the domestic market.

This occurs notwithstanding the existence of demand. And there can be, additionally, a mismatch due to the price. The price at which the product and service is available may be out of reach for the consumer, so the items are not produced or imported and supplied in the domestic market. Labor and financial capital may be abundant, but market idiosyncrasies can turn them into scarce resources. People striving for desk jobs may not feel attracted to menial jobs even when the wages are higher for the latter. Or, despite a surplus of idle capital in the bank, many entrepreneurs still cannot obtain financing for perhaps profitable undertakings due to, for instance, lack of information.

Having an abundance of resources like mineral deposits does not mean that the country has the ability to use these resources to produce products and services to match market demand and generate economic growth to provide an adequate standard of living across the population. Some countries can achieve a level of well-being without having some of the required resources. As an example, the Netherlands in Europe and Japan in the Far East became major exporters of products using minerals and raw material imported from abroad. This helped in producing an average income of sufficient size to create a satisfying level of consumption, material possessions, individual savings, and national saving that could be continuously applied to reinvestment in manufacturing of exportable products and services. These countries used available domestic entrepreneurship and labor resources to obtain economic growth.

Scarcity in resources compels countries to make choices of what can be produced and supplied domestically versus what has to be imported to respond to what is demanded, given that the country wants to obtain an increased standard of living for the population. In the absence of one or more resources, a country may import the missing factor of production and still use some of the available resources to produce directly for the home market or for export.

Price and Availability

The choice with respect to the use of available water for any purpose is dependent on the price and the willingness of the consumer to pay the asked price. The price also influences how much the supplier is willing to offer for the product or service relative to the cost of production. The cost of producing water through the process of desalination using large machinery and sophisticated technology is generally prohibitively high. Even where rainwater is plentiful and stored in cisterns, the land area available to produce for the market may not be sufficiently large to produce competitively.

The several uses of the same commodity influence the choice to exploit that commodity. Water is used for the production of alcoholic and nonalcoholic beverages, for general drinking and household purposes (hygiene and health-related), for industrial production, for agricultural production (such as growing tomatoes), and in the hospitality sector. There is demand for water from a variety of sources, and the lack of supply of this commodity from rainwater and deep wells literally forces innovative processes to convert seawater to potable water for use by the various constituents.

Opportunity Cost

If there is abundance in all resources, there is little need for hard choices. Air is still abundant and no one thinks of it as a resource. Although the islands are surrounded by water, potable water is scarce. The scarcity condition implies the need for choices to be made. If there is scarcity and X is provided for you, then there may be fewer resources available to provide Y for someone else. If an island uses the scarce land for hotels, industry, and residential purposes, there will be little left for meaningful agriculture. It means that you have to make choices; you may have to give up some things to gain others. That which you give up is called an *opportunity cost.* Opportunity cost is discussed in chapter 7.

With the domestic economy open to the rest of the world, much of domestic decision-making will be affected by factors external to the domestic economy. If the population of the island has a source of income or wealth, local demand for goods and services is matched with what is supplied in another country. This creates the possibility for obtaining a great range of items that could have otherwise been out of the reach of the population. At the same time, this matching may create imbalances in the domestic economy that cannot be matched by export of goods and services produced locally to the rest of the world.

Supply and Demand

This takes us to the question of how the demand and supply of resources can work toward the achievement of satisfaction of needs and wants in society and as a result toward a better quality of life. One can hypothetically state that the proper use of the internal resources versus the demand for the internal resources can lead to a condition where the two are in equilibrium. For instance, if there is a demand for labor for production purposes and the community supplies this labor, there will be a condition where supply meets demand. Generally, this equilibrium is achieved at a price to which the two sides agree.

Equilibrium of supply and demand

Supply-and-demand questions are observable for skills, jobs, money, goods, services, and so forth. In the area of tourism, the demand is for beaches, services, hotels, restaurants, nightlife, transportation, gifts, and all kind of leisure activities. The supply of those goods and services needs to match what the tourist demands in terms of price and quality. As we saw in the history chapter, the islands had to supply a combination of factors, like political and economic stability, convenient taxes, tax treaties, and so on to meet the demand by foreign investors in the offshore finance industry. This is similar for the tourism industry. The combination of services supplied is a necessary feature that enhances the use of the natural resources: sea, beach, and natural surroundings.

So supply-and-demand relates to the factors of production, to the economic sectors, to the products and services, and to individual wants and needs. Resources of an individual are time, money, and skills. If the individual does not have sufficient money (scarcity), this will affect how much he or she can demand or supply relative to the price of that which he or she demands or wants to supply.

Disequilibrium between supply and demand can exist from direct and indirect causes. For instance, the disequilibrium between supply of workers and demand for workers can be directly related to price issues or skill issues.

When the Curaçao Oil Refinery (now called Refineria di Korsou) started up the Built Own and Operate project (CRU) in the late 1990s to early 2000s, foreign workers were imported, seemingly bypassing much of the 15 percent of locally unemployed. The reasons most often cited were lack of the necessary skills in the short term and the competitive price of the foreign supply of labor. This was a direct cause of the disequilibrium.

Disequilibrium in labor demand and supply can also come about through economic activities that produce revenue but do not necessitate local input. With offshore medical education, both students and teaching staff come from outside the island. Supply and demand for these services is matched outside the jurisdiction. Such interaction is good for the island, as the new people will be making use of the retail trade, housing facilities, recreation facilities, and other services on the island.

The matching of supply and demand for domestic labor occurs in the latter sectors.

A mismatch between supply and demand of labor persists when the expected wages do not conform to the wages offered by the industry, allowing immigrants to settle for jobs at lower wages, closing the fallback position for domestic workers. This mismatch of domestic demand for labor and domestic supply of labor and subsequent substitution by foreign labor supply tend to have consequences for growth as measured in the national statistics, with locals unemployed or active in a shadow economy.

Theory of Supply and Demand

The theory of supply and demand is about how supply and alternatively demand react to price changes and how this produces a match between what is demanded and what is supplied.

Law of Supply

One speaks of a law of supply, reflecting the behavior of suppliers relative to a price in the market as indicated in figure 5.1. The higher the price shown on the y axis, the higher the quantity that suppliers want to offer. This is indicated on the x axis. Changes in supply shown as a positive sloping curve mean that suppliers are willing to supply more of a product to the market at consecutively higher prices. This is shown as a movement along the curve.

Figure 5.1 Law of Supply

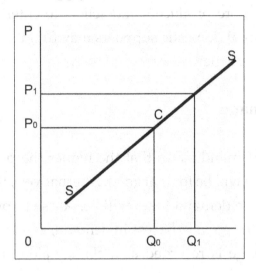

This law is based on the expectation that suppliers behave rationally. At a certain price P_0, suppliers are willing to supply a quantity Q_0 of goods. At a price lower than P_0, they will supply less of that good. At a higher price, more of that same good is supplied. There are a number of reasons for this. One is the scarcity of raw material, scarcity of production facilities, and the risk of not being able to obtain an acceptable return on the investment and operations. Looked at from the domestic suppliers' market perspective, there is also the price competitiveness with foreign suppliers and substitute products.

Take, for example, the supply of eggs to the buying market. Suppliers in general (domestic and foreign) are willing to supply Q_0 eggs to the market at a price P_0. They will not supply the same quantity if the price is lower than P_0. But at a higher price, say P_1, they will supply more. This happens on the assumption that their production costs do not rise in such a way as to wipe out possible gain. A higher price would often entice more producers and sellers to enter the market. Thus, additional domestic suppliers may find it interesting to participate at the new price.

Law of Demand

The law of demand states that the higher the price, the less demand there will be for that good. Alternatively, the lower the price, the more demand there will be. A rise in price from P_0 to P_1 causes the good to be less in demand, as shown in figure 5.2. The change is recorded as a change along the demand schedule DD.

Figure 5.2 Law of Demand

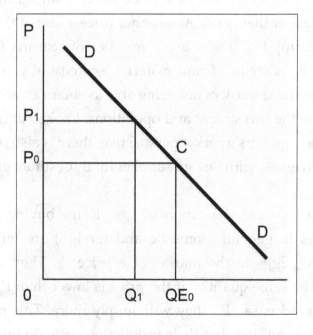

Interaction of Supply and Demand

The interaction between supply and demand tends to take the market to a point of equilibrium where the quantity supplied is equal to the quantity demanded at a given price. This is shown in figure 5.3 where the supply curve and the demand curve intersect at PE_0 and QE_0. The law of supply and demand implies that a change in price will cause a movement of supply or demand along the respective curves. Eventually these interactions will remain stableat one point, bringing equilibrium between the price of the suppliers and the price the market is willing to pay.

Figure 5.3 Supply and Demand Interaction

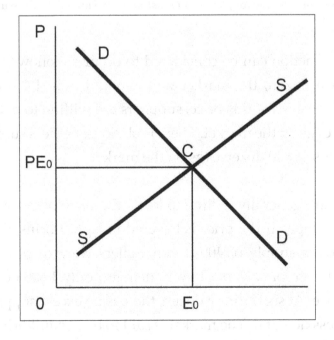

Referring to the example of egg production and supply used earlier in this section, table 5.1 shows how the demand and supply schedules interact.

Table 5.1 Schedule of demand and supply of Eggs

Example of demand and supply interaction		
Eggs price	Dozens of Eggs demanded	Dozens of Eggs supplied
florins		
10	1,400	2,200
8	1,600	2,000
6	1,800	1,800
4	2,000	1,600
2	2,200	1,400

This example is only for purpose of illustration, the numbers are assumed.

The interaction can be considered to occur as follows: At ten florins a dozen, the market will demand only 1,400 dozen eggs. However, at this price, suppliers are willing to put 2,200 dozen eggs on the market. There is obviously excess supply, or a surplus of 800 dozen eggs on the market.

Sellers are generally willing to lower the price because of the excess supply. If the price is lowered to eight florins, there is still excess supply of 400 dozen. Sellers want to place only 2,000 dozen for sale, but buyers demand only 1,600 dozen at that price. At six florins a dozen, there is no excess supply and no excess demand. The market is said to be in equilibrium. At a lower price of four florins there will be excess demand, or a shortage of 400 dozen eggs. At that price, sellers only want to supply 1,600 dozen eggs to the market.

Figure 5.4 Equilibrium supply and demand of Eggs

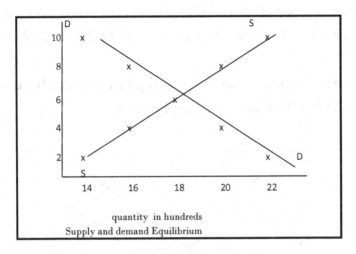

quantity in hundreds
Supply and demand Equilibrium

Shifts in Demand and Supply

If for some reason people decide to buy more of the same good without any substantial price change, a shift occurs in the demand schedule. The demand curve will shift to the right. This occurs often when there is a change in taste, change in income, change in expectations, or a change in the number of buyers.

Supply of a product or service also increases due to changes in technology and/or a lower cost of production. Suppliers can then deliver more products at the same or lower price without compromising their income. In such a case, there will be a shift to the right in the supply schedule at the same price. This could happen when there are changes in the cost of resources for the supplier. These events cause a shift in the supply curve to the right when it senses that the market can buy more of the product or service. Supply shift may also change due to the introduction of price controls by the government, or the introduction of direct taxes on a product, or changes in price expectation. The latter can shift the supply curve to the left if suppliers perceive lower demand due to higher cost of living.

Figure 5.5 illustrates a shift to the right in the supply curve.
Figure 5.5 Shift to the right Supply curve

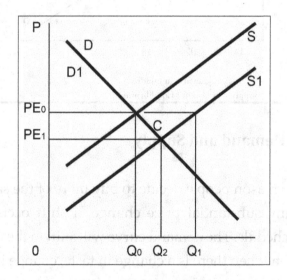

If increased supply occurs because of the reasons cited earlier and price stays the same at P_0, then the firms can sell quantity Q_1. But if demand does not shift out too, there will be excess supply, and eventually equilibrium is obtained at Q_2, where the demand curve and the supply curve intersect and the product/ service sells at PE_1.

Similar conditions apply when changes in demand occur due to factors other than price. If demand increases, the curve shifts to the right; if it decreases, there is a shift to the left. Figure 5.6 shows a shift to the left in the demand curve from DD to D_1D_1. The shifts may occur differently for individual subsectors within a sector, but the final outcome for the whole sector may be either positive or negative.

The introduction of a speedy and technologically advanced transportation system that increases ease and frequency of connection between the Dutch islands and Venezuela and Colombia can have several effects on the travel and transportation market. This new service brings about a relative change in total demand for transportation, boosting sea travel and lowering air travel some. If at the same time more regional business is generated, the supply curve of the different sectors that can use the new mode of transport will shift to the right. The demand curve for the airline business shifts to the left if the number of passengers and parcels declines. Under conditions of rationality, this will force the price of air travel down.

This in time will force a new equilibrium if the airlines are sensitive to the changes in the environment. As the number of passengers using the airlines diminishes, this causes a shift in the airlines' demand curve to the left from D to D_1. This is because the travelers want to purchase only Q_1 of airline tickets at the existing price. If the price stays the same, travelers will purchase Q_1 number of tickets.

Figure 5.6 Shift in Demand

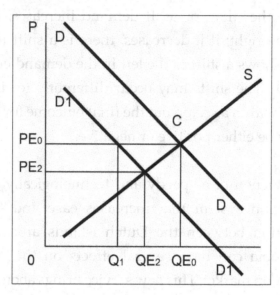

This mismatch between demand and supply is corrected when the price of air travel goes to PE_2. At that point, QE_2 tickets for air travel are demanded. For sea travel, a shift in the supply schedule occurs similar to the one shown in figure 5.5. A shift to the right occurs in the supply curve. Note that, in case this new mode of transportation increases the number of travelers in the country as well as exports of goods and services beyond past numbers, increasing the total income generated in this sector after subtracting the loss in air travel, this entails an expansion of production in the transportation sector. The topic of production possibilities is treated in chapter 7.

Price Elasticity of Demand

The interaction between supply and demand is affected by the degree to which demand reacts to changes in price. This is referred to as *price elasticity of demand*. Generally, goods that are seen as of more necessity to the individual are less sensitive to price changes. Products that are seen as of less necessity are generally more sensitive to the price.

The price elasticity of demand is expressed as the percentage change in quantity divided by the percentage change in price. If the result is equal to one, economists refer to this as unitary; if greater than one, the demand for the product is said to be price-elastic. If less than one, the product is considered to be price-inelastic. Price inelasticity occurs when demand is less sensitive to price increases or decreases.

Point elasticity

One method of determining elasticity is by determining elasticity at one point in the demand schedule. This is referred to as *point elasticity* and is obtained by dividing the change in quantity caused by the change in price by the change in price.

$$\frac{\text{Percent change in quantity}}{\text{Percent change in price}} \times 100 \text{ percent}$$

So in the numerical example used earlier to determine equilibrium, when price goes down to 8 florins from 10 florins, quantity demanded goes up from 1,400 to 1,600.

The percentage change in quantity is

$$(1{,}400 - 1{,}600) \div 1{,}600 = -.1250.$$

The percentage change in price is

$$(10 - 8) \div 8 = .25.$$

The point elasticity of demand, using absolute amounts and ignoring the minus sign, is

$$.1250 \div .25 = .50.$$

As the result is less than one, the price elasticity of demand is said to be inelastic.

Midpoint elasticity

By using a midpoint elasticity calculation, one can avoid the difference that may occur between a rise in price and a decrease in price when computing point elasticity. In the example above, the rise in price from 8 to 10 is 20 percent, and a decrease in price from 10 to 8 is 25 percent. So with the midpoint elasticity, the average of the initial and final levels is applied.

The following is an example illustrating the approach.

$$\text{Price elasticity of demand} = \frac{(Q_2 - Q_1) \div [(Q_2 + Q_1) \div 2]}{(P_2 - P_1) \div [(P_2 + P_1) \div 2]}$$

With the same example above, this gives, for the changes in quantity,

$$(1{,}600 - 1{,}400) \div [(1{,}600 + 1{,}400) \div 2].$$

The result is divided by the price effect:

$$(8 - 10) \div [(8 + 10) \div 2].$$

The numerator comes to

$$200 \div 1{,}500 = 0.133$$

and the denominator comes to

$$-2 \div 9 = -.222.$$

The resulting elasticity, using absolute amounts and ignoring the minus sign, is

$$.1333 \div .222 = .60.$$

Note that when the percentage change in quantity is greater than the percentage change in price, demand is price-elastic.

Income Elasticity of Demand

Elasticity of demand is also perceived with incomes. The perception with regard to one's income may change in the case of substitutes (with similar types or brands of coffee, teas, bread) or due to the amount of income available to spend or extra time available. For example, when income increases, this generally leads to more demand for goods. One can then determine the income elasticity of demand. This is expressed as the percentage change in quantity of a good purchased now and at a time before, divided by the percentage change in a new income to that of a point in time earlier.

For example, Antonio travels five times a year from Sint Maarten to Aruba. He used to make ANG 70,000 a year, but lately his salary was increased to ANG 80,000 a year. Now he intends to travel seven times a year. Is he income elastic or inelastic with regard to traveling? This is calculated as follows:

$$[(7 - 5) \div 5)] \div [(80 - 70) \div 70)].$$

If the result is greater than one, Antonio's travel decision is based on his income elasticity of demand. In this case, the result is 2.82.

It is also possible that although income rises (or the price of the product falls), the consumer spends less on a particular good. Such a good is considered in economics an *inferior good*.

Aggregate Expenditures

The economic behavior by the members of society is summed up in an aggregate demand and aggregate supply picture. Aggregate demand takes into account the overall spending behavior by all members of society. Table 5.2 shows a spending/consumption pattern per month for the microeconomy of an island with 15,000 inhabitants.

The data is solely for illustration purposes.

Table 5.2 Expenditures

Household Expenditures						
			Expenditures	Expenditures	Expenditures	Expenditures
	Number of Households 15,000		Average Household Expenditures per month	Aggregate Household Expenditures per month		Aggregate Spending per year 12
Expenditure Category			Forins	Florins		Florins
Shelter			938	14,070,000		168,840,000
Transport and Communication			832	12,480,000		149,760,000
Food			547	8,205,000		98,460,000
Clothing and Footwear			211	3,165,000		37,980,000
Household Expenditures			230	3,450,000		41,400,000
Healt Care			90	1,350,000		16,200,000
Beverage and Tobacco			56	840,000		10,080,000
Recreation/Education			313	4,695,000		56,340,000
Other			455	6,825,000		81,900,000
Total Spending				55,080,000		660,960,000

Adapted from Household Expenditure Survey CBS 2005

The items represented by the categories of expenditures are produced locally or imported at a cost that is generally lower than that which the consumer pays. The table shows average demand or expenditures by all members of society for various categories of goods and services.

The Factor and Product Market

In effect, there are two markets operating. One is the factor market, not shown here, where there is demand for and supply of factors of production like labor, land, and capital to produce and have available the various goods and services shown in the table above. The other is the product/ service market that regulates the interaction between those demanding and those supplying the final goods shown in the table. When the expenditures by the factor market are known, it is incorrect to add these to the data above, as this will constitute double-counting in certain areas. The way individual supply and demand plays out at the aggregate level is discussed in the next chapter, where I will also discuss how to avoid the problem of double-counting in the value-added statistic used to compute the gross domestic product (GDP). Consumption expenditures will be one of several expenditure components necessary to produce the GDP. For the purposes of this chapter, table 5.2 illustrates the demand for final goods, with the understanding that those products and services shown were supplied by producers of goods and services to the buying market.

Final Remarks

This chapter discusses the supply and demand concept and the obstacles on the road to achieving the major goal of an island-country of insuring an adequate standard of living for the population. People on the islands generally know the shortcomings in the economic environment and engage in certain economic behavior to overcome the limitations and obtain a standard of living within reach. This in certain ways constitutes a particular economic thinking that guides the economic processes, as shown for instance by the constant recurrence of international financial support.

While the population has unlimited wants for all kinds of goods and services, the islands often do not have the resources on their own to satisfy these wants and needs. The resources are capital, land, labor, and entrepreneurship. Scarcity requests choices in the sense that using a resource to produce X makes it difficult to produce product Y.

The exploitation of resources to attain an environment within which the people can satisfy their needs is contingent upon the interaction of demand and supply and to a certain extent on how the economy is managed. Demand and supply determine the value of a product or service in the marketplace. The lack of sufficient domestic entrepreneurs and capital is compensated by allowing immigrants and foreign direct investors to set up business, or by obtaining international financial assistance.

[1] Kenneth Abraham, from *Free Enterprise in Curaçao*, eds. M. F. Hasham and D. Dare (Curaçao Chamber of Commerce and the University of the Netherlands Antilles, 1992).

CHAPTER 6

MACROECONOMIC PERFORMANCE

In this chapter, the reader will obtain an understanding of the measurement of economic performance from several perspectives. The short treatment of value-added with the production approach to measurement provides, together with the corrections of market GDP to real GDP and the economic indicators related to business cycles, additional input to understand reports on macroeconomics and even perhaps do a quick analysis of how the current trends and events affect you. The chapter also introduces the Human Development Index (HDI) model as an alternative to measure the performance of the economy.

Introduction

This chapter introduces the concepts that are generally utilized for the analysis of macroeconomic performance. Topics to be discussed include:

- Measurement of economic performance from the expenditure side and the output or earnings/income side. This section also treats the value-added concept.

- The adjustment of the expenditure data to correct for inflation
- Introduction of the business cycles concept and economic indicators to create insight with regard to factors affecting or explaining the economic performance.
- The Human Development Index.

Measurement of Economic Performance

The system that records and measures the economy's output or overall performance is referred to as the *national income accounting*. The results are published in the Annual National Accounts (or Nationale Rekeningen). The broadest of these measures is the gross domestic product (GDP). There is a similar measure, the gross domestic income (GDI), which measures the incomes earned in the production of the GDP. A third way of measuring the national income is through the output or production method using a value-added approach. GDP measures output as the sum of final expenditures on consumer spending, on private investments, on government consumption and investments, and on net exports.

Measuring the Expenditures

The GDP can be obtained by summing up all the expenditures made by society during a year. This is generally referred to as the *fiscal year*. The expenditures concern all the purchases of goods and services that people in a country and others living outside the country demand. The list of goods and services at the end of last chapter gives an idea of what people spend money on.

Dividing up the total spending into components makes it easier to appraise and analyze how the economy is performing.

The components used traditionally are consumer expenditures (C), investment expenditures (I), and government expenditures (G). Since locals buy goods and services abroad, imports (M) are also an important component. People and businesses in foreign countries also buy goods and services, or exports (X), from the local economy. The latter expenditures are generally combined in a net figure, referred to as net exports (Xn), which stands for exports (X) minus imports (M).

Table 6.1: Components of GDP and GNP

		FLS
1 Personal Consumption expenses	C	200
2 Gross domestic Investment	I	150
3 Government Consumption/Inv	G	100
4 Export of Goods and Service	X	25
5 Import of Goods and Services	M	75
6 Income by local citizens abroad	L	75
7 Income of foreigners earned here	F	45

The GDP is calculated by summing up the amounts on the right, reflecting final expenditures for each component. The components numbered 1 to 5 are necessary for calculating the GDP. Component 5 is generally subtracted, as it represents purchases outside the domestic economy. As a result, the GDP from the data in table 6.1 would be

200 + 150 + 100 + 25-75 = ANG 400.[1]

The next measure is the gross national product (GNP), which measures the economic performance of the whole economy. As seen above, in calculating the GDP we did not take into account the income received abroad or payments made to citizens from another country. These expenditures are often termed *unrequited* transfers. By adding and alternatively subtracting these numbers from the GDP one obtains the GNP. So the GNP is made up of the GDP plus income received by the citizens of an economic unit for factor production supplied abroad, less income paid to foreigners for contribution to domestic output. The income is from property income based on dividends, interest, and profits, as well as the payments based on the same items.

Numbers 6 and 7 in table 6.1 are used to obtain the GNP.

$$GNP = GDP + 75 - 45 = 400 + 75 - 45 = ANG\ 430$$
$$GNP = C + I + G + Xn + unrequited\ transfers$$

There are exclusions and shortcomings in the preparation of the GDP and GDP measures.

Exclusions
Certain expenditures are excluded from the calculation of the GDP and GNP.

- *Transfer payments.* Transfer payments are excluded because they are not a government expenditure on goods and services of the current year. They are not payments for current productive services.

- *Interest on public debt.* Interest on public debt is also excluded. The argument is that it is a transfer and not a payment for current goods and services.

Shortcomings

Although governments try to include all items of production in the national accounts, there remain some shortcomings to GDP in the sense that some production is excluded from the calculations. Household production—the work done by homemakers—is excluded. Illegal production (drug trade, prostitution, and gambling if not legalized) is generally ignored in the development of the GDP. In the Dutch Caribbean, gambling at the casino and via the numbers game is legalized, and is supervised and counted in the GDP by the government. In the United States, more and more states are adopting state lotteries, and as a result this area of gambling becomes more and more controlled and a part of the GDP. The underground economy or informal economy does not report its sales; as a result, it is not included in the GDP. In many countries, it is assumed that the informal economy makes up close to 15 percent of total economic activities. It could be even more, considering the rise in the number of illegal immigrants as part of the work force, possible money-laundering activities, and part of the production by offshore business operating in the economy.

Net National Product (NNP)

By refining the GNP statistic, we obtain the NNP, which accounts for depreciation of a portion of the value of the capital available for production. The depreciation refers to that part of the total capital investment that is written off during the accounting year. One deducts this cost or depreciation from the GNP. The difference is the NNP._So, GNP = NNP + depreciation, which reflects the total money value of the flow of final products in the economy.

National Income (NI)

The NI represents a money measure of the overall annual flow of goods and services into an economy. Or, alternatively, it is the total income payment to owners of human and physical capital during a period. It includes both domestic and foreign income. NI also includes:

- production costs like employee compensation and net interest received by business, and
- profits, which are the corporate profits, proprietorship and partnership profits, and rental income of persons.

The NI is arrived at by deducting indirect taxes (sales taxes, revenue taxes, excises, and property taxes) from the NNP. The taxes are transferred from the private sector to government units. This results is the NI. In the Dutch islands, the majority of indirect taxes are from property taxes, turnover taxes, customs duties, and excises. In the special municipalities, the Algemene Besteding Belasting (ABB) or expenditure tax is used instead of the turnover tax or revenue tax, which is utilized in the autonomous islands.

Table 6.2 Earnings Income Approach

Determining GDP from the Income Side		
Fls xxx		
GDP 1999		4,819.3
Less: Primary Income paid abroad	180.7	
Primary Income received from abroad	217.3	
Gross National Product		**4,782.7**
Consumption of Fixed Capital	555.2	
Net National Product		**4,227.5**
Indirect business Taxes (less subsidies)	399.1	
National Income		**3,828.4**

Source: Adapted from National Accounts Netherlands Antilles 1996-1999
Central Bureau of Statistics

One can appreciate from table 6.2 that it is possible to calculate the GDP, GNP, NNP, after determining the National Income.

Earnings/income approach to calculating NNP

The income or earnings approach adds up the aggregate sum of final income from rent of property, wages, salaries of employees and income of self-employed, interest on capital, and profits. As with the expenditure approach, it excludes transfer payments like welfare benefits and private transfer of money.

To calculate the NNP, first determine the NI:

NI = W + R + I + P (or loss), where

W = wages of labor,

R = imputed rental income based on payments from use of property, housing, office space, license, and so forth,

I = net interest income, excluding government and household interest payments, and

P = income of proprietors and shareholders after paying wages, rent and interest.

Next, add indirect business taxes to NI, and this will sum up to NNP.

Adding depreciation to NNP will provide the GNP as a result. Consequently, to determine GDP, one has to take into consideration the effect of income received abroad and income sent abroad.

Output and Value Added
The national accounts also show GDP by sector, applying the output method. The output method has the additional advantage of making it possible to dissect vertical and horizontal relationships for further input-output analysis. Input-output analysis is treated in chapter 16. This approach presents the value that is added by each sector to produce the output for the year. In the table below, the International Standard Industry Classification (ISIC) scheme is used to present the proportion of value added at market price for the several sectors of the economy. The sectors in this table are grouped in a discretionary way to highlight the contribution by sectors to value added.

Table 6.3 Value Added by Sector

				Netherlands Antilles				Currency: ANG xxx xxx	
Value Added from 1996 to 2004				Proportion of value added by sector and year					
Neth. Antilles ceased to exst as country in 2010									
Year	1996	1997	1998	1999	2000	2001	2002	2003	2004
At market prices									
Productive Sector									
Agriculture,fishing and mining	0.01	0.01	0.01	0.01	0.01	0.01	0.01	0.01	0.01
Manufacturing	0.09	0.06	0.06	0.06	0.08	0.07	0.07	0.07	0.07
Electricity, water, gas	0.04	0.05	0.05	0.05	0.05	0.05	0.05	0.05	0.05
Construction	0.07	0.06	0.06	0.05	0.05	0.05	0.05	0.05	0.05
% of Total value added	**0.20**	**0.19**	**0.18**	**0.16**	**0.19**	**0.19**	**0.18**	**0.18**	**0.18**
General Services Sectors									
Trade	0.15	0.15	0.17	0.15	0.17	0.16	0.18	0.18	0.18
Hotels and restaurants	0.04	0.04	0.04	0.05	0.05	0.04	0.05	0.05	0.05
Transport, storage, communication	0.12	0.12	0.13	0.12	0.10	0.11	0.10	0.10	0.09
Non-profit and real estate renting	0.14	0.15	0.13	0.18	0.11	0.11	0.12	0.11	0.11
% of Total value added	**0.45**	**0.46**	**0.47**	**0.50**	**0.42**	**0.42**	**0.45**	**0.44**	**0.44**
Financial Sector									
Financial intermediation	0.19	0.20	0.20	0.19	0.21	0.21	0.20	0.21	0.21
% of Total value added	**0.19**	**0.20**	**0.20**	**0.19**	**0.21**	**0.21**	**0.20**	**0.21**	**0.21**
Social Services Sector									
Education private	0.09	0.09	0.09	0.08	0.09	0.09	0.09	0.09	0.09
Education government	0.00	0.00	0.00	0.00	0.00	0.00	0.00	0.00	0.00
Health and social work private	0.07	0.06	0.06	0.07	0.08	0.09	0.08	0.08	0.08
% of Total value added	**0.17**	**0.15**	**0.15**	**0.15**	**0.18**	**0.18**	**0.17**	**0.17**	**0.17**
Total value added	**4005.4**	**4097**	**3884.3**	**3885.4**	**3647.7**	**3822.2**	**3848.5**	**4005.3**	**4121.5**

After calculating the value added, add taxes less subsidies on products and then subtract indirectly measured financial intermediation to obtain GDP.

Avoidance of double counting

When using the output method, caution is taken to avoid double-counting in the determination of the GDP by insuring that expenses that appear on the income statements of firms doing business with each other are not stated more than once.

The following example shows the phases of production and sales of johnnycakes. Each phase is carried out by another company. The wheat is imported and turned into flour locally. As we can see, domestic value-added starts with turning the imported wheat into flour. In this process, the financial value reflected by the price paid, indicated as sales receipts, is turned into economic values. There is in the first phase an amount that is paid abroad where local currency escapes our economy. In the expenditure approach, this amount is included as import.

The process that takes place to convert wheat into flour is shown by the sales receipt of 11 cents. What was paid to buy the wheat abroad is entered at the intermediary level as 8 cents. Consequently, there is a value added of 3 cents at that point in the process.

This would be different if wheat was produced locally. Imagine that the Maishi Chiki (sorghum is a local produce) is used in the process. Then we would start off with 8 cents as value added. The company processing the flour into dough bought the flour for 11 cents but charges 20 cents to the firm that is going to bake the bread or johnnycake. So, by subtracting all intermediary values from the total sales receipts in the process, without considering the balance of payments effect, we obtain a total value added of 32. If wheat was cultivated and processed domestically, *ceteris paribus*, the value added would have been 40, which makes the case for greater attention to lowering the cost of imports in selected areas. Net value added represents GDP at factor cost.

Table 6.4 Value-added Calculation

	Sales Receipts	Intermediate Products	Value Added
Totals	**79**	**39**	**32**
Bread	40	20	20
Dough	20	11	9
Flour	11	8	3
Wheat	8	0	0

The value-added process of measuring GDP performance creates insight into what contributes more toward total sales receipts and to net value added by industry. A very short chain—with, for instance, the direct import of cars or other items by the end-user—will contribute little to a trickle-down effect in national value added, although it does contribute to the satisfaction of the buyer. Of course, if the imported item needs further processing (taxes, repairs, and so on) after importing, some direct economic value is attached.

If a large part of the value added is based on wages, profits, rent, and interest income, any further multiplier effect will depend on the way this income is spent in the economy. If income is plowed back through new domestic investments and economic activities, the effects will bring a horizontal multiplier effect due to the lateral investments. If income is saved with local financial intermediaries and is used (in a second round) for domestic investments (loans), this will also have a further positive effect on economic growth. The income received directly from these transactions could alternatively be saved abroad or invested in economic activities abroad. This will happen if there are no apparent worthwhile investment opportunities domestically. In this case, until these sums and the accumulated interests and dividends are repatriated, the economic impact of these activities occurs abroad.

Correcting for Inflation

This section concerns one of the aspects that can bring imbalance in economic performance affecting the equilibrium between supply and demand.

Real GDP

GDP is generally recorded at nominal or market prices. With inflation, the purchasing power of a florin decreases. To correct for inflation in the determination of the GDP, countries use a GDP deflator or the consumer price index (CPI). The resulting figure is referred to as constant (GDP) florins or real (GDP) florins. The CPI is calculated for the goods that are relevant for consumer, investment, and government spending on goods and services.

Governments often use an implicit GDP deflator. This deflator reflects both changes in prices and changes in the composition of output, and it is generally referred to as an *implicit price index* because it is derived from estimates of real and nominal GDP. The CPI measures the price change for a fixed market basket of goods and services of constant quantity and quality purchased for consumption. The samples and weights are updated periodically to reflect changes in consumer spending patterns. The CPI is usually applied, with a base year selected for comparison purposes. See chapter 15 for a more in-depth treatment of the subject matter.

To compare the GDP for 2010 with that of a base year—in this case, the base year is 2009—we deflate the 2010 GDP with respect to 2009 as follows:

$$\text{Real GDP2010} = \text{CPI (or GDP deflator for 2009} \div \text{CPI current year)}$$

The CPI for the base year 2009 is 100. If nominal GDP of 2010 is ANG 4,500 and the CPI at end of 2010 relative to the base year 2009 is 115, then real GDP for 2010 is found by the following calculation:

$$(\text{ANG } 4{,}500 \times 100) \div 115 = \text{ANG } 3{,}913.04$$

If 2009 was not a base year and the general price level due to inflation and with respect to an earlier base year was, say, 110, then real GDP for 2010 relative to 2009 would be:

$$4{,}500 \times (110 \div 115) = .9565 \times 4{,}500 = 4{,}304.35 \text{ (rounded)}.$$

The CPI of the year in consideration is expressed in an earlier year's currency value. Imagine this was your take-home pay this year. It means that the 4,500 you received can buy the equivalent of what you can get with 4,304.35 last year.

Business Cycles and Economic Indicators

For those trying to appraise the performance of the economy, the knowledge of business cycles provides some support. A business cycle portrays GDP results at several points in time, which gives us a way to interpret the current condition of the economy. The GDP is shown as a series of consecutive data on a trend line. If there is a trend upward, this is seen as a period of expansion. During an expansion period, resources are often overextended. This takes the expansion to a peak, after which the economy starts to adjust itself. Then a general contraction is visible. If this contraction is prolonged and deep—for instance, the trough occurs at a level of GDP that is way lower than the previous GDP and stays that way for a while—the country can be said to be in a recession.

Figure 6.1 Business Cycles

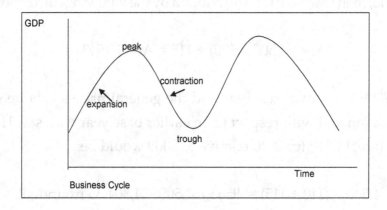

If the GDP declines for a period of six consecutive months or more, the economy is said to be in a recession. If the GDP decreases for several consecutive years and unemployment grows above 15 percent, this is considered to be a depression. The business cycles are typified by periods of expansion, contraction, peaks, and troughs.

Regular cycles

Business cycles[2] [] differ with respect to duration, intensity, and scope, and the cycles recur at irregular intervals. During expansion, employment generally increases and more new firms are started. In manufacturing, output would increase as production becomes more profitable. Interest rates are generally favorable, attracting people to invest. During such a period there tends to be much optimism, and consumer spending increases. Due to capacity constraints and shortages, the raising of prices and wages, and rising interest rates, the expansion tends to recede slowly as profit margins diminish. At this point, the economy starts to contract as production decreases pull employment downward. The mood generally becomes more pessimistic. During this period, there is a tendency toward more bankruptcies.

Economic Indicators

There are some useful indicators with respect to business cycles that help individuals, businesses, and governments understand the economic environment and perhaps foresee major changes. These economic indicators are usually divided into three types: *leading, coincident,* and *lagging.* They are selected and categorized on the basis of those features that impact the economy most or relate best to business cycles in the economy. The individual components of each indicator type can be grouped together to form an index of the underlying indicators.

If the changes in some indicators reflect a negative trend, one can forecast a recession; alternatively, one can forecast an expansion. As each economy is different, the strength of the indicators will also vary. In the next paragraphs, an effort is made to list a selection of parameters as leading, lagging, or co-incident indicators. Use is made of a mix of indicators from foreign countries, data from the central bureaus of statistics, and components applied by the Curaçao Chamber of Commerce to indicate the health of the economy.

Leading indicators

Leading indicators are, as one would guess from the name, those factors that occur before a certain trend is visible in the business cycle. They are useful to predict future economic activity. The following list contains examples of economic factors that can indicate ahead of time that changes can be expected in the economic environment.

- *Changes in the money supply (M2).* Money supply information is useful as an indicator of expansionary trends or contraction trends and is provided by the quarterly bulletins of the central banks.

- *Building permits requested.* Permits are available on a monthly basis from the office in charge of spatial planning and housing development. The number of building-permit requests gives a feeling for possible housing starts and construction activities in the future.
- *New order for consumer goods and durable goods.* These are found in the quarterly statistics bulletin published by the central bureau of statistics, and the data mostly reflect imports.
- *Changes in sensitive material price.* These could be found in price changes with regard to building materials; oil and oil products; water and electricity; communication and transportation; and consumer products.
- *Appreciation or depreciation in currency values of countries supplying materials and visitors.* An appreciation in the value of the euro vis-à-vis the US dollar has allowed more Europeans to travel to areas with an advantageous conversion rate and encouraged more spending. Similarly, depreciation in the value of the bolivar has had an influence on the number of tourist from Venezuela.
- *Changes in the rate of inflation* in the country of origin of imports and changes in labor cost per unit in trading partner countries.
- Changes in stock market data. In an economy where publicly traded stocks are prevalent, widespread changes in the prices of stocks will reflect expectations about future earnings and overall business conditions. Usually the majority of shares traded will come from the large domestic firms. Coincident indicators

These are factors that vary directly and simultaneously with the business cycle. Some examples are:

- *Employment.* This concerns changes in domestic employment, unemployment and the unemployment rate that provide an impression of the condition of the economy at each location on the business cycle.
- *Foreign-exchange reserve.* The foreign-exchange reserve is managed and policed by the central bank. Decline in the reserve indicates decline in the ability to cover short-term foreign indebtedness.
- *Trade balance.* A widening trade deficit most often reveals slow growth of the economy.
- *Trends in personal income spending* on durable and nondurable goods and services. Retail sales and automobile sales are important sources of information, as is consumer borrowing. A household-budget survey allows insight as to distribution of personal consumption expenditures.
- *Exports.* These include free-zone exports, container transportation services, tourist transportation services, and tourist accommodation services.

Lagging indicators

Lagging indicators are those factors that change after a new trend is visible in the economy. These lagging indicators generally are manifested four to six months after the beginning of an upturn or a downturn of the economy. Some components are:

- average duration of unemployment (an important measure to indicate how strong or how weak the economy is),
- ratio of consumer installment credit to personal income, and
- change in pattern of migration, emigration, or immigration.

Use of indicators

An understanding of the indicators can help business and government leaders track the business cycle and make estimations about the economic performance of the country in the future, and can assist in determining countercyclical measures. The government can calculate potential output by considering business-cycle characteristics and measuring labor input, hours worked, and productivity level. This is helpful in estimating potential GDP.

Businesses can track the business cycle to determine effect of employment, prices, consumer spending, financial markets, and international trade on their activities. Dutch Caribbean businesses can access, with some ease, data on employment, automobile sales, trade balance, consumer-price index, durable-goods order, housing starts, and building permits.

Most of the data is available from monthly publications by the bureau of statistics or from quarterly publications by the central banks and the offices concerned with physical planning and housing development. The central bureau of statistics conducts regular qualitative surveys to determine what the investment climate is like through opinions of individuals and business representatives. The Curaçao Chamber of Commerce produces a short-term economic review (STER).

The Human Development Index

The UNDP (United Nations Development Programme) developed the concept of a human development index. The HDI measures the wellness of the population in terms of education, health, and income. The index provides insight as to the capability of the country to be competitive globally. The index in that sense allows countries to compare their progress from year to year and against other, more developed nations.

The HDI[3] uses the parameters of education, health, and income to determine the internal capabilities of a country and allow comparison with other countries. Health is measured by looking at longevity based on life expectancy at birth. Education or knowledge is measured considering adult literacy rate and the combined primary, secondary, and tertiary gross enrollment ratio. Gross domestic per capita income is used as a proxy to indicate the accessibility to an acceptable standard of living. These parameters are combined in an index where a lower index score indicates that the country scores well on the requirements for growth. If a country is lacking in one of these dimensions, as reflected by the components of the HDI, it could make the necessary efforts to improve in this area. The HDI reflects the basic capability of a country to put in place those conditions that will enhance its competitiveness in world markets.

Although the HDI implicitly recognizes deficiencies with regard to variables like crime, housing, and poverty, it is possible to develop and integrate these factors with the formal HDI. The UNDP also produces the gender-related development index, the gender empowerment measure, and the human poverty index. These instruments can be used at the national level, regional level, and subnational level for analyzing policy, measuring progress, or promoting change.

Selected Rankings

According to Francis Vierbergen the Netherlands Antilles ranked close to Barbados on the HDI ranking in the "high human development" column[4]. Barbados appeared as number 38 in the "high human development" ranking, which goes from 1 to 70. Medium human development is ranked from 71 to 146 and low human development from 147 and up.

Summary

The chapter introduces the reader to various tools to measure macroeconomic performance. The first measuring instrument is the GDP, using the expenditure, income, and value-added approach. The GDP illustrates performance in a given year. A real GDP is calculated using the CPI or alternatively the GDP deflator. The real GDP makes it possible to compare the current

GDP with the GDP in previous years by factoring out the effect of price-level increases.

The understanding of the business-cycles concept and the use of leading, coincident, and lagging indicators enhances the performance analysis and the ability to forecast future performance or what can affect future performance.

The chapter also throws light on the HDI as an additional performance measure. The HDI uses national data on education, health, and income to determine the "wellness" of the population. This set of data also serves to indicate whether or not the country has the internal capacity to be competitive internationally.

---

[1]   ANG is used to indicate Antillean guilder or florin, the official currency of the Netherlands Antilles until the breakup of the union. AWG is the abbreviation for the Aruban florin. The US dollar is the official currency in the special municipalities of Bonaire, Saba, and Saint Eustatius. However, it is also a substitute currency in Sint Maarten. US dollar bills are accepted on all the islands as a medium of exchange.

[2]   Paul Wachtel. *Macro-economics: From Theory to Practice*; MacGraw-Hill, NY 1989. . . .

[3]   Gerald M. Meier and James Rauch, *Leading Issues in Economic Development* (Oxford University Press, 2004).

[4]   Francis Vierbergen, MODUS publication, 2011 by the Central Bureau of Statistics of the Netherlands Antilles.

CHAPTER 7

PRODUCTION POSSIBILITIES
AND GROWTH

This chapter offers the reader an indication of the link between the pursuit of production possibilities by members of society and the achievement of a national level of production that employs the available factors of production most effectively.

Introduction

Countries can make choices in the development of economic activities that, notwithstanding scarcity of natural resources, can still contribute to employment of the local labor force. These choices can result in a new or additional orientation and enhanced production activities in nontraditional sectors. The selection of production possibilities requires efficient operations in the areas of choice to increase the potential of the country to produce higher output. This is confirmed by increased gross domestic product (GDP) and increased employment.

There are a variety of influential factors at play in the process of reaching a production level that achieves full employment and GDP growth. Some of these factors are contingent on the type of political economy pursued by the country. This includes market vs. non-market price determination, competitiveness, and comparative-advantage considerations. Factors of a socioeconomic nature include the societal attitude toward self-reliance.

Economic Potential

Economic potential can be defined as a state in which the country experiences sustainable full employment of labor and capital at a level that promotes a degree of well-being to members of society. If this level is not reached, additional efforts are made to expand production. For instance, if there is high unemployment with GDP growth, this could imply that the GDP growth came from just a few sectors, leaving job vacancies in other sectors or regions. Or if there is GDP growth with a large deficit in the balance of payments, this shows shortcomings in international trade or negative effects due to exchange-rate fluctuations of the US dollar relative to other currencies. When the latter conditions are present, the country is not meeting its economic potential, at which it would be employing its resources, especially labor, entrepreneurs, and capital effectively and efficiently.

Production Possibilities

A country can develop its economic potential by using the available resources to produce products and services that can be traded domestically and/or internationally. The resources in most simple terms are the stock of capital; land and natural resources; and labor. The resources are, in principle, exploited using a certain level of technology. In that sense, technology is also a resource. Economic goals then will be to produce products and services while insuring that the resources are employed as fully as possible. This is appraised as increase in economic growth that gradually affords the population a sustainable level of comfort and standard of living.

The objective is to use capital efficiently and at capacity level. For labor, this implies attaining a level of production and productivity utilizing labor resources fully. The output produced will result in income sufficient to cover the cost of resource inputs and further allow distribution of income to those in society who cannot participate in the labor force. The savings in the private sector and in the public sector from the production activities should contribute partially or fully to support reinvestment in enterprises and in the physical infrastructure—roads, streetlights, airports, hospitals, and so on.

The production possibilities include all kinds of economic activity—the services and products that are sold in the market as well as the hotels, offices, and factories built and used for production purpose or for administrative and regulatory purposes. Infrastructure, government buildings, and government services are included as possibilities for achieving the economic potential of the country.

Each island of the Dutch Antilles offers a unique potential to develop suitable economic activities that make use of existing resources. A simple way to illustrate the suitability of economic activities is by considering a production-possibilities curve for just two products or service sectors. The production-possibilities curve concerns how much output a country can produce, given the way it uses its resources. The more efficiently and productively the resources needed for a chosen production possibility are employed, the greater the opportunities for economic growth and development.

Example

The following example illustrates a hypothetical production-possibility curve for a very small island. Imagine the island has a two-product economy of tourist services and fisheries, both of which are export products. The population is at about 2,000 people in the current year. The labor force is about 40 percent of the population. The production processes under these circumstances do not need any other resources than the sporadic pieces of flat land to build hotels and fishing facilities. For both these economic activities, domestic labor is used. The capital used is represented in the fishing boats and equipment for the fishing industry and by hotels, buildings, and facilities for the tourism industry.

The production possibilities for this island are with regard to these two economic activities. If the people decide to focus completely on tourism, they cannot fish for export purposes, because all capital and labor is employed in tourism. Alternatively, the island can devote all the resources and gear all its investments and operations to fishing for export. The results of these choices are shown in the production schedule below. The schedule shows choices and trade-offs between the two products at various production levels. The people on the island—the entrepreneurs—will make choices either spontaneously or in a planned fashion with regard to the use of the resources at hand to develop the economic potential. These choices are explained using the production-possibility schedule and production-possibility curve.

Table 7.1: Production Schedule

	Fish (tons)	Tourist (rooms)
1	0	2000
2	1	1500
3	2	1250
4	3	1000
5	4	500
6	5	250
7	6	0

So, if all the available resources are devoted to producing tourist services, the island will not produce any fish for export. Then it can provide 2,000 rooms to visitors. Alternatively, if there are zero rooms for tourists' services, this automatically indicates that the island cannot cater to any stayover tourist arrivals. But it can produce six tons of fish for export.

Opportunity cost
The production schedule pinpoints an important concept used in economic theory. Looking at table 7.1, it can be noted that if the island people decide to produce one ton of fish, they will have to sacrifice five hundred tourist-room service units because of the fact that some of those working in the tourist

sector will move to work in the fishery sector. This means that there is an opportunity cost of one ton of fish against the provision and servicing of five hundred tourist rooms, as the resources, in this case labor resources, need to be used in the fish-production process.

The country theoretically would want to choose the level, or combination of resources, that employs the available resources more fully. Additionally, it makes sense to maintain both production units, because it brings some degree of diversification that could support economic stability when slumping sales in one sector can be offset by higher production and sales in another sector.

The data on the schedule can be transported to a production-possibility curve showing the tons of fish that can be produced on the vertical coordinate and the tourist rooms on the horizontal coordinate. The negative sloping curve on the right represents the trade-off between the two products/ activities using all available resources. Or else, on that curve, all available resources are fully employed. Efficient production occurs when all firms operate on the production possibilities curve, which is also referred to as the efficiency frontier.

Figure 7.1: Production Possibility Frontier—Fish vs. Tourism

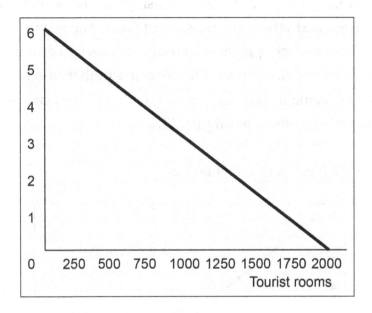

However, if the requirements for full employment of resources are not met, the country will be searching to introduce other activities that can increase its possibilities for attaining the economic potential.

To take this example further, the island in mind still has some people unemployed and is able to expand the production possibilities by allowing the establishment and operation of another basic economic activity. This generates spillover effects in the economy, leading to the establishment of other enterprises that cater to the expanded economy. In such a way, the island gets closer to attaining its economic potential. The expansion is instrumental in creating economic diversification with new sectors. The expansion can also require additional labor beyond the domestic full-employment level.

When the economy is not operating on the production-possibility curve, the trade-offs using the resources most effectively and efficiently are not obtained. The island is, for instance, producing eight hundred tourist-service units vs. two tons of fish for export. The economy in that case is most probably facing a recession, in that neither of the activities is employed effectively. See figure 7.2.

Figure 7.2 Inefficient use of factors

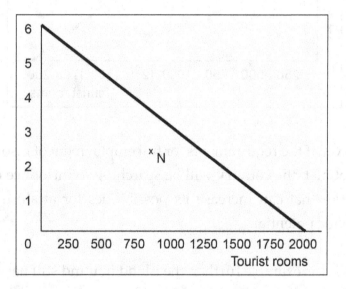

In the given situation, the combination of fish and hotel rooms meets at point N on the graph. At this point, the economy is not at full employment of capital and labor. The efficient combination would be three tons of fish and 1,250 hotel rooms, using the schedule of production above. So production has to increase. If it is not possible to meet the level of production that satisfies the efficiency criterion operating on the transformation curve, the country will be searching for alternative ways to obtain the economic potential.

The problems can be plentiful. There are not enough savings to turn into new investments and maintain employment, and the government is not receiving sufficient tax revenue for redistribution. In fact, if part of the workforce is employed by the government, this condition creates a budget deficit as long as it persists. The government may have to seek external assistance to maintain an acceptable standard of spending. Furthermore, if the island cannot find a solution to this problem by stimulating activities in basic sectors, it will most probably be facing frequent economic crisis even after incidental budget assistance from abroad.

One can conclude from the above that there is an output level, the potential GNP, that can be reached if enough activity can be generated to employ the applicable resources. Generally, a microisland will need, in comparison to a larger state, only a few midsize investments in a growth sector to create the environment for an increased and sustainable standard of living.

Figure 7.3 shows a selection of services and products to illustrate the ongoing pursuit to expand the production possibilities. It is possible to diversify the economy in any of these areas.

Figure 7.3 Employment of resources

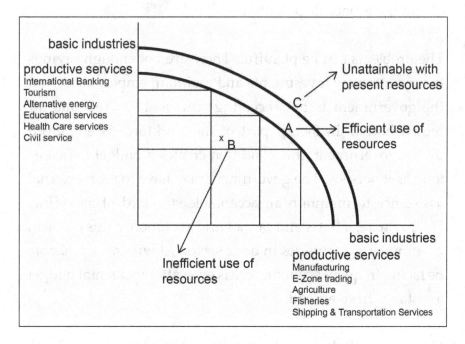

If the combined production and output of goods and services in the various sectors does not take the economy to the efficiency frontier, as indicated at B in figure 7.3, this is an indication that the resources, labor, and capital are not adequately employed. A reason could be existing indivisibilities with regard to capital goods whose costs are not recuperated, or underemployment of labor and equipment in the production of goods and services because of lack of market. It is also possible that certain industries operate as monopolies, dominating the resource market and consequently lowering opportunities for new investments in a sector.

When these conditions are present, adequate positive stimuli is necessary to get the economy to move in the direction of the efficient frontier. This can be achieved by attracting direct foreign investing or through upgrading the domestic processes, and government regulation or legislation to facilitate financing of local ventures. The most favorable outcome involves a shift outward in the production possibility curve, accompanied by additional production capabilities, expanding the economic potential.

Foreign investments are contingent on the investment climate and ease of establishment. There are many contrasting elements in a small island economy. A surge in investments in a sector that has as a consequence increase in demand for labor may require foreign labor due to the lack of needed skills that are not immediately available or developed among the local population. The economic expansion in the given sector can shift the current frontier outward with the utilization of the imported capital and labor.

As is observable on the several Dutch islands, one or just a few sizable investments in a sector quickly create an environment for increased standard of living. Although this can be the case, the economy remains fragile if the economic diversification is limited, lacking other industries that generate stable employment, foreign exchange, and tax revenues. A downturn in the business cycle affecting the growth sector creates new recessionary conditions, and this occurs now with a labor force that has swollen to a size beyond that of the pre-expansion level and possibly generating excess capacity in physical capital.

179

This constant pressure due to negative economies of scale and shortcomings related to home and foreign-market factors affects the ability of the small developing state to maintain long-run stable growth conditions. To get out of the apparent doldrums that take the nation from one crisis to another, the pursuit of economic expansion requires a positive attitude toward self-reliance by the population, especially in the private and public sectors, and a notion of the need and ability to produce at home and compete beyond its borders. Stable economic growth does not only depend on the improvement of the economic infrastructure, education, and investment financing, but also on the degree of self-reliance and willingness to develop the capability to produce, export, and compete abroad.

Self-Reliance

Self-reliance comprises the degree to which the residents of a country believe in the ability of the different institutions to contribute to the general welfare, by themselves or jointly, as is or with improvements. This belief is supported by a conviction that the island, as small as it is, can develop a production system that generates full employment. It does not mean that foreign investments are avoided, but that foreign investments and foreign financial assistance are used to fit the long-term goals toward a stable standard of living and quality of life.

There are a number of factors that can inhibit the feeling of self-reliance. One such factor is the time aspect of domestic circulation of the funds employed in economic activities. The cycles are fairly short, as a great part of domestic funds is quickly translated into foreign exchange and used to pay for imports. The islands generally import close to 100 percent of the goods consumed and raw materials used in production processes.

Another factor that can inhibit self-reliance and self-determination is the easy escape of know-how, creating a brain drain toward especially Europe whenever an economic downturn occurs. For those who do not leave, past experience and perception of smallness of the island can discourage innovative ideas. While the opportunity to leave and experience a higher standard of living somewhere else remains a necessary condition for the inhabitants of a small economy, a continuous and large-scale exodus leads to lower production and productivity. In the period 1998 to 2001, according to the International Monetary Fund (IMF) mission report of September of 2011, close to 12 percent of the population left the Netherlands Antilles. The positive net migration in the following years was mainly due to the influx of immigrants from the region, while unemployment remained for a long time at 15 percent.

Government and competitiveness

Government can play a major role in the positive stimulation of this self-reliant attitude, leading to an increase in productive capacity. An example is the several rounds of industry protection instituted in the 1970s and the 1980s in the Dutch Caribbean. These were with the intention of creating an environment conducive to import-substitution and outright exporting.

There are arguments that shed doubt on the ability of the government to attain efficient operations and adequate pricing

181

while operating in the private sector. One concerns the ability to operate without distorting the operational efficiencies through political pressures. The other concerns the (in)ability to allow the pricing mechanism balancing supply and demand to reflect the intrinsic value of a good or service.

The Caribbean Common Market (CARICOM) countries proposed in the 1991 West Indian Commission report that if the market participants have freedom to act, they will seek opportunities in the market, which would in a spontaneous way lead to the attainment of the economic potential of the country. The West Indian Commission recommended that for CARICOM countries to make progress, they have to "summon their determination to increase their adaptability, resilience, innovation, and international competitiveness; to be successful, governments should become less involved in the direct production of goods and services and concentrate on catalytic, facilitating, supportive, and regulatory functions, and that all parties ensure the removal of biases against and obstacles to export-led growth."[1]

This same thinking was voiced in 1776 by Adam Smith in his publication "An inquiry into the Wealth of Nations," in which he pointed to the fact that in a market economy, products and services generally appear spontaneously in the market:" as if guided by an invisible hand, and as individuals pursue their selfish ends, this will promote the wealth of society more effectively than when he (the person) sets out to promote wealth for everyone[2]" If people are out for themselves, they will work harder and produce more.

Efficiency and competitiveness

The efficiency referred to in the discussion of the production-possibility curve is gained from efficiency in production and efficiency in allocation. With *productive efficiency,* resources are used as efficiently as possible in the production process and so insure cost advantages that can be transferred to lower prices. With *allocative efficiency,* distribution is as efficient as possible, so that consumers around the world can maximize their utility or satisfaction by purchasing the products and services offered by firms in a country.

These efficiencies contribute to extra value for the consumers. As explained in microeconomic theory, efficiency is obtained when price and marginal costs are at least equal, or price exceeds the marginal cost. Marginal cost is the unit cost for producing an extra unit. If the productive units in a country can achieve increases in efficiency, profit can be maximized by producing and selling more units of the products and services. In principle, it should not matter whether a producing unit is owned by the government or not, as long as it can achieve the efficiencies mentioned.

Achievement of the economic potential by productive units

B.G. Malkiel and E.F Fama[3] and Jack Hirschleiffer describe efficiencies as a result of the pursuit of wealth by individual firms. [4]Firms, as explained for the whole country with the production-possibility curve, face a set of productive opportunities and will go after the ones that (for them) dominate all others. The production possibilities curve for the individual firms is expressed as a transformation curve between Time 1 and Time 2. Utilizing an example from Edwin Neave and John Wiginton 1981 will help us understand the wealth pursuit of the individual firm. In this case, the firm invests funds in Time 1 with the purpose of creating added value in Time 2.

Figure 7.4 shows the transformation curve, with K_1 representing funds available to invest in Time 1 and K_2 representing the value of the investment at Time 2. The productive set is constrained by a transformation curve that has a general form where $T(K_1, K_2) = 0$. The negative slope indicates that the transformation curve shows equal present values at each point. So an efficient investment occurs when the investment at Time T_1 equates with the corresponding value at T_2 on the transformation curve.

Figure 7.4: Transformation Curve

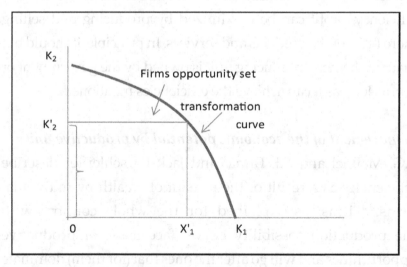

Adapted from *Financial Management: Theory and Strategies* by Neave and Wiginton[5]

In the figure above, $0K_1$ (read "zero to K_1") represents the current market value that a firm has in available resources. The firm chooses to use X_1-K_1 of the available resources to invest. This provides a return $0K_2$ when the resources are used efficiently as shown by being on the transformation curve. If the firm uses all the resources available, the value of the investments at Time 2 will be $0K_2$. This achievement of efficiency and increase in wealth by individual firms will be manifested as contributing to economic growth.

Comparative Advantage

If island states can be efficient in producing and distributing their products and services notwithstanding the typical distance from markets, this increases the possibility for an island to be better integrated in the world economy. To be successful in external markets, each island confronts the question of how to make use of or create competitive and comparative advantages.

The idea of comparative advantage is that a country is to specialize in the production of a good or service in a particular area, for export, if total output in that area is greater and achieved at a lower opportunity cost than if another product were to be produced. This allows that two countries producing exactly the same products can still trade with each other if there is a situation of relative advantage. In that case, both benefit.

Absolute and relative advantage

Assume that Country A can produce more aloe and more beer with fewer resources than Country C. Therefore, Country A has an *absolute advantage* in the production of both aloe and beer. This is not really the incentive for specialization. The incentive is, as explained long ago by David Ricardo[6], due to lower opportunity cost in production of one product versus another product. This creates a comparative advantage.

To compute opportunity cost, take the following example:

Country A produces 12 units of aloe products versus 5 units of beer. Country C produces 10 units of aloe versus 4 units of beer.

Country A's opportunity cost to produce one unit of an aloe product is through giving up 5/12 unit of beer (or .42). Country C's opportunity cost of producing 1 unit of aloe product means giving up 4/10 (or .40) units of beer. So Country C has a comparative advantage in producing aloe, as its opportunity cost of sacrificing on producing beer is less than it is the case for Country A.

If we use labor as a resource, we can state that if Country C can use less labor input than Country A to produce an additional unit of aloe, then it has comparative advantage in producing aloe. Imagine that Country A uses 4 units of labor to produce 1 unit of aloe products. Country C needs 6 units of labor to produce 1 unit of aloe products. With regard to beer, Country A needs 6 units of labor to produce 1 unit of beer, and Country C needs 5 units of labor to 1 unit of labor.

Table 7.2 Cost of labor input

		Country	
		A	C
Products	Aloe	4	6
	Beer	6	5

Although one country seems to have an absolute advantage over the other in the production of one of the two products, due to the lower number of labor input per unit, the importance is based on the understanding of the comparative advantage from increasing production in the areas in which each one has lower opportunity cost. Imagine that there is full employment and that no workers can be attracted from outside the country. Also assume that wages remain constant. Then, if country A wants to produce one extra unit of aloe, it needs to only add 4 units of labor. If A wants to produce an extra unit of beer, it will need 6 units of labor (attracting labor from the aloe sector). This relationship in the labor market where the production of an additional unit of aloe products in Country A is less expensive than for an extra unit of beer indicates an opportunity cost.

This can be expressed in ratios, as shown in table 7.3 for each country.

Table 7.3 Relative cost of production

		Country	
		A	C
Products	Aloe	4/6	6/5
	Beer	6/4	5/6

These ratios indicate the relative cost in the production of the two products. For country A, the relationship of aloe to beer is 4/6 < 6/4, meaning that the opportunity cost of producing aloe is lower for Country A. So Country A has a comparative advantage in producing aloe to beer. For Country C, the relationship for aloe to beer is 6/5 > 5/6. It follows that Country C has a comparative advantage in producing beer, where the opportunity costs of units used to produce beer to aloe are lower. So the country would benefit if it increases the production of the commodity in which it has the lowest opportunity cost and continues to do this as long as this discrepancy exists. This increase in production is regarded as specialization.

If Country A specializes in the production of aloe products, it does not stop Country C from producing aloe products, but people in Country C can benefit from importing the product from Country A where the aloe product has been produced more cheaply. It also shows at the same time that it is worthwhile for Country C to consider specializing in the production of beer. Even though A is also producing beer, the people on that island may find it less expensive to buy the beer from Country C.

With the pressures to grow the economy and the diversity of possibilities that exist in the global economy, one often does not have the luxury of pondering over these comparative-advantage thoughts. Rather, for private citizens and firms, what provides relative advantage (to establish) are those sectors they are accustomed to. Or the government provides incentives to a sector it considers a growth sector, generating revenues and employment.

Over time, relative advantages seem to erode with changes in the technological environment. Changes in the mode of transportation and lower cost of air transport have eroded the relative locational advantage Curaçao had in the past as a bunker harbor for ships traveling between Europe and Asia going through the Panama Canal. The increasing use of containerized shipping of goods with mammoth container ships changes the requirements of an island as an entrepôt or transfer harbor. The changes in the cost of air transport make every island more accessible to a foreign visitor, which widens the competitive environment and asks for a thorough search for ways to boost efficient allocation and increase specialization in the areas that offer a relative advantage.

Economic growth[7] is supported by the factor endowments of the country in labor and capital or through technical progress. If a country is highly endowed with labor, it will need to increase the production of labor-intensive goods and reduce the production of capital-intensive goods to maintain or affect a measure of economic growth. If growth occurs through capital-intensive production, this could lead to higher economic performance and higher per capita income, but not necessarily higher distribution of income that increases general welfare.

Another growth stimulant is technical progress that leads to an increase in marginal productivity of labor because of capital savings, as less capital is employed per unit of labor. Alternatively, there is labor-saving technical progress. As discussed earlier in this writing, the islands in some cases do not have sufficient skilled labor to develop a capital-intensive industry. Under those circumstances, the island will have to import labor to meet the demands of the industry.

Value standards

While the cost of living and concomitant price of goods and services can be relatively high in some islands, a comparative advantage and specialization in given areas as shown in the beer versus aloe example earlier provide an edge in trading. This is further enhanced if the market recognizes so-called value standards for the product or with regard to surrounding features. For the prospective buyers, it will be quality or other enticing features other than price that provide value.

The tourism sector is a case in point. High labor prices in many islands can act as a constraining factor lowering competitiveness with other islands and countries in the region. The relatively high level of personal income permits the importation of expensive foreign goods. The cost of living is translated to a relatively expensive proposal for visitors when compared to islands where the cost of living is lower, and reflected in lower cost of accommodation. Still, many tourists frequently return to, for instance, Aruba and Sint Maarten or buy property there. In Sint Maarten, for instance, the price of labor in infrastructure construction is almost 80 cents more expensive for every guilder/florin of a similar production or service in Curaçao. Still, the island of Sint Maarten receives a flow of long-term visitors who buy real estate at astronomical prices on the island. The foreign market obviously recognizes certain value standards, which helps the island to remain competitive. *Value standards*[8] are elements of a product or service that remain attractive to a buyer notwithstanding the price.

Comment

The above paragraphs show a set of aspects that are to be considered in the pursuit of achieving the economic potential of a country, which include exploiting the production possibilities that members of society can identify and, at the same time, determining and using relative advantages to boost trade. Coming out of a colonial system with foreign domination of the production arrangements, it takes time and effort to create and sustain new comparative and competitive advantages without a dose of self-reliance and determination to specialize to increase efficiency in production and allocation in selected sectors.

Reading

"Time for Action"

The CARICOM in 1991 produced a document for discussion and implementation concerned with deepening and widening the CARICOM with the objective of improving the lives of all West Indians. Deepening will be first of all with regard to the member states, where a community of sovereign states exercises the sovereignty in very specific respects collectively. Widening is with regard to wider cooperation with countries in the Greater Caribbean. The 1991 report of the West Indian Commission, "Time for Action,"[9] recommended that:

> In order to make progress in the conditions of today's world the CARICOM countries have to summon their determination to increase their adaptability, resilience, innovation, and international competitiveness

> Governments become less involved in the direct production of goods and services and concentrate on catalytic, facilitating, supportive, and regulatory functions, and that all parties ensure the removal of biases against and obstacles to export-led growth.

> The governments are to pursue sound overall policies which generate current account surpluses, avoid borrowing from the Central Banks, curb the rate of inflation to levels no higher than those prevailing

in their principal trading partners, advance systematically toward stabilizing a common currency and demonstrate an unmistakable commitment to the maintenance of parity of the currency

1   West Indian Commission Report/ Time for Action; 1991 CARICOM

2   Smith, Adam; Wealth of Nations; 1776. W. Strahan and T. Cadell publishers, 1776; Republished by Random House in 1937.

3   E. Fama and B.G. Malkiel; *Efficient Capital Markets: a review of theory and empirical work*; Journal of Finance 25 (2) p 383-417; 1970.

4   Jack Hirschleiffer; *Efficient allocation of capital in an uncertain world*. American Economic Review, Vol 54 No3 pp 77-85, 1964

5   Edwin H. Neave and John C. Wiginton, *Financial Management: Theory and Strategies* (Prentice Hall, 1981).

6   David Ricardo, The Principles of Political Economy and Taxation; Publisher J.M. Dent, London, third edition, 1929. See also Notes on Malthus, Principles of Political Economy, by David Ricardo, ch. 10; edited by Jacob Hollander et al. published by John Hopkins Press 1928.

7   B. V. Yarbrough and Robert M. Yarbrough, *The World Economy: Trade and Finance, 2nd Edition* (Dryden Press, Harcourt Brace Jovanovich College Publishers, 1991).

8   Ibid 5. B.V. Yarbrough and Robert M. Yarbrough.

9   West Indian Commission Report/ Time for Action; 1991 CARICOM pp 95-112

CHAPTER 8

NATIONAL DEBT AND PRODUCTIVITY

~—•—~

When cyclical downturns occur, island governments tend to use fiscal policy to maintain the level of spending and employment. Governments then borrow domestically and internationally and pay these liabilities back when the economy improves. If the government is facing a budget deficit, increasing of debt levels may become unsustainable and can force a sovereign debt crisis. Additionally, national productivity goals can be compromised by a large civil-service apparatus requiring relatively high expenditures to contribute to the solution of unemployment problems.

Introduction

This chapter deals with two aspects that directly affect the performance of the economy. One part concerns how the increasing use of government debt can make the country vulnerable to outside forces, even loss of sovereignty. The vulnerability is higher when the borrowing is used on projects that have insufficient returns to pay the interest and the principal, or the returns do not occur before the maturity of the loan, or no consideration is given to unforeseen events when calculating the amount of debt that is acceptable.[1]

The other part concerns the productivity of the working population. Low productivity has as a consequence lower returns to the economy, which translates to lower growth in gross value added and gross domestic product (GDP). The purpose of the chapter is to bring these two issues in the macroeconomic discussion regarding economic performance.

Level of Debt

With continuous high levels of government debt, the economy tends to fall into a vicious circle, with a substantial part of the income generated by the government through taxes and fees going to service the debt. In the face of a continuing budget deficit and a weak economy, governments typically sense a responsibility to borrow time and again to maintain the spending level in society. The expenditures of the government are primarily with respect to the civil-service apparatus, public goods and merit goods, debt-service agreements, and transfer payments that the government feels obligated to. If no sufficient revenue is obtained, the country has to borrow to close the gap between revenue and expenditures. While tax increases can lead to unrest among the population, debt financing to maintain spending generally occurs without much ado. The government borrows from international sources or from local sources.

The strategy to maintain spending and purchasing power can, however, take an economy into a vicious circle with a debt-reduction strategy under those circumstances that is ineffective as long as no substantial addition to production and exports can be achieved.

Degree of indebtedness

The degree of indebtedness and the seriousness of the situation can be established by looking at the categories of debt and the degree to which the indebtedness is tied. External indebtedness is tied to debt to other countries or institutions. In this writing, I'm focusing on public debt. Internal debt is government debt to individuals and organizations in the private sector or in the public sector. The degree of indebtedness can be estimated by calculating various types of ratios. Total debt to GDP is a ratio that shows the relationship of the debt to the size of the economy.

Typically, corporate and government debt is categorized with regard to the risk of default. A triple-A rating (AAA) is the highest rating representing investor grade. This means that the borrower is healthy and shows very little risk of default. With an average of a 40 percent debt-to-GDP ratio, the country may be awarded a BBB investor-grade classification. Generally, a C rating expresses higher risk of default, which discourages investors from participating in a bond issue. The classification is done by a rating agency. Two well-known rating agencies that operate worldwide are Standard & Poor's and Moody's.

To gauge the riskiness of the external portion of total debt, countries also relate external debt to international reserves (gold, foreign exchange, and SDRs) and to exports, and current account deficit to exports. The latter indicates the proportion of the current account deficit that must be financed by other sources than export earnings, if it becomes necessary. An external debt to GDP ratio shows the linkage of the size of the external debt to the size of the economy.

Experience in the Region

Many small economies in the Caribbean region and Central America have fallen in the vicious circle alluded to above, which took them to a situation of financial crisis that had to be attended to in order to forestall complete bankruptcy, with relative loss of sovereignty where other countries or domestic private lenders get influential power over the government.

As presented at a conference of the Association of Caribbean Economists in 1989,[2] the crisis is manifested as follows:

- high illiquidity of the debtor with frequent renegotiation of the debt and increasing dependency on bilateral debt to fund and achieve government objectives for which there are no sufficient government savings or private savings.
- Involuntary accumulation of arrears on debt-service payments.

Alternative measures

Among the multiple reasons for the rising debt to external creditors and widening budget deficits one finds the following:

- possible swings in primary commodity prices and inflationary conditions
- a revenue base that is gradually getting smaller due to sector contraction, with accompanying contraction in population and labor contingent through emigration
- constant official and informal flight of capital from the private sector for long-run investments in overseas assets and for speculative purposes, pursuing stable investment opportunities abroad that are not offered domestically
- an increasing reliance on official credit with frequent renegotiation

When a small state government borrows to finance its deficits in the face of a debt crisis, it is with the purpose of forestalling a worse downturn. But the debt crisis will get worse if domestic production and exports to obtain enough revenue and foreign exchange to pay back the external debt is not sufficient.

The increase in debt to maintain spending power can lead to stagnation of the economy and make the country vulnerable to outside forces. This could occur to such a degree that the sovereignty of a country that has major national and international commitments and becomes insolvent is threatened. In the case of the Netherlands Antilles, a major and prolonged debt crisis contributed to the breakup of the existing political union, with the islands belonging to that union searching for more economic stability in other political-economic configurations.

Efforts to Solve the Debt Crisis

The independent countries in the region that experienced a debt crisis typically used International Monetary Fund (IMF) arrangements or other sources of debt, together with adjustment strategies that include devaluation, expansion, structural reform, or a combination of the following, to come out of the crisis:

- *Deflationary adjustment.* With this, the country's currency is devalued by adjusting the exchange rate with the expectation that this will support economic growth. However, devaluation of the national currency generally results in inflationary spirals that tend to cripple economic activity instead.
- *Expansionary adjustment.* With this strategy, it is expected that export will take off based on internal policies to stimulate production and export. In this case, the results are dependent on the economic health of the trading partners. Furthermore, the pace of recovery through export-led expansion does not necessarily synchronize with the timing of the debt repayment.
- *Structural reform.* With this strategy, the country attempts to change its economic structure with emphasis on the promotion of market competitiveness.

The structural adjustment programs generally require reforms that include currency devaluation, privatization of public enterprises, reduction of trade barriers, greater emphasis on indirect taxes, and deregulation of business. The social and human cost to the country has proven to be immense, as this approach generally requires slimming down of the government apparatus, which in turn has direct consequences on the private-sector businesses.

Standby Agreements

Independent countries that are members of the IMF can make use of the standby agreement, which depending on the country's status could be the standby credit facility for low-income countries payable in ten years' time or the standby arrangement (for middle-income countries) payable in five years.

The arrangements are to help a country deal with a short-term balance-of-payment problem. Another alternative is to obtain financing from, for instance, the Inter-American Development Bank (IDB). In this case, the IDB assumes the external and domestic debt of commercial banks and the public. The nonindependent countries cannot make use of these arrangements nor can they independently approach the IDB or USAID or World Bank for a credit arrangement.

If no standby arrangements are possible or the policy/strategies have been exhausted with no positive result, countries can use their gold reserves as a final measure for a one-time correction of a balance-of-payment problem. This, however, does not necessarily constitute a solution to the debt-service problem with respect to domestic commercial banks and individual investors. A trend can be observed lately with international lending institutions to involve the government (borrower), the domestic creditors, and taxpayers in an eventual restructuring process. In case the country confronts a situation where an unsustainable sovereign debt needs to be restructured,[3] it is becoming commonplace to include these collective-action clauses in loan agreements to enhance the speed of negotiations between creditors and borrowers.

Alternative Measures

Countries also pursue debt-reform proposals targeting interest rates and amortization rates through rescheduling of the debt and by lowering the trade deficit by increasing exports. In the case of the Netherlands Antilles, these alternatives seem to be exhausted, and the central government approached the Netherlands for assistance. The Netherlands assumed the domestic debt of the central government of the Netherlands Antilles in a debt-to-debt swap and did debt forgiveness for the outstanding debt of the Netherlands Antilles to the Netherlands. A great portion of the Curaçao and Sint Maarten island-level domestic debt stayed on the books of the respective islands after the breakup of the Netherlands Antilles political union, with the Netherlands assuming complete financial and economic responsibility of the islands of Bonaire, Saba, and Saint Eustatius.

Debt Ceilings and Benchmarking

A debt crisis can worsen if major retrenchment occurs in basic sectors thinning out the production capability of the island state. When the crisis compels a further downsizing in the private sector, the island government will consider policies and strategies that will help avoid the situation in the future. Hugo Radice, for instance, argues that when intended savings in the private sector greatly exceed intended investments, the excess savings are absorbed through the sale of government securities and the proceeds are used to sustain aggregate output and employment.[4]

Alternatively, ex-ante controls and regulations can be set up to guard against further increase in borrowing in relation to the carrying capacity of the economy. This asks for the determination of an upper limit of debt beyond which the debt service cannot be honored without jeopardizing the financial potential of the country. An upper-limit or ceiling is exceeded when the country cannot continue with the agreed-upon debt service and has to continually refinance the debt while the country is facing a budget deficit. This strategy can be flanked by an industrial policy, which identifies growth sectors for investment and financing.

Benchmarking

A rapid increase in the level of debt with no major sector decline often illustrates the absence of a yardstick and/or benchmark for evaluation of possible variance from an acceptable standard.

Benchmarks help to determine a healthy relationship between borrowing and production capacity. An example of a yardstick is the European Union (EU) budgetary criteria that was agreed to with the Maastricht convention[5] and stipulates that the government budget deficit is not to exceed 3 percent of GDP and the government debt should not exceed 60 percent of GDP.

Historical data of the Netherlands Antilles is shown in table 8.1 to illustrate the worsening conditions several years before the breakup. The data is compiled from several sources—quarterly bulletin of the Netherlands Antilles Central Bank, IMF country statistics, and Central Bureau of Statistics annual reports—and illustrates the financial situation of the Netherlands Antilles for an eight-year period. The GDP is at market prices. Data on export of goods and services (XGS) reflect the ability of the country to produce foreign income to pay for imports and foreign debt service.

The table shows that this economy has stepped up the borrowing from domestic sources over the years. Total domestic debt to official creditors in Year 1 was 635 million Antillean guilders. By Year 8 in the table, total domestic debt grew to 2 billion, and 129 million florins. Total debt,[6] including foreign debt, during the eight consecutive years has increased quickly up to the point that it became 83 percent of the XGS and 57 percent of the GDP by the end of the eighth year. With a persistent budget deficit, it becomes increasingly more difficult to pay back the debt, and the government will have to resort to new strategies to turn the situation around.

Table 8.1: Debt, GDP, and Export

Example of Debt Accumulation				Relation of Debt to Export and to GDP			
Years	1	2	3	4	5	6	7	8
Population (thousands)	190	190	190	195	200	200	205	210
GDP million florins	3090	3255	3410	3560	3815	4110	4445	4885
Foreign debt	632	725	712	698	636	684	724	662
Total Domestic Debt	635	709	864	1077	1243	1425	1940	2129
Total domestic and foreign debt	1267	1434	1576	1775	1879	2109	2664	2791
Foreign Debt Service	49	49	51	54	52	53	53	20
Export of Goods and Services [XGS]	2590	2855	2955	3179	3156	3299	3648	3358
% of foreign debt per XGS	0.24	0.25	0.24	0.22	0.2	0.21	0.2	0.2
% of foreign debt service per XGS	0.02	0.02	0.02	0.02	0.02	0.02	0.01	0.01
Total Debt/XGS %	0.49	0.5	0.53	0.56	0.6	0.64	0.73	0.83
Total Debt/GDP %	0.41	0.44	0.46	0.5	0.49	0.51	0.6	0.57
Per capita Debt Fls	6,668	7,547	8,295	9,103	9,395	10,545	12,995	13,290
Per capita GDP Fls	16,263	17,132	17,947	18,256	19,075	20,550	21,683	23,262

Note: XGS is based on BOP Exports of goods and services

With a widening budget deficit, it became clear a few years later (by 1999) that repayment of the domestic and foreign debt principal and interest was impossible.[7]

The structure of the economy of the Netherlands Antilles provides limited capacity to compress imports without affecting internal production. Although the economy showed growing specialization in offshore finance and tourism, the structural external payment pressures were already present (as was the case in Jamaica, Trinidad, and Barbados) from the 1960s with the development-assistance-related borrowings. The mixture of growth-sectors income with the foreign funds, based on a debt that was misinterpreted as an internal kingdom-relations aspect (which ought not to bring sovereignty threats, it was thought), brought rapid growth in imports. This created a widening balance-of-payments deficit and augmented the exposure to external shocks, like the increases in primary commodity prices and the closing of the refineries. Evidently, the fast growth in official domestic debt was as a countercyclical measure to compensate for the contraction in the traditional export sectors (petroleum refining and offshore financial services), which led to additional contraction in population and labor through emigration. In the addendum at the end of this chapter, a proposal is made for debt monitoring.

Closing a Fiscal Gap

When facing a budget deficit, government could use debt to cover the deficit or raise taxes (or fees) to be able to cover the outlays in given civil-service sectors. With an economy producing at a level below the warranted GDP level to sustain a debt level of 60 percent of GDP or more, tax income or debt is typically used for consumptive purposes. As a result, as long as there are no increases in private-sector investments and/or other contributions to GDP or outside (budget) financing, a fiscal gap will remain.

To close this gap and produce a turnaround in the economy, there is evidently need for policies that stimulate activities in economic sectors that show growth and export possibilities. These are so-called "industrial" policies.

Industrial policies

Dennis Pantin[8] indicated that a focus on industrial policy will help those dealing with the question of how to change a situation that leads to national debt. Industrial policy helps with identifying and financing competitive exports. An industrial policy, Pantin says, is necessary to gauge the resources required for financing, marketing, and providing support services when a competitive edge is identified. Financing of the identified projects will require an investment policy that, among other things, defines criteria with regard to acceptance of domestic and foreign participation.

The production base is increased by instituting policies that affect the behavior in the private and public sectors. This includes the following, among other things:

- incentives to the private sector for innovative solutions that add to increased revenue

- controlling growth in public-sector costs by restricting wage increases
- gearing government borrowing toward productive investments, and as a result engaging local businesses
- redefining the use of low-interest or no-interest international subsidies for upgrading of the infrastructure and capacity building so that a part of the customary foreign financial assistance retains a development-assistance status
- redefining and focusing use of given external assistance grants as a complement to the yearly budget for transfer of funds to forestall growth of poverty

The goal is that economic growth produced this way will gradually lead to lowering demand for international assistance, bringing it to a manageable level.

Remarks

A healthy economy, for the purpose of this section, is one where the government has sufficient income to cover the going expenditures; one where there is full employment; and one where the general price level does not show major inflationary tendencies. Containing the increase in total debt will depend on the ability of the small country with a limited domestic market to determine an acceptable growth in debt, given the capacity of aggregate production and exports. There is a habitual behavior to turn to borrowing, either internationally or locally, to solve financial problems, and this could easily become the persistent way to maintain short-run stability in the economy.

The expectation with government loans is that they act as leverage factors for national economic growth. The creation of a greater production capacity for export purposes requires substantial financing and marketing. Growth will be achieved if the investments in capital equipment and technology and subsequent production increase domestic productivity. The next section discusses productivity as a strategic objective to achieve increased performance of the economy.

Productivity and Production

Productivity is about how much value-added is obtained from the input of labor, technology, and capital in the production process. Increased productivity occurs when the same quantity of labor, capital, and technology produce a higher aggregate value-added. For that reason, one could say that the standard of living of a country depends on the country's ability to produce goods and services, and on productivity.

The increase in labor productivity from year to year is a result of use of improved capital equipment, new technology, and training and education. A simple way to derive productivity is by dividing gross value-added by the number of persons employed during a year. This so-called "partial productivity" leaves out other possible factors that can contribute to productivity, like capital, technology, and management. Total productivity is obtained by considering all other factors that contribute to the increase in production.

So labor productivity is the average output per fixed labor input. In most calculations, the fixed labor input used is labor hours. Using labor hours gives a better view, since parttime work or very short-term employment may not be counted in calculating productivity based on number employed. The production function, as shown in figure 8.1, illustrates the relation between labor input and GDP.

The graph shows that GDP increases along the curve producing GDP1 as more labor is added to the production process. The second curve producing GDP2 is due to the rise in productivity. With the rise in productivity, the production function shifts upward.

Figure 8.1

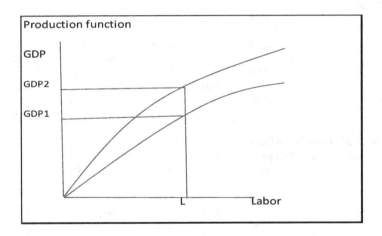

The shift upward could be a result of new equipment, new technology, or more efficient input with regard to progress in time and motion handling, improvements due to additional experience and training, or other behavioral factors.

Monitoring National Debt

National productivity is a result of the output (value added) for the country. If correct, the changes in the year following the first data year should show that production and productivity resulted in higher output. Table 8.2 shows the number employed, real value added, and partial productivity using the formula provided above.

Table 8.2: Labor Productivity

Gross Value Added 2005-2008			Selected Dutch Caribbean Islands				
Year	2005		2006		2007		2008
Real Terms/ millions	FLS		FLS		FLS		FLS
Curacao	3775.6	0.053793	3978.7	0.057406	4207.1	0.044948	4396.2
Bonaire	305.3	0.036358	316.4	0.054362	333.6	0.056055	352.3
StMaarten	1087.1	0.080029	1174.1	0.065497	1251	0.041087	1302.4

Employed people							
Year	2005		2006		2007		2008
Curacao	51342		52050		54049		56535
% increase		0.01		0.04		0.05	
Bonaire	4334		4661		5646		6407
% increase		0.08		0.21		0.13	
StMaarten	15495		16200		18072		20720
% increase		0.05		0.12		0.15	

Partial productivity based on labor							
Gross value added/Number employed							
Year	2005		2006		2007		2008
Curacao	73538		76440		77839		77761
% incr Curacao		0.04		0.02		0.00	
Bonaire	70443		67882		59086		54986
% Increase Bonaire		-0.04		-0.13		-0.07	
StMaarten	70158		72475		69223		62857
% increase StMaarten		0.03		-0.04		-0.09	

Increase in labor productivity according to the results shown in the table seems inconsequential for all islands, leading one to assume that real gross value added rose most, probably due to other factors.

Factors Affecting Productivity

National productivity increase is dependent on the aggregate productivity in the individual units in society that contribute to GDP. Productivity is related to the tools available and used by the working population to increase production in the respective sectors. An economy can become highly capital-intensive using advanced technology. For the particular industries involved, this could result in high levels of productivity at the expense of work opportunities for domestic labor. While the long-term answer is sought with expansion of private-sector activities, in the short term (which could last forever if there are no set goals) in the several islands the government tends to use tax revenues from the growth sectors to curb unemployment.

The civil service and public enterprises generally concentrate on nontraded services and products, where the production is not directly tied to export and, as a result, the actors are not always urged to stick to global competitiveness. The public enterprises are generally not directly involved in insuring a continuous flow of external funds to pay for imports. Besides, where monopolistic market conditions prevail, they, the public enterprises, are cushioned to some degree from the rapid and drastic changes in the global economic environment.

In pursuing the economic goals, countries with a microsize economy are generally faced with a dilemma to balance the productivity requirement with full employment aims. Hereby a high rate of participation in the workforce is seen as important to the social economic well-being of society, over and above productivity. In effect, the country can be seeking efficiency in use of raw material and other costs of production, but not in work opportunities for the population.

In Conclusion

This chapter indicates that if national debt is allowed to grow past a certain limit, it becomes unmanageable and a negative force in the economic performance. When the level of government debt goes beyond a point where the repayment of principal and interest cannot be guaranteed by the aggregate output and the budgeted income, the country finds itself in a situation that require harsh policies that often do not give the desired results and may in fact take the country to a situation where even its sovereignty can be threatened.

Debt is used to create leverage in the economy and obtain higher revenues. This leverage has to be supported by greater efficiency and productivity. If in the process of the achievement of the economic potential the efficiency requirement is traded off in favor of a full employment requirement, this can result in lower-than-expected growth as productivity is sacrificed.

Addendum

The Reason for Structural and Functional Adjustments

Owen Arthur, former prime minister of Barbados, refers in the publication "Contending With Destiny: the Caribbean in the 21st Century"[9] to economic vulnerabilities faced by the islands in the Caribbean as coming from a debt crisis of overwhelming proportion, overwhelming dependence on custom revenue, economic activity focused on trade preferences, heavy concentration on the agricultural sector, prevalence of state and private monopolies in critical service sectors, and narrow specialization in the production of a few goods and services. This is the reason why a structural and functional adjustment is needed. The gap between the current conditions of the region and what is required to support sustained and sustainable development, according to Arthur, is evident at the turn of the century, which becomes more pronounced with the emerging global economy, with a change of focus away from the North Atlantic.

Monitoring National Debt
The eventuality of a debt crisis, as experienced in the 1980s and 1990s by the Netherlands Antilles, prompts a closer look at strategies to follow to improve the economy given present resources and debt level, and to introduce control measures to restrict excessive increase in the debt level. In this section, the 60 percent to GDP debt limit as proposed by the EU is

used to monitor unbalanced growth in foreign and domestic component of debt in relation to national output.

Finance and economic coverage

Debt is most often used as a way to leverage economic growth. International borrowing is usually geared to financing investments in infrastructure. Domestic borrowing often occurs to maintain economic stability.

Foreign debt characteristically cannot be easily renegotiated. In the crisis years in Latin America, the foreign debt was often renegotiated by exchanging the debt for equity, in a process known as equitization. The kind of foreign debt held by the Dutch Islands originates from the Dutch government and is not renegotiated the same way. On the contrary, and hypothetically, it is possible to renegotiate and refinance domestic debt externally.

For this reason, the coverage to insure repayment of the external debt is termed *financial coverage*. Finance coverage entails insuring on-time repayment of the interest and the foreign debt to lower the exposure that can quickly lead to sovereign debt risk. *Economic coverage* entails that the domestic debt can be renegotiated and rescheduled over a longer period of time as long as the economy permits. These coverage conditions presuppose that there is a way to indicate that the debt is still within an acceptable range, or a debt ceiling.

A debt ceiling

Imagine a debt ratio policy with a ceiling of 60 percent of GDP and expected total debt of 3 billion florins. Under these circumstances, the island state is compelled to strive for a GDP of at least 5 billion florins, otherwise the debt is not sustainable, according to the policy. Since part of the debt is to external creditors, the nation's output should cover both external and domestic debt. The 60 percent marker regards foreign and domestic debt. If the foreign debt portion in the total debt is 25 percent of total debt of 3 billion florins and domestic debt 75 percent, this means that theoretically, and using the 60 percent benchmark, 1.25 billion florins in the expected GDP relates to the foreign exposure. With the foreign debt at 750 million, the corresponding exposure of 750/1,250 is 60 percent. The exposure to domestic debt of 2,250/3,750 is 60.0 percent, and 3.75 billion florins in GDP covers this exposure.

Assessment of exposure

Subsequently, one is to evaluate what additional steps need to be taken in case the 60 percent debt limit is reached or exceeded. Two situations are presented next to illustrate the need for efforts that could take the economy back to a sustainable level. The interest-payment requirements are omitted in this discussion.

Situation A

The first situation that the country faces is that domestic production can only obtain a GDP of 4 billion of the local currency, while the outstanding debt is at 3 billion.

If due to circumstances—some of which could be the low multiplier effect of major capital investments made abroad or the lower-than-expected impact on value added due to intermediate goods import and lower-than-expected net export—the economy does not grow past a GDP of 4 billion, then the exposure to creditors (based on 3 billion debt) is magnified, and the debt service conditions deteriorate. While the foreign debt portion is at 25 percent of total debt (750), theoretically the coverage also deteriorates from 1,250 to 1,000, *ceteris paribus*, and following the line of thinking in the paragraph above. The finance coverage ratio of 750/1,000 is now 75 percent, way above the 60 percent, and as a result indicates increased risk of default and sovereignty risk.

If it were possible to forecast the lower GDP on time, under strict conditions, the country should only have total debt of 2.4 billion and not 3 billion.

The foreign debt portion at .75 billion is now 31.25 percent of acceptable total debt and should be trimmed back to 25 percent, which is equal to 600 million, or else the domestic debt is to be reduced to 1.65 billion. As a result, the country needs to make efforts to lower the debt exposure to achieve sustainable debt.

Situation B

The country experiences increase in foreign debt and the foreign-debt portion in total debt increases beyond the expected current foreign debt. In that case, a higher sovereignty risk exposure occurs. Consequently, the GDP has to rise correspondingly to maintain the debt-to-GDP ratio of 60 percent.

If in a new arrangement the portion of external debt rises to 1 billion and domestic debt remains at, say, 45 percent of GDP, total debt is now 65 percent of GDP given the expected 5 billion revenue level. Now the coverage ratio for external debt of 1,000/1,250 is 80 percent, because theoretically 1.25 billion in the GDP covers the external exposure.

The new total debt situation is 3.25 billion florins. As a result, the GDP to sustain this growth in debt exposure has to be, *ceteris paribus*, 3.25/.60, which is equal to 5.417 billion, more than the present productive capacity. This level of debt is not sustainable with the present productive capacity of the economy.

The two examples illustrate how the combination of external and domestic debt forces government to curb deficit spending and/ or increase domestic production to stay within a predetermined limit of spending. Without increasing the production base, it becomes a major challenge to maintain the standard of living and cover the growing expenses of government.

[1] Beth V. Yarbrough and Robert M. Yarbrough, *the World Economy: Trade and Finance* (Dryden Press, 1991), 350-352.

2   Norman Girvan, Mariano Arana Sevilla, Miguel Ceara Hatton, and Ennio Henriquez, in special issue on Caribbean Economy, Institute of Caribbean Studies, *Restructuring and Debt in the Caribbean*, 2nd Ace Conference Barbados, 1989.

3   Chris C. Carvounis, *The Foreign Debt/National Development Conflict: External Adjustments and Internal Disorder in the Developing Nations* (Quorum Books, 1986). See also: Randall S. Krozner, "Enhancing Sovereignty Debt Restructuring," *The Cato Journal*, Volume 23, No. 1, Spring-Summer 2003.

4   Hugo Radice, "Cutting Government Deficits: Economic Science or a Class War?" *Capital and Class*, February 2011.

5   The Maastricht Convergence criteria stipulates maximum values of annual government deficit and government debt to GDP as a budgetary criteria. The treaty also stipulates long-term interest stability, not higher than two percentage points above average returns in the three EU states with best price stability and an inflation criterion with a ceiling of 1.5 percent above a reference value.

6   The constant increase in debt is mainly due to new bond issues and refinancing of old debt on the domestic market, increasing the debt burden from 635 million in Year 1 to 2.129 billion in Year 8. The relation of debt to GDP provides an indication of the capability of the economy to grow without obstacles—that is, to maintain the sustainability of government debt.

7   See report "Commissie Nationaal Herstelplan" (National Recovery Plan) of June 1999 by Dr. E. D. Tromp, Jr., G. Wawoe, and I. De Windt RA. "Op eigen kracht zoekend naar herstel van de bestuurlijke kracht en verstevigen van de financiale basis in de Nederlandse Antillen." The total budget deficit was estimated for 1999 at ANG 316 million. The budget deficit for Curaçao and the central government stood at ANG 124.2 million and ANG 150 million respectively. These two had

debt service requirements of, respectively, ANG 202.4 million and ANG 98.8 million for the year.

[8] Dennis Pantin Into the Valley of Debt; An Alternative to the IMF/ World Bank Path in Trinidad and Tobago (Dennis Pantin, Gloria V. Ferguson Ltd. Printers, 1989).

[9] Dennis Benn and Kenneth Hall; Contending with Destiny; The Caribbean in the21st Century; Ian Randle Publishers, 2000.

CHAPTER 9
ISLAND STATE PROBLEMS AND OPPORTUNITIES

~─•─~

This chapter points to a focus in the islands on economic growth through investing in construction and on application of external financing to develop an infrastructure to stimulate economic activities. The size of the islands, the small internal market, the lack of natural resources, and the high thresholds with regard to exporting lead to this behavior by government and private citizens to grow and safeguard material possessions. This situation puts continuous pressure on the ability of the islands to obtain export currencies (inflow of foreign exchange) to import and at least retain the level of well-being achieved in previous economic cycles. The capability is enhanced by introducing new perspectives for growth based on domestic strengths. Such a new stance is increasingly possible with the rapid advances in technology (not discussed here) and the growing tendency for establishment of free trade agreements in the region and globally.

Introduction

Numerous factors tend to lead to diseconomies of scale and make small developing economies, particularly islands, vulnerable to outside forces. The attention paid to islands as developing states, starting particularly with the Lomé and Cotonou agreements, also brought a new dimension in the cooperation with organizations like the United Nations (UN), the International Monetary Fund (IMF), and the World Trade Organization (WTO) in terms of development assistance and special consideration for the islands with regard to rules and directives by these organizations.

It is now widely recognized that island nations confront problems typical mostly to insular or very small continental developing territories. As open economies, they are vulnerable to conditions placed by players in foreign markets. Small islands are also exceptionally vulnerable to physical environmental conditions. Furthermore, because of the small size of the economy, a dependency condition often develops with larger economies when the island experiences limited exports or fluctuating exports from only one or two sectors. The dependency is often related to foreign development assistance from colonial parents or other foreign countries or institutions.

Consequently, this chapter presents an overview of factors that are of micro and macroeconomic importance for the economic management of the islands. The content is divided in three parts. One part concerns issues of size, infrastructure, resource limitation, and the need to sustain the level of material wealth obtained, as illustrated by the possessions and import/export characteristics. The next part regards the requirement to concentrate on the use of local resources, the need to reduce a one-sided focus on hedging, and benefits of giving more attention to local legislation deficiencies and capital needs. The last section contains a description of the various institutions in the region and globally that can be of socioeconomic-development importance to the islands.

Size, Infrastructure, and Resource Limitation

Islands tend to be referred to as micro, very small, small, intermediate size, and large territories. The economies of the very small and microterritories tend to be so small that the traditional production processes using plants and equipment utilized in large and advanced economies to create products for the domestic market entail indivisibilities that make production for the small home market inefficient and expensive relative to imports.

Smallness

From the several definitions of what can be considered a small territory, it is obvious that much depends on personal views. Charles Taylor[1] in 1969 defined a microstate as a land area of less than 142,822 square kilometers, a population of less than 2,928,000, and a GNP of less than 583 million US dollars. Elmer Plitschke[2] considered both smallness and viability, defining

> *small states* as those that have populations ranging from 300,000 to one million, and *micro states* as those that have population of less than 300,000, with *sub micro states* having a population of less than one hundred thousand. These Islands can be demographically

economically viable when the human populations of islands can mobilize the potential of the physical and biological environment for their own benefit.

The ability to mobilize the potential will depend, according to Plitschke, on their numbers, the density, their distribution, and their biological dynamism. Other aspects of viability concern cultural developments and economic opportunities. This approach is an important one because it establishes the possibility for criteria to be classified for financial development assistance.

In 1982, the Caribbean Commonwealth secretariat proposed a population of 1.5 million as the threshold for a small economy, to qualify as a "small island developing state" or SIDS for foreign financial assistance. But Jamaica and Haiti have a much larger population and qualify as a SIDS. They are considered exceptions. There are several other proposals regarding how SIDS is to be defined. By 1996, economies in general were being categorized by global institutions on the basis of income to measure socioeconomic development. Low-income economies have per capita gross national income of $750 or less and high-income economies of $9,320 plus. In that year, the per capita gross national income for Aruba was at $15,663 and for the Netherlands Antilles $14,362. It is evident that per capita income does not portray how income is distributed among the domestic population. Besides, the small islands are generally much more vulnerable to external shocks, either due to location or due to trade disadvantages. The Committee for Development Policy of the UN devised an Economic Vulnerability Index to determine the exposure and "capacity of countries to withstand external shocks to gauge this vulnerability from island to island"[3].

Complementary criteria for development financing

It is increasingly felt that size or income is not sufficient as criteria for apportioning external financing support among SIDS. Instead, the following factors should also be recognized as determining the size and type of support that can take the developing island to a level that could help it achieve greater autonomy in implementing development efforts[4]:

- the conditions in a microeconomy, where the population cannot mobilize natural resources (both physical and biological resources) from their own savings to enhance production capacity
- the situation where the economic activities displayed on the island are insufficient to promote economic growth, contributing to large-scale incidence of absolute poverty
- the higher-than-normal vulnerability to ecological disasters due to geographic location and size
- a continuously displayed need for outside assistance for finance and technical assistance as a result of the size of the population, the size of the domestic market, and lack of skills

A review of these factors for an island will reveal the direction of efforts for external financing of activities that promote economic development and growth. The first factor clearly shows need to attract foreign direct investments by the private sector. The second factor relates to circumstances that need to be addressed domestically as proposed later in this chapter to improve the environment for investments. The third and fourth factors indicate more permanent conditions that require consistent and continuous outside assistance. Consequently, foreign assistance will remain a requirement for the time being but is related to the internal capabilities of an island.

Internal decision power

There is an apparent process visible in most of the islands in the Caribbean region to get more personal control over their destiny to enhance their own capabilities. Several very small islands— like Grenada, Saint Kitts and Nevis, Antigua, and Barbados to name a few, have achieved a status of independence, which exerts pressure on developing this internal capability. In the politically dependent islands, there is also a move toward more internal decision-making power, including power to be able to control the size and flow of foreign assistance and relate this to local efforts for development. In the recent past, Saint Martin on the French side of the island voted to become a separate collectivity of France instead of a *communité* and the Dutch section of the island, Sint Maarten, voted in a referendum to gain a separate status from the Netherlands Antilles within the Dutch kingdom, similar to the status Aruba gained years before the political union of the Netherlands Antilles was disbanded.

Size and Replicated Infrastructure

Small developing island states develop a similar economic infrastructure to larger continental states, albeit on a smaller scale. However, the financial impact per head of population or square kilometer is many times higher. This is most visible with island groupings like the Dutch Antilles or the eight islands belonging to the Organization of Eastern Caribbean States (OECS). Each island will make great efforts to develop the necessary infrastructure facilities with harbors, airports, government offices, hospitals, utilities, and other amenities to serve the inhabitants and to ensure greater possibilities for socioeconomic development.

The Dutch Caribbean consists of two sets of islands at a distance of approximately 500 miles from each other, a population on each island of 150,000 people or less, but has technically six "international" airports, though of varying sizes. The Netherlands has fewer international airports on a population of 16 million. Besides, the Dutch islands have two central banks and three monetary systems, with the Antillean guilder, the Aruban florin, and the US dollar as legal tender. The small size of each operation and the scattering of investments serving the same purpose from island to island, although necessary, tends to run counter to efficiency, requiring relatively more financial input for construction and maintenance.

Limited Resources, Limited Sectors

Although the limited resource base of an island state includes he natural resources and the human and financial resources that the country has at its disposal, it is not simple to turn these into productive and efficient use to compete in global markets. One complication with regard to the financial resources argument is, according to DeLisle Worrell (1991), due to the fact that investments in the islands of the Caribbean are predominantly in construction and other nontradable goods. This influences the amount of funds available to cover investment-financing needs for tradable commodities that can be competitive in external markets. Tradable goods are products and services that can be sold outside the country. A small domestic market, typical for the islands, often works as a deterrent to competitive production at home.

Standard of living

The level of economic development of an island is to a certain extent illustrated by the material standard of living. This material standard of living creates a reliance on imports for the goods and services demanded, which in turn creates a requirement for exports that make the imports affordable and to maintain a purchasing power utilizing foreign exchange. Table 9.1, produced by the bureau of statistics of the Netherlands Antilles (data for Aruba is not included), shows a select number of products that indicate to some degree the standard of living in the Dutch Caribbean. It also reflects the need for a variety of products that are not produced on the island.

Table 9.1 Imports and Standard of Living

Percentage of Households with	Bonaire	Curacao	Saba	St.Eustatius	St. Maarten
Refrigerator	97	97	97	95	96
Deep Freezer	20	20	27	28	14
Washing Machines	87	87	68	79	76
Telephone	53	76	78	57	44
TV	94	96	90	92	92
Video Recorder	46	60	43	50	60
Cable TV	73	31	79	79	69
Personal Computer	29	33	38	25	25
Internet Connection	16	21	26	14	15
Airconditioning	40	38	23	23	22
Cencus 2001					

The above data reflects only partially the reality of imports guaranteeing a given standard of living. While the telephone category above only represents landline connections, mobile-phone possessions are closer to 100 percent. The list does not include, for instance, food and food products, clothing and footwear, furniture, beverage, and tobacco, which are all imported. The standard of living and quality of life also include the possibility of relying on imported cars and ease in travelling abroad for vacationing, for medical services, and for educational services. The conditions illustrated above as well as a given level of income to afford these are, according to DeLisle Worrell (using an example from Trinidad and Tobago), particularly due to

the expectation of the general population that a continuous supply of consumer goods can be made available. Government was carried along by the insistent demand for more goods and services, contributing to overall expenditure levels that strained domestic productive capacity and precipitated a cascade of imports. When the brief era of prosperity came to an end in the 1980s, the citizens of Trinidad and Tobago had acquired habits of spending which could no longer be sustained by the slower growth of output."[5]

Worrell also observes that "the machinery for economic management in the Caribbean is rudimentary with its principle defects being the lack of good systems to produce and disseminate economic information and decision making that is unstructured and predictable."[6]

Balance of Payments

The societal demands and activities influence the results of the current account of the balance-of-payment statistics. The current account is made up of the balance of trade of goods, services, labor and investment income, and current transfers. The balance-of-payment data provides some insight as to the import demands to maintain the lifestyle indicated with the items in table above.

Next to the current account, the balance of payment also has a capital account that describes mainly changes in capital transfers and foreign-exchange reserves and bank deposits at the central bank. In this section, the focus is on the current account and trade balance. The trade balance is the difference between merchandise exports and merchandise imports. If there is a trade imbalance—that means more imports than exports (in monetary units)—then in the long run the situation leads to major economic incapacity to maintain the standard of living obtained on an island. The reliance on imported goods that reflect the standard of living also creates a condition whereby foreign inflation and other anomalies cannot be avoided, and these tend to affect domestic economic activities. Below is a current account as it was reported in a given year.

Table 9.2: Current Account in the Balance of Payment

CURRENT ACCOUNT *in florins xxx.xxx*	8.42
TRADE BALANCE	*-1820.7*
MERCHANDISE EXPORTS	1171.2
MERCHANDISE IMPORTS	2991.9
SERVICE BALANCE	1590.98
LABOR AND INVESTMENT INCOME BALANCE	-12.8
CURRENT TRANSFERS BALANCE	250.9

Adapted from the Central Bureau of Statistics of the Netherlands Antilles

In the example above, the island has a small but positive current account balance in the balance of payments. The trade balance shows that merchandise imports exceed merchandise exports by 1,820.7 million florins. If it were not for the services balance—which in the case of the former Netherlands Antilles is predominantly from income from the international finance sector and oil-refining sector as shown on the (balance of payments of the Netherlands Antilles during consecutive years)—the result would be devastating. The current transfers balance consists mainly of transfers of taxes and workers' remittances.

Table 9.2 shows the situation at year end. However, it is possible that during the year, scarcity of foreign currencies occurs due to late deposits by, for instance, the refinery for refinery services. Similarly, when activities in a sector providing either service or product exports fluctuate or are abandoned, this has a direct negative effect on the current account balance and the ability to service foreign purchases and debt. Alternatively, if imports increases to the extent that both trade and service balances are negative, pressure is exerted on the value of the local currency and on the reserves of the country. Cash differentials between imports and exports are revealed by the inflow and outflow of cash statistic shown in the quarterly reports of the central bank.

Inflow and outflow of cash

Payments for international transactions require the availability of foreign currencies. These foreign currencies are mainly obtained from exports of goods and services. Foreign currencies may also be obtained from foreign investments and foreign-development funding. A minor part of the foreign currencies may come from unrequited transfers by workers and organizations operating abroad. When a gap exists between inflow and outflow in favor of outflow, the size of the gap and the length of time the gap persists can lead to inability to pay foreign purchases or debt even though the importer or debtor has sufficient income in the local currency.

Table 9.3 gives an impression of the inflow and outflow of foreign exchange in millions ANG for selected years for the combination of islands of the then Netherlands Antilles. The data is presented according to currency areas and indicates that some form of synchronization of the cash outflow and cash inflow of foreign currencies is particularly important for importers to pay for the purchases they make abroad, or for paying foreign debt. A three months' reserve of foreign exchange is often used as a criterion of a safe minimum throughout a year.

Table 9.3: Inflow and Outflow of Foreign Exchange

Cash Inflow and outflow of foreign exchange				
Netherlands Antilles		2003	2004	2005
		ANG	ANG	ANG
Inflow	U.S. Dollars	5,399.70	5,589.20	5,997.80
Outflow	U.S. Dollars	5,645.50	6,211.00	6,497.40
Netflow	US Dollars	-245.80	-621.80	-499.60
Inflow	Euro	594.7	603	766.9
Outflow	Euro	872.6	826	879.7
Net flow	Euro	-277.9	-223	-112.8
Inflow	Aruban Guilders	32.7	32.4	22.5
Outflow	Aruban Guilders	132.6	95.7	98.8
Net flow	Aruban Guilders	-99.9	-63.3	-76.3
Inflow	Other currencies	19.7	28	35.1
Ouflow	Other currencies	50.8	50.2	57.6
Net flow	Other currencies	-31.1	-22.2	-22.5
Total inflow		6,046.80	6,252.60	6,822.30
Total outflow		6,701.50	7,182.90	7,533.50
Net total flow		-654.70	-930.30	-711.20

Adapted from Quarterly Bulletin of the Central Bank of the
Netherlands Antilles

There is a visible deficit in each currency area. Since the Netherlands Antilles has not existed as a political unit since 2010, these figures are only for illustrative purposes. However, they tell the story of the constancy of the dominance of imports over exports, which are still likely true for Curaçao, Bonaire, and the Windward Islands.

Economic growth, either through investment-led or export-led expansion strategies to achieve maintenance of the spending power, remains heavily reliant on imports. The manufacturing sector imports close to 100 percent of its machinery, equipment, and raw material to be used in the local processes. Only water and electricity and a few other commodities are to be considered products with a high local content used in manufacturing (and general consumption). The construction sector imports equipment like trucks, loaders, asphalt, lumber, cement, and so on for the construction of buildings, roads, and other infrastructure needs. Foods, materials, and supplies are generally imported to support the growing tourism activities. The general public and all economic sectors buy an amazing quantity of imported products like books, electric and electronic equipment, gasoline, office supplies, cars, clothes, household appliances, petroleum products, and food products. Some goods are durable and last longer than one year. Other goods are nondurable, meaning they are used up during a relatively short period of time and consequently are imported over and over again during an accounting year.

Lowering the Dependence

There are several aspects in the domestic economy that contribute to a dependency on imports. These include the natural outsourcing of raw material production as proposed in the section on value added in chapter 6 or the hedging attitude to mitigate risks by investing in construction, the investment in expensive economic infrastructure to attract investments, and of course the demands by society to maintain the material standard of living obtained.

Changing the economic environment to lower the pressures due to the dependence on imports and as a result on the balance of payment and on GDP requires adjustment to the normal way of dealing with the economy. Often new ideas are proposed, and as often they disappear. Perhaps this occurs due to difficulty with implementation. The problems related to low economic performance, however, do not disappear. The ideas by Anthony Dolman and Hernando de Soto[7] in the next paragraphs are used as examples to address a change of focus toward more viable domestic production and a change toward the development of domestic and not imported institutions and legal parameters.

Use of Local Resources

The dependence on imports can be mitigated, as noted by Anthony Dolman, by placing emphasis on meeting food and energy requirements through local resources and indigenously generated processes. In small island developing countries, it will be impossible to overcome 'growing' food and energy dependence without the reconstitution of local food systems, the rediscovery of the sea, and the imaginative integration of marine and land-based resourcesFurther, Dolman observes that:

the colonial heritage is one that has undervalued the sea as resource. . . . Countries have traditionally stressed exploitation of land-based resources to the exclusion of much else . . . it is becoming increasingly clear that many of the concerns of island governments, not only food and energy but also industrialization, transport and tourism, need in large measure to be defined in terms of relationships to the sea. This should be more feasible under the provisions of the New Law of the Sea of the United Nations that extend national jurisdictions with an economic zone of around 166,000 sq. miles. Within this zone, the island government has a set of rights which are virtually complete with respect to the exploitation of the living and non-living resources of the seabed, and very substantial with respect to the exploitation of the living resources of the water column.[8]

Legal and Administrative Deficiencies and Undercapitalization

Small islands the size of those in the Dutch Caribbean often face demand from society to speed up socioeconomic development.

As a result, economic policies and legislation are borrowed from the former parent country and slightly adapted to fit the requirements of the moment. The islands often seem to lack the institutions, with financial and manpower capacity, to do original work. Besides, original work could be seen as rediscovering the wheel. But this borrowing is becoming more and more a debatable issue, and this kind of built-in mechanism can constrain real development. Hernando de Soto[9] characterizes the situation whereby an underdeveloped country does not develop the proper institutions to support its development efforts as follows:

> Underdeveloped countries often try to emulate the most recent achievements of the developed countries. The underdeveloped countries tend to import legal parameters from overseas, which on paper look perfect but do not necessarily fit the local circumstances. Consequently, we [the *underdeveloped countries*] set aside the various efforts the developed countries made to get to this point where they are now. The origin of capital and importance of the way capital has to play a role in this process is often underestimated, as is the importance of a good system of property rights that underlies the proper utilization of capital. It is this fact that helps to constrain development. The lack of a legal system that is anchored in the beliefs and principles of the society and can administer property rights appropriately will lower the opportunities to provide capital to business ventures

and subsequently cultivate the needed foundation for economic development. As long as these aspects are not taken care of properly, the underdeveloped countries will face huge under-capitalization of their (investment) efforts, and an expansive array of dead capital, notwithstanding the great efforts by the countries to enhance their economies., As long as the legal system and the administrative system do not provide an adequate base to increase the effectiveness and efficiency in dealing with capital creation, this tend to perpetuate the underdevelopment.[10]

The inhabitants of a country seek to maintain or improve the current standard of living and utilize the most recent laws and policies from the developed countries, some of which may be perfect for another economy and social environment but do not necessarily match the needs of the developing country at the stage at which it is in its development. This outward look and openness to supplies from abroad often work as a restrictive factor in giving proper attention to better use of the land for agriculture and the surrounding sea for fisheries and mariculture.

The Regional and Global Challenge

This section looks at the cooperative efforts in the region and globalization realities as recent phenomena that can have an influence on the support of uninterrupted growth for small islands in the Caribbean region. While in the past a few developing economies were haphazardly "blessed" by the establishment of one or more major multinationals, in time various islands and regional mainland countries vie for the settlement of the same foreign industries in their respective territories. Additionally, rapid advances in technology make it possible for the smallest of islands to globally market local products and services.

There is an almost natural cooperation among nearby countries. For instance, the Windward Islands in the Eastern Caribbean work together with neighboring islands in marketing to foster growth in tourism. In the Leeward Islands, Bonaire, Curaçao, and Aruba form to a degree a regional economic zone with Venezuela in connection with the oil industry, notwithstanding the constitutional ties to the Netherlands. This cooperation takes place in principle on the basis of sector-level agreements. There are various forms of alignment in the region, ranging from loose alignments to bilateral or multilateral agreements with stringent conditions.

Loose Alignments

The islands in the Caribbean Region also collaborate through the organizations listed below to foster socioeconomic growth and stability. Some are supranational organizations covering the whole Western Hemisphere, others are a Caribbean-United States connection or are based on Caribbean-Latin America cooperative activities, while others are industry-specific. While the Netherlands Antilles has ceased to exist, the functions, where they exist, are still carried on for or by the specific Dutch Caribbean islands.

Western Hemisphere cooperation

* *Organization of American States.* The OAS is a United Nations regional agency for the whole Western Hemisphere, with the intent to settle controversies between countries in the region by peaceful means. The Dutch Caribbean islands, as nonindependent countries, are formally represented by the Netherlands on behalf of the kingdom. The Netherlands Antilles had a status as permanent observer with the InterAmerican Drug Abuse Control Commission of the OAS.
* *Pan American Health Organization.* Officially, the kingdom of the Netherlands is member of the PAHO, since the Netherlands conducts international relations for the Dutch Caribbean. The Netherlands Antilles and Aruba together with the PAHO consult with the Dutch kingdom for closer regional collaboration. The Curaçao and Aruba PAHO offices operate in strict alliance with the PAHO center in Venezuela.
* *Inter-American Development Bank.* The IDB, established since 1959, is a regional organization that has as its goal to help combat poverty and inequality in the region. The IDB has two distinct memberships. One is the developing countries of the Caribbean and Latin America and the other is nonregional countries, one of which is the Netherlands. The Dutch Caribbean islands are not entitled to direct financing from the IDB due their dependence status. However, the islands can make use of the expertise of IDB.

Caribbean-United States collaboration

- *Caribbean Basin Initiative.* The United States launched the CBI based on the Caribbean Basin Recovery Act (CBERA) of 1983 in an attempt to assist in the development of Caribbean economies by facilitating trade expansion through easier market access. This market access became possible through duty-free entry of eligible products, with at least 35 percent of the value of the products produced in an eligible CBERA country. The CBERA was reviewed in 1990, and the CBI-II has become a permanent one-way free-trade program. The opportunity for the Caribbean is that any product that matches the requirements of the CBI can be exported to the United States, and several products that were first exempted from duty-free entry can, with CBI-II, be imported at a lower tariff or obtain preferential access if nontariff barriers are present.

Research and development

- *Economic Commission for Latin America and the Caribbean.* The ECLAC (or CEPAL for the Spanish speaking nations) was established in 1948 as a United Nations agency. Its tasks include supporting economic development and integration in the region. The main office is in Chile, with subregional headquarters in Trinidad and Tobago and Mexico. The Netherlands Antilles and Aruba are associate members. The ECLAC produces a wide range of publications that are of interest to the region, like the

Economic Survey of the Caribbean, the *Caribbean Millennium Development Goal*, and yearly Caribbean development reports, with one of the last ones having the topic of *Economics of Climate Change in the Caribbean*.

- *Regional Coordinator for Economic and Social Research.* The CRIES, established since 1982, is headquartered in Buenos Aires, Argentina, but has a vast network of research organizations in Latin America and the Caribbean. CRIES promotes research in economics, politics, environment, and social sciences. This organization tries to involve the civil society in the regional and global agenda.

Regional economic cooperation

- *Association of Caribbean States.* Curacao, Aruba and St. Maarten are associate members of the ACS. The ACS was founded in 1994 to promote consultation and cooperation and concerted actions among the countries of the greater Caribbean. The ACS wants to promote sustainable development in the greater Caribbean, which stretches from Mexico down to the Guyanas with a total population of about 250 million. The ACS additionally wants to strengthen the regional cooperation and integration process, and to preserve the environmental integrity of the Caribbean Sea.
- *Allianza Bolivariana de las Americas.* In 2004, Cuba and Venezuela established the ALBA, which had as its aim the exchange of medical and educational resources and petroleum. The membership nowadays comprises

Bolivia, Ecuador, Nicaragua, Honduras, Dominica, Saint
Vincent and the Grenadines, Antigua, and Barbuda.

- *Caribbean Forum.* The islands in the Caribbean belonging
  to the ACP (African, Caribbean, and Pacific) group of
  countries face lately new conditions in their dealings with
  former parent countries. The European Union (EU) is
  changing the existing agreement based on the Cotonou
  convention with single ACP countries to one that comprises
  a free-trade area made up of regional and subregional
  countries. In this process, the trade preferences will only
  be retained for the poorest ACP countries. The Caribbean
  ACPs formed the CARIFORUM-EU Economic Partnership
  Agreement in 1997 to comply with the changed stance
  of Europe. CARIFORUM pulls together the countries
  Antigua and Barbuda, the Bahamas, Barbados, Belize,
  Dominica, Dominican Republic, Grenada, Guyana, Haiti,
  Jamaica, Saint Kitts and Nevis, Saint Lucia, Saint Vincent
  and the Grenadines, Suriname, and Trinidad and Tobago.
  This new form of cooperation increases the opportunity
  for further integration of the independent islands in the
  region.

Industry-specific cooperation

- *ITU, CTO, and CCA.* The International Telecommunication
  Union for the Caribbean (also a United Nations Agency)
  and the Caribbean Tourism Organization are industry-
  specific organizations in the Caribbean region that
  help intensify regional cooperation. The Caribbean
  Conservation Association works closely with the

Caribbean islands to help improve awareness of the natural environment to insure sustainability.

- *Caribbean Rim Investment Initiative.* The Organization for Economic Cooperation and Development (OECD) initiated a process in the early 2000s to help countries in the Caribbean basin improve their investment climate to attract interisland and foreign investments. The Caribbean Rim Investment Initiative is also helping to establish a dialogue between international organizations and national governments and to avoid duplication of work already done by governments or international organizations.

Official Regionalization

Regionalization in the sense of closer economic cooperation of countries in a region can be explained from several perspectives. One is to improve the material well-being of the citizens through concerted efforts, lowering possible dis-economies of scale. In this way, it is able to construct a larger playing field for human activities. Another view is that it allows the individual country to muster strength to deal with the increasing push toward flexible production systems using "created assets" to produce wealth instead of or next to traditional resources, land labor, and capital. The created assets, as explained by Helen Nesadurai, are based on information, technology and management, and operational competencies, with technology and skills as crucial elements. With cooperation, the countries can preserve the domestic agenda by resisting the negative effects of globalization.[11]

Certain official regional agreements among countries can encourage or alternatively discourage trade with outsiders. When regional concessions are also awarded to nonmembers, one speaks of open-regionalization.

Formal Regional Alignments

Countries may enter into agreements to establish a free-trade area, a customs union, and a common market. A free-trade-area agreement technically establishes the conditions of free movement of goods and services between countries at zero or low customs duties. With a customs union, the participating countries institute an external tariff that is common for all the member countries to the free-trade agreement within the customs union. A common market is a step higher and allows capital and labor movement across borders within the customs union. An even higher level of integration occurs with an economic union, when all kinds of border checks and the market and monetary systems are unified.

Most of the time, these agreements are among countries in the same region, but free-trade agreements can exist between any number of countries without necessarily a regional proximity. Regionalization indicates a conscious effort by adjacent countries to form regional economic blocks.

European Union

The importance of the EU comes from the formal arrangements between the various Caribbean islands and Europe and the lessons that can be learned. Some islands are extraperipheral territories of Europe through a territorially integrated status with a European country.

The EU was many years in the making before it was instituted officially in 1992. In 1952, six West European countries created the European Coal and Steel Community. In 1958, the European Economic Community (EEC) was created to reduce trade barriers, streamline economic policies, remove measures restricting free competition, and promote the mobility of labor and capital among member nations. Negotiations among the EEC members led to the adoption of a single European Act in 1987 to create the EU, which seeks further cooperation by removing border checks, tariffs, customs, and capital and labor restrictions.

Shortly after the creation of the economic union, the EU made a decision to go further toward monetary unification. The EU is, since 1992, an economic and monetary union, with a single market and a single currency. This monetary unification, according to Christian N. Chabot, "brings several benefits to the participating countries. The exchange rate risk is eliminated with the introduction of a single currency. Transaction costs of currencies when traveling or doing business across borders is also eliminated. Besides having a single currency, prices become more transparent for the participating countries. . . .

It was also hoped that the single currency can lead to more macroeconomic stability and lower interest rates."[12]

CARICOM

In the Caribbean region, several nations started a movement toward a regional economic bloc in the 1960s with the development of the Caribbean Free Trade Area (CARIFTA) in 1968 and the Caribbean Common Market (CARICOM) in 1972. This development was patterned after the European Economic Common Market and included first mainly the former British territories. Later on, other nations like Haiti and Surinam were accepted as members. The common market established a common external tariff and a common protective policy. This allowed control over aspects of external economic policy that would have been made independently by each participating country before the establishment of the common market.

The coming of the CARICOM also made possible enhanced cooperation in noneconomic fields and in the establishment of common services. For the Dutch islands, the CARICOM offered possibilities as associate members to participate in areas of functional cooperation, international trade negotiations, and common services. In a 2001 ECLAC report on the possibilities of closer cooperation by the Netherlands Antilles with CARICOM, it appeared that a Partial Scope Trade Agreement could be negotiated with CARICOM.[13] The CARICOM format in this way becomes more open to nonmembers.

Andean Community and Mercosur Custom Unions

In South America, the Andes Pact and the Mercosur are examples of customs unions. The members of the Andean Community are Bolivia, Ecuador, Colombia, and Peru. Mercosur consisted originally of the countries of the southern cone—Argentina, Brazil, Uruguay, and Paraguay. Lately, this customs union has been expanded to include Venezuela and Bolivia. These associations of countries to a certain extent are designed to obtain lower tariffs in trade among the member countries. These two organizations decided recently to combine efforts by establishing a *Union de Naciones Sur Americanas* (UNASUR) with the purpose of establishing free trade on the entire South American continent and a single currency area, next to other objectives like democracy and integration. Other members are Colombia, Chile, Ecuador, Peru, Surinam, and Guyana

Free Trade Areas

The region also has a number of free-trade cooperation agreements among adjacent countries and islands.

North American Free Trade Area

NAFTA has similar goals as those proposed by the EEC, the forerunner of the EU, and is formed by Canada, the United *States, and Mexico.*

Central American Free Trade Area

The United States in August of 2005 signed free-trade agreements with the Central American countries Costa

Rica, El Salvador, Guatemala, Honduras, Nicaragua, and the Dominican Republic. The participation of the Dominican Republic in the CAFTA and possibly in the Central America Common Market (CACM) illustrated the many opportunities in the immediate and greater Caribbean region for enhanced free trading arrangements in a much wider territory.

Free Trade Area of the Americas

In 1994, negotiations were started among thirty-four nations in the region to establish a FTAA, including the stretch of nations from Canada to Argentina. Although the negotiations stalled in and around 2005, work is still being done by the members of the Trade Negotiation Committee, which is spearheaded by the United States and Brazil. During the several deliberations, a Hemispheric Cooperation Program (HCP) was established to help smaller economies in the region participate in the process and guarantee technical assistance, financial support, and transparency.

While this grand strategy is stalled, it has not stopped the progress in the signing of bilateral free-trade agreements in the region. Chile already had an FTA with the United States. Colombia and Peru recently signed a similar free-trade agreement with the United States, and CACM has trade agreements with Mercosur and the Andean Community and is also entering a bilateral agreement with Chile.[14]

Globalization

Globalization is according to Joseph Stigler[15] a closer integration of the countries and the peoples of the world that has been brought about by the enormous reduction of cost of transportation and communication and the breaking down of artificial barriers to the flow of goods, services, capital, knowledge, and (to a lesser extent) people across borders. What characterizes globalization, though, says Soumyen Sikdar[16], is the increasing pace of technological innovations shortening the economic life cycles of processes and products. The IT revolution has made possible a scattering of production facilities over several countries, leading to more market-friendly economic structures worldwide. These changes allow countries to participate more greatly in the international flow of resources.

The increased interaction between nation-states through the flow of goods, ideas, and information tends to create the illusion of a borderless world. From this perspective, island countries like continental states react to preserve their autonomy within this new interdependence. On the one hand, they go into economic cooperation agreements to serve the interests of the individual island state, and on the other hand they compete more openly with each other to attract foreign direct investments from China, Europe, North America, and South America

Global institutions

In this globalized world, several institutions—including the World Health Organization (WHO), the World Trade Organization (WTO), the World Bank, and the International Monetary Fund (IMF)—have assumed, as mentioned in other chapters, prominent roles to promote economic stability globally. These international bodies have brought new perspectives but also new challenges with regard to insertion in the world economy. The WTO, for instance, brought great promise to the underdeveloped countries as it sets rules for international commerce and market access. At the same time, certain issues like trade in services, protection of intellectual property rights, and trade-specific investment measures can be more in favor of the developed economies. Countries feel pressure by the WTO to change from a protective strategy at relatively great speed to one of reciprocity with free trade and limited tariffs as cornerstones. So the individual island faces new situations that require more know-how to survive in the international economic and political arena.

---

[1]   This is referenced by Edward Dommen in a United Nations publication "States, Micro States, and Islands," edited by Dommen and Philippe Hein.

[2]   Elmer Plitschke; Microstates in World Affairs; Policy Problems and Options; Washington: American Enterprise Institute for Policy Research; 1977.

[3]   Philippe Hein. *Is a special treatment of Small Island Developing States possible?* Small Island Developing States; Origin of the category

and definition issues; United Nations Conference on Trade and Development; UNCTAD/LDC/2004/1 UN 2004

4 This concept is first treated in the feasibility study for the 9th European Development Financing directed to improvement of conditions in low-income communities in the Netherlands Antilles, 2007.

5 Delisle Worrell, *Small Island Economics: Structure and Performance in the English-Speaking Caribbean Since 1970* (Praeger, 1987), 143.

6 Worrell, *Small Island Economics*, 173.

7 Dolman, Anthony; Paradise Lost? The past performance and future prospects of Small Island Developing Countries; In: States, Microstates and Islands; edited by Edward Dommen and Philippe Hein; Croom Helm Ltd. 1985 pp 40-69. The reading also makes clear that industrialization efforts are difficult. Hernando De Soto, *The Mystery of Capital: Why Capitalism Triumphs in the West and Fails Everywhere Else* (Basic Books, 2000).

8 Dolman goes on to cite other constraints or vulnerabilities. Small island countries, because of their relative affluence and geographic situation, tend to be high-cost producers. They have tiny internal markets. They lack physical infrastructure and are deficient in technical, managerial, and sometimes entrepreneurial skills. They do not have the critical mass required to first initiate and then sustain processes of technological innovation. "The additional cost of small island industrialization (transport costs, supervisory salary costs, energy costs, etc.) are such that they cannot generally be compensated for by lower wage rates, tax holidays, exchange rate adjustments and similar measures. Viewed from the standpoint of an industrial entrepreneur, the setting up of even a modest operation in a small and remote island does not make much economic sense, and there is little an island government can do to change the overriding logic.

[9] Hernando de Soto, *The Mystery of Capital: Why Capitalism Triumphs in the West and Fails Everywhere Else* (Basic Books, 2000). Underdeveloped countries (and de Soto mentions the former Communist countries as well) try to emulate the developed countries by employing present features that represent the level of economic development of the industrialized countries, without being aware of the process these developed countries have gone through and the origin and importance of capital in this process. Therefore, notwithstanding the efforts by the undeveloped countries, they still often face huge undercapitalization of their (investment) efforts and an expansive array of dead capital.

[10] Hernando De Soto Ibid 9. pp

[11] Helen S. Nesadurai, *Globalisation, Domestic Politics, and Regionalism: the ASEAN Free Trade Area* (Routledge, 2003).

[12] Christian N. Chabot; Understanding theEuro; The clear and concise guide to the New Trans-European Currency; McGraw-Hill, 1999

[13] Economic Commission of Latin America and the Caribbean, "The Netherlands Antilles: Trade and Integration with CARICOM," *LC/CAR/G.681*, December 21, 2001. The study made a thorough comparison of the trade regimes of the CARICOM and the Netherlands Antilles. The report lists CARICOM tariffs on imports from Curaçao and Bonaire, exports to CARICOM, and tariffs in general to CARICOM countries. These act as barriers. The lack of export credit and insurance facilities seem to weigh negatively against exports in the Netherlands Antilles. Transportation and high port charges also have negative effects for trade.

[14] Norman Girvan and Miguel Ceara Hatton, *CARICOM, Central America, and the Free Trade Agreement of the Americas* (Friedrich Ebert Stiftung in collaboration with the Association of Caribbean Economists, 1998).

[15] Joseph E. Stigler; Globalization and its Discontent; Norton and Co. 2002

[16] Soumyen Sikdar; Contemporary Issues in Globalization. An introduction to Theory and Policy in India. P. 13 Oxford University Press; 2002.

CHAPTER 10
MACROECONOMICS, EQUILIBRIUM, AND ECONOMIC PERFORMANCE

This chapter first introduces the concept of equilibrium and economic stability and next the variety of ideas and concepts proposed by economists over the course of time as to what can insure stability and equilibrium as well as how internal forces can distort the conditions that generate stability and equilibrium of supply and demand. The reader is introduced to views by classical and neoclassical economists on what produces value, utility, and general welfare. This discussion provides additional insight with regard to possible imperfections within the free-enterprise system, which can add to inefficiency in the economy.

Introduction

The chapter is to present some thoughts regarding the aspects that affect or can be used to affect the achievement of a condition where supply and demand of goods and services are in equilibrium and produce full employment of the resources applied. The small island states are typically open economies where supply and demand issues generally transcend the home borders, forcing the players in the economy to participate globally in free enterprise. On the other hand the small size of the economy does promote monopolistic conditions at home, where one or just a few firms represent an economic sector. The openness to outside forces and the limited domestic economic activities tend to affect the achievement of economic growth and an acceptable level of societal welfare. It is in this context that contributions to economics, in this chapter essentially by classical economists, are reviewed as to their possible influence on macroeconomic practice in the islands, on how equilibrium is maintained and with regard to those aspects that either generate or prevent economic growth and equilibrium.

Equilibrium Between Supply and Demand

A general idea about economies is that there has to be growth, and this needs to occur with a degree of stability. Stability is upset if supply and demand of goods and services are not synchronized, or discrepancy in supply and demand of labor due to scarcity of skills demanded has as result unemployment that affects economic stability in the economy. Additionally, increases in the general price level can produce inflationary spirals that also affect the purchasing power in the economy and so upset economic stability, lowering real spending and even increasing unemployment. There are a number of factors that cause balance or imbalance between product and factor markets. In an economy it is expected that output by firms and household income are continuously in tandem.

A simple economy can be characterized as follows:

Y = household income

O = output produced by the firms

C = consumption by households of that which is supplied by the firms

S = that part of Y that is not consumed by the households

I = that part of S that is turned into investments by firms and individual in productive enterprise.

Based on the above, equilibrium would occur if O = Y.

Similarly, and from the side of the firm, O = C + I.

Investments occur in capital goods, machines, equipment, and plants. In economics, the I is also indicated as K (capital investment) plus the stock of inventories produced (g). So I = K + g.

And on the household side: Y = C + S, as Y is disposed of through consumption and savings.

Savings are turned into investments through bank intermediation providing productive loans, through stock and bond markets over the counter or via an exchange, or through direct use of savings, like those from retained earnings.

The economy is in equilibrium if Y = O.

For Y to be equal to O, it is expected that C + S = C + I.

Thus, S = I.

What if I and S are not equal?

Table 10.1 illustrates the results of the circular flow of income where S is 10 percent of Yt-1.

Table 10.1 Consumption investment and Income

T	Yt − 1	S	C	I	Y1
1	4000	400	3600	400	4000
2	4000	400	3600	400	4000
3	4000	400	3600	0	3600
4	3600	360	3240	0	3240
5	3240	324	2916	0	2916
6	2916	292	2624	0	2624

Expenditure in the current period t depends on the incomes received in the preceding period, t-1. As long as S and I are equal, Yt-1 and Y1 will remain equal.

If I falls to zero, eventually income will fall to zero.

It falls because the amount allocated to investment is less than the amount allocated to savings. (I-S = 0). I reflects investments in stock of goods and material and in capital equipment. The investments and the size of investments depend on the firm's expectations about the future and dependence on technology.

In table 10.1, we see that at Y = 4,000 and C = 3,600, automatically S = 400. If investment I = 600 on capital goods, then income earned is C + I or 3,600 + 600 = 4,200.

Note that I could be 600 (200 more than savings)—for instance through foreign autonomous investments. Consequently, in a dynamic economy, increasing injections of financial capital to boost economic activities will lead to an increase in income for the country. If savings are not invested and no alternatives are found for investments, then it follows that the economy runs the risk of falling into a downward spiral, because the conditions of Y = C + I in the first period of stagnation would be represented by 3,600 + 0 = 3,600.

Injections and Leakages

In the circular flow is also embedded the influence on the economy from savings, exports, and imports. Economists typically use such terms as *leakages* and *injections* to explain the likely effect of investments, savings, exports, and imports on the economy. Savings and imports are, for instance, seen as withdrawals or leakages from the circular flow.

The following example explains this relationship: The national income (Y) is 4 billion. Consumption is 3 billion. Households save 300 million and import 700 million. The firms invest 200 million and export 500 million in goods and services.

For $Y = O$, it follows that $C + S = C + I$.

In this example, $C + I = 3 + .2$, and $C + S = 3 + .3$, which shows that the economy is not in equilibrium.

The overall economy reflects these injections and leakages as follows:

$$C + I + X - M = 3 + .2 + .5 - .7 = 3.0$$
$$C + S + X - M = 3 + .3 + .5 - .7 = 3.1 \text{ billion}$$

There is a deficit in the trade balance, with X being less than M, or the leakages due to import exceed the injections from export. Alternatively, the total amount of leakage from the economy is given by the amount of withdrawals (savings and imports) versus the amount of injections, or $S + M = 1$ versus $I + X = .7$ This simple illustration of the economy provides further insight as to where actions can be taken to bring the economy in balance.

The Quest for Equilibrium and Economic Stability

There are many explanations as to why a country can be experiencing recessionary conditions with supply and demand for goods and services and for labor not balancing. For instance, insufficient aggregate spending and investments or a decline in technological progress or decline in efficiency[1] while the economy is at full employment can be causes. These can lead to falling output, which takes the country into a recession.

The e following sections introduce thoughts on how macroeconomic behavior influences equilibrium and economic stability.

Thoughts on Equilibrium

Francois Quesnay around 1756 presented the concept of the *tableau economique* in France. [2]This tableau describes the "equilibrating" relationship between supply of work, production, income, and demand for goods. Figure 10.1 below illustrates the circular flow of ncome. It typified for the first time how supply of jobs in a producing firm provides income and, with this income, those in households can buy that which is produced by the worker (coming out of the households) from the firm.

Quesnay interpreted the economic performance in his time as based mainly on agricultural activities. This was due to the fact that agriculture was seen as the more important contributor to the economy. The group of people who shared this concept as a point of reference for their publication was referred to as *physiocrats*. The term *laissez faire, laissez passer* was first used by the physiocrats and indicated that the economy performs best when it is left to the market.

Figure 10.1: Circular flow of income

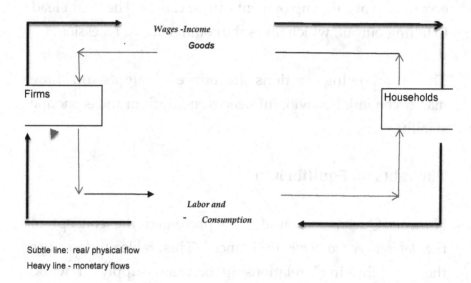

Subtle line: real/ physical flow
Heavy line - monetary flows

The equilibrium concept is illustrated by the circular flow of income, a concept introduced by Francois Quesnay. Equilibrium occurs between product and factor markets.

There are two loops of exactly the same size. Households provide business firms with resources. In turn, business firms pay out rent, wages, and interest to members of households. Profit (or loss) is the residual that takes on the size needed to make the lower loop, via productive services, exactly match the upper loop, via flow of goods. Alternatively, households purchase the goods and services that are made by business firms with the income that they receive through the factor services that they render. To simplify this, the balancing factor will occur when factor income, represented by output (O), is equal to household income (Y). O is income created by firms (wages, interest, profit) in the production process. This was possible through investing and producing goods that are purchased by Y households with the wages and interests that they receive. The simple economy model used as an introduction to this chapter is clearly derived from this thinking.

Mercantilism

Gradually, the governments of mostly European countries changed their focus to trade, amassing silver and gold, the latter which came to symbolize economic growth. A country that did not have its own mines to obtain silver and gold would instead try to increase its exports over imports to obtain gold. This period is characterized as the era of mercantilism, and it is typified on one hand by the gold rush and grand-scale colonialism (and slavery) around the world and on the other hand by a surge in international trade.

Equilibrium: A Natural Condition

With the industrial revolution starting in the late eighteenth century and beginning of the nineteenth century, societies were becoming more complex and the emphasis went to manufacturing and exporting, which greatly expanded the economic potential of the participating countries in Western Europe and North America. The new conditions prompted a number of studies and publications about the economy from people like Jean Baptiste Say, Adam Smith, David Ricardo, Thomas Malthus, and John Stuart Mill. The basic tenet of these writers is that wages and prices will automatically bring supply and demand equilibrium in a free market.

These writers, who are categorized as classicists (belonging to the classical school), believed that equilibrium is a natural condition, always occurring at a point of full employment. If a recession were to occur, it would generally be preceded by a large decrease in money supply, which also decreases total spending. The classicists mentioned above expanded the performance measures to include the effective and efficient use of land, labor, and capital. The proponents of the classical school and later of the neoclassical school generally have in common that money supply in circulation determines what is produced and demanded, as well as the value of products for use and the value that products and services gain in the process of exchange. For the classical school, the equilibrium will be distorted if, say, government is to intervene in the process.

Jean Baptiste Say

Jean Baptiste Say, a French economist, is generally noted for the statement referred to later as Say's law: "Aggregate supply creates its own aggregate demand."[3] It means that the economy regulates itself. He also argued that an increase in the amount of money in the economy would increase the price of other goods, bringing about inflation. However, the relative price related to the relative quantity of the products remains the same. These ideas formed the root for the quantity theory of money that became well-known later on through publications by other economists like Ludwig Von Mises in Austria and Irving Fisher in the United States, indicated as MV = PT or MV = PQ.

The equation suggests that whatever money one does not spend directly is borrowed anyway by businesses to expand productive capacity. *M* stands for money, *V* is velocity, *P* is price, and *Q* is quantity. Thus, the velocity with which money turns over in the economy is supposed to equate with the quantity of products and services supplied, times the price of these. And this automatically insures full employment. Simply put, supply creates its own demand.

For the classical economist, markets should operate freely, seeking equilibrium, without government intervention. Full employment is that level of employment that the economy can absorb at that level of demand that is generated by a given level of supply.

Adam Smith

Adam Smith recognizes in the 1776 publication "An Inquiry into the Wealth of Nations"[4] that there can be a difference in the demand and supply balancing process because of the possible difference between value in exchange and value in use. Value in exchange is determined through pricing and scarcity. Value in use can be greater than value in exchange, so the two values can differ. This is illustrated by the fact that a two-liter bottle of water will not get a similar price as a diamond the size of a quarter, while the value in use of the first item is much higher. There is a difference in value in the use of diamonds and of water and the value in exchange of these two items. This value of products (and services) is determined by the market through the exchange process.

Smith and David Ricardo, another classical economist of the time who is known for the concept of comparative advantage in economics, accepted that there is also a "real" value that comes from the labor used to provide the product or service that is reflected in the wages paid. As a result, one can accomplish efficiency by lowering the cost of labor or production. Smith applied the concept of real value to manufacturing, stating that through greater division of labor more efficiency is achieved in the production process.

Neoclassicals

Economic thought from the late nineteenth century to recently that falls under the umbrella of neoclassical economics upholds the economic thinking of a free market, stressing that for the economy to prosper, there has to be individual liberty, the right to private property, freedom of contract, and a free price system. For the neoclassical school, the free market with free competition is the only way to enhance economic growth, since the free market is held to be more efficient in the allocation of resources given that the means are scarce and the needs multiple.

Great contributors are William Stanley Jevons, Carl Menger, and Leon Walras. They are grouped together as members of the Austrian School who helped explain the concepts of supply, demand, and price equilibrium we discussed in chapter 5. The members of the Austrian school were instrumental in advancing the concepts of marginalism in economics. They hold that the individual makes decisions rationally and on the margin. The concept is simply that an individual will make a decision on an extra unit of production on the basis of benefit versus cost.

The discussion on the labor theory of value shifted to value as being dependent on the utility that the individual ascribes to a good. Other contemporaries who elaborated on utilitarianism are Alex Hume, John Stuart Mill, and Jeremy Bentham; they explained that consumers make purchase decisions based on usefulness, a theory that was further expanded on by Alfred Marshall with ideas about economies of scale and the concepts regarding increasing and decreasing cost industries.

Collective Economic Welfare

These constant discussions and propositions enhance the understanding of how an economy works, what produces general equilibrium, and what is to the benefit of the society as a whole. Vilfredo Pareto (1848-1923) established that a situation can be created where the majority of the population can benefit with the proper allocation of goods (and services) in society. Pareto makes the point that any change that increases the welfare of at least one member of the collective society without reducing the welfare of one or more members of society is a change that improves the collective economic welfare.

The proper allocation of resources occurs with free competition and free exchange that has as a result cost minimization, which leads to an economic maximum and contributes to the greatest welfare. If some individuals are left out of benefiting from the allocation, reallocation of resources will eventually lead to a situation where the majority in society benefits from the improvements. This condition is referred to as the Pareto Optimum.

Marxism

Karl Marx and Friedrich Engels in the late nineteenth century also focused on exchange theory of value like the classical school but came to the conclusion that in the end, the exchange value should produce greater general welfare, and this is not apparent with the capitalist system. Value for Karl Marx is based on the value of the labor that goes into making a product or giving a service. The wages are an artificial construct. The wages by themselves do not provide for a real equilibrating situation.

This focus led to the interpretation of the economic environment as one where labor is exploited to the benefit of owners of capital, thus rendering welfare to a small group. To achieve a state where both the owners and labor benefit, Marx realized that a process had to unfold in such a way that the existing conditions of exploitation by the owners of capital would slowly erode through a series of conflicts that in the end would allow everyone in society to benefit.

Marx was apparently influenced by the philosophy of G. W. Hegel that civilizations go through a process beginning at an existing state, called the *thesis*, to another state that builds on conflicts within the existing state, the *antithesis*, and to a final state, *synthesis*, where order is restored. Consequently, and according to this reasoning, capitalism—which is the thesis—will eventually evolve into socialism and finally into communism. This final stage will be classless and everything will be owned by the "people."

This was alternative thinking, and socialism was embraced in the twentieth century by several countries as their economic model. The Soviet Union, mainland China, Vietnam, Cuba, and North Korea have introduced versions of such an economic model, which is predominantly a command economy with all or most factors of production owned by the state. The importance of private property rights, free-price system, and individual liberty were sacrificed for a system where the state (in the name of the people) assumes all or most of those rights. By the end of the twentieth century, many countries that subscribed to this line of thinking retracted on their rigid position, allowing more free participation of individuals and firms in the economic process.

Caribbean Experiments

In the Caribbean, several countries in addition to Cuba tried out a socialist solution Jamaica introduced Democratic Socialism in the 1970s, and Grenada wanted to achieve development by following a noncapitalist path toward development. Unemployment in Jamaica had grown to 24 percent, while the major sectors of the economy were to a large extent under foreign ownership. In Grenada the government felt that:" the level of industrialization was low, that there was significant unemployment of resources, and that the price/market system did not yield profits commensurate with their fullest utilization."[5] Guyana (formerly British Guiana) established the Cooperative (Socialist) Republic of Guyana, with the development of the economy based primarily on resources like sugar, rice, and bauxite-alumina cooperatives. Guyana nationalized these industries with the intent to "assert more national control over the economy." It was Guyana's intention to get the basic needs of the population tended to with the profits from the sectors. With the new economic structure putting most industries in government hands, a socialist foundation was to be created with the private profit motive substituted by the social goal.[6]

As pointed out by Patrick R. Liverpool: "cooperativism in the context of Guyana] is a variant of socialism—an economic system guided by socialist principles—in which the major means of production in the society are owned and controlled by cooperative institutions."[7] This is different from democratic socialism, where para-statal organizations have control over the economy and managed capitalism, as in the case of the United States, where large-scale private and public organizations seem to have the de facto control.[8]

The efforts in the Caribbean toward socialism in the 1970s were to lower the external dependence of the economy, reduce the exploiting capacity of domestic monopolies, and get better control on serving the basic needs of the country. To take just one example,[9] the objectives in Jamaica were to:

1. Enhance redistribution of income
2. Change the structure of economic power
3. Change the social relations of productions
4. Secure economic growth and development

For the small Caribbean countries and island nations, these objectives constituted a way to foster development and sustainable growth as they emerged from having been colonial outposts for many centuries, facing major market imperfections. There was a continuous search for which economic model served the country best to take an island from underdeveloped to more developed. Most countries that followed socialist principles in the seventies and the eighties have changed to a different model since the 1990s.

Market Imperfections

Notwithstanding the settled ideas about free markets by the neoclassical school in the first part of the twentieth century, it was acknowledged in the 1930s that the market is not completely free, as the freedom itself can generate monopolistic behavior by the participating firms without any government involvement. Edward Chamberlin (USA) and Joan Robinson (Great Britain), who published in the same year,[10] noted that the market is not necessarily free if one firm can dominate the market with regard to supply or demand of a product or service. Chamberlin and Robinson brought forward that ideologically perfect competition would be best for the market, but there were many instances where monopolies affect prices, production capacity, supply of products and services, and ultimately demand.

Michal Kalecki[11] discussed the weaknesses that monopolies and monopolistic competition bring to the economy, saying that monopolies tend to engage in a process that is increasingly biased toward overaccumulation and stagnation. This behavior has an effect on the distribution of national income, on economic power, and on stagnation. Josef Steindl[12] also weighed in on this discussion and mentioned that giant firms, able to control to a considerable extent the levels of their price, output, and investment, would not invest if large portions of their existing productive capacity were already standing idle. If there is a downward shift in final demand, monopolistic or oligopolistic firms would not lower their prices as would occur with competitive systems but rely on cutbacks in output, capacity, utilization, and investments. They would try to maintain existing prices and prevailing profits.

When large firms acting as a single firm in a single industry are owned and operated by the government, government agencies, or through concessions for operation, Paul A. Baran and Paul Sweezy suggest that such economy can be characterized as *monopoly capitalism*.[13] They added that left to itself, in the absence of counteracting forces, monopoly capitalism would sink deeper and deeper into a bog of chronic depression.[14] Baran and Sweezy contend that monopolies can have far-reaching effects on the economic performance of a country due to the fact that with giant firms, there is concentration and centralization of capital and little to no price competition; investments are regulated by the level of excess capacity instead of by competition. These conditions can distort the ability of a country to improve its economic performance.

Evidently, there are sometimes valid reasons for the existence of some fashion of monopoly in a small economy. Natural monopoly exists when the size of the country makes only one or a few companies viable due to, for instance, indivisibility of capital. National interest motives for political and economic benefit will also lead to the establishment and maintenance of specific domestic monopolies, to forestall foreign participation that can be detrimental to the continued health of the nation state.

Joseph Schumpeter

New thoughts on macroeconomics are continually appearing, and Joseph Schumpeter argued that developments in the market economy bring changes that affect prior thoughts held by classicists. Great corporations, he claimed, contribute with constant technological improvements and innovations to economic development. This happens through a process of "creative destruction." With the changing structure of business, more people may have joint ownership of property and appointed officers run companies based on power that comes from their status and not based on property ownership. As a result, the concept of property as applied by the classical economists does not provide the same "overriding argument to economic development anymore."[15]

Rebirth of the Neoclassical School

Monetarism

Milton Friedman of the Chicago School of Economics published his thoughts on the importance of the free-market economy at approximately the same time the Keynes concepts was becoming widely adopted around the world using national income statistics and carrying out monetary and fiscal policies to correct shortcomings in the economy. Milton Friedman questioned the value of a far-reaching involvement of the government in the market. His thesis, as it was for the classical school, was that the money supply is determinant of the nominal value of output, and that inflation can only be controlled by the central bank through controlling the amount of money that circulates in the financial system. A fixed rate of monetary growth is a better stabilizer than fiscal policy. According to his thoughts, policymakers cannot maintain low unemployment while permitting inflation to soar. The markets should be left to operate freely, with little government intervention.

Rational expectations

This doubt about the real value of government intervention keeps lingering, and Robert Lucas and contemporaries at the University of Chicago referred to as the Rational Expectation School remain of the opinion that the marketplace works better on its own than with intervention. Besides, if there is intervention by the central bank, say by a given percentage increases in the money supply to ward off recession, businessmen tend to in time expect these increases and respond in their price system to these policies. As a result of these rational decisions, the policies of the government will not be effective.

Supply-side economics

The supply-side concept introduced during the years of President Reagan in the United States and referred to as Reagonomics focuses on increasing aggregate supply by increasing the production of goods and services. To increase production of goods and services requires reducing taxes and reducing the effect of all other factors that could impede increase in production. This would raise aggregate supply.

The market remains important. Economic growth is seen as dependent on the supply of goods and services. As shown on the graph below, increase in production of supply of goods and services increases output and lower prices. As we discussed in chapter 5, the lower price will have as an effect that demand increases along the demand curve, obtaining equilibrium between supply and demand at higher quantities of goods and services.

Figure 10.2 Equilibrium and Supply Side theory

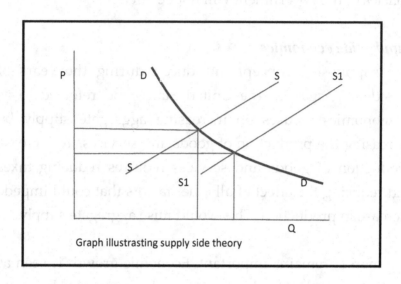

Graph illustrasting supply side theory

It is always a question of how such a strategy would work in a minute economy. The Structural Adjustment Program (SAP) suggested by the International Monetary Fund (IMF) in the late 1990s for the Dutch Caribbean islands within the Netherlands Antilles was to have this effect of increasing production and productivity. The small population and the limited individual and aggregate savings that are characteristic for the small and microstates, but also the historic dependency on a colonial past, requires more involvement by the government and financing from foreign countries for investments of the size required in the economy to increase supply. These circumstances bring imperfection to the market and consequently influence rationality in decisions on consumption and production that are not a result of government interference but due to market anomalies.

Remarks

The classical school and the neoclassical school consider the equality of "Money times Velocity" and "Price times Trade" as the equilibrium situation that creates full employment. Thus, full employment is the number that can be employed at the MV = PT level that exists at a certain moment. Equilibrium is seen as a result of the application of the resources, the technology and individual preferences. According to these schools, if there is any distortion, this is due to government meddling.[107]

[1]   Walter J. Wessels, *Economics,* 3rd ed. (Business Review Books, Barron's, 2000).

[2]   Francois Quesnay; Tableau Economique; presented in 1756 and 1757 but officially published in 1758.

[3]   J.B. Say (1767-1832) published "A Treatise on Political Economy" in 1803, in which he treats the various ideas on aggregate supply and aggregate demand, including aspects of purchasing power and the roles of the circulation banks and deposit banks in the economy.

[4]   Adam Smith, An inquiry into the Nature and Causes of the Wealth of Nations; W Strahan and T. Cadell, publishers; 1776. Also republished by Random House in 1937.

[5]   Clive Y. Thomas, "The Next Time Around: Radical Options and Caribbean Economy," In *Development in Suspense: Selected Papers and Proceedings of the First Conference of Caribbean Economists,* eds. Norman Girvan and George Beckford; pp 291-296; (Friedrich Ebert Stiftung in collaboration with the Association of Caribbean Economists, 1989).

[6] Clive Y. Thomas, "The Next Time Around: Radical Options and Caribbean Economy," In *Development in Suspense: Selected Papers and Proceedings of the First Conference of Caribbean Economists*, eds. Norman Girvan and George Beckford pp 306-310; (Friedrich Ebert Stiftung in collaboration with the Association of Caribbean Economists, 1989).

[7] Patrick R. Liverpool, "A Note on Dilemmas of Cooperative Development in Post-Colonial Guyana," in *Studies in Post-colonial Society*, ed. Aubrey Armstrong (Cameroun: African World Press, 1975).

[8] Liverpool, "A Note on Dilemmas of Cooperative Development in Post-Colonial Guyana," 59. This comparison of systems is adapted by Liverpool from John Elliot's *Comparative Economic Systems* (NJ: Prentice Hall, 1973).

[9] Norman Girvan commenting on Clive Thomas paper. Ibid 5.

[10] Edward Chamberlin, with the "Theory of Monopolistic Competition" in 1933, and Joan Robinson, with the publication "The Economics of Imperfect Competition" in the same year.

[11] Kalecki published his notions about the influence of monopolies on the economic crisis starting in the 1930s (in Polish). In this chapter, I refer to his book *Theory of Economic Dynamics* (1952).

[12] Josef Steindl (1952), in the publication "Maturity and Stagnation in American Capitalism."

[13] Paul Sweezy and Paul A. Baran, *Monopoly Capital* (New York: Monthly Review Press, 1966).

[14] Sweezy and Baran, *Monopoly Capital*, 125.

[15] Joseph Schumpeter: Capitalism, Socialism and Democracy; 3d ed. Harper Torch Books; 1962.

Chapter 11
Keynesian Analysis

This chapter is about the use of the Keynesian model to analyze economic performance. This approach is different from the classical and neoclassical approach in that government has a role to play in maintaining economic stability and equilibrium between aggregate supply and aggregate demand. The new approach introduces a number of handholds to determine how the economy can be manipulated to get it back on track. Among these are, on the demand side, the aspects of disposable income, the average propensity to consume, and the marginal propensity to consume, and on the supply side, the economic potential based on what the output of the economy can be when all resources are used effectively and efficiently. With this approach, aggregate spending for the period is evaluated against aggregate production.

Introduction

The classical economists subscribe to the automatic-adjustment principle, where supply creates demand without government intervention. Still, historically, even where nations have maintained the liberal market economy concept, government intervention and oversight have become commonplace to cure problems due to recession or depression or due to excesses during a period of economic expansion. As shown in chapter 3, the government could even set the stage for private enterprise to be active with the government condoning slavery, wars, and conquests by free enterprisers for "national" gain. Furthermore, "without government intervention" does not mean that monopolies cannot exist in a free-enterprise environment and have similar effects as those that classical economists would denounce.

The Keynesian approach proposes government intervention when needed to maintain a desired national spending level that helps to generate full employment. This is based on the tenet that a mismatch of supply and demand can occur because of issues in the economic environment or because of a catastrophic event produced by a hurricane, earthquake, or volcanic eruption. Although supply is acknowledged, the emphasis is laid on spending to maintain economic stability. This is where the government can influence the match between supply and demand. In fact, even if supply and demand were to coincide, if there was a situation of unemployment, government might be able through economic policies and strategies help to boost spending, which can bring about increase in supply with the economy operating at a higher level.

The expenditure components of the gross domestic product (GDP) addressed in chapter 6—consumption, investments, exports and imports, and government expenditures—provide details necessary to analyze economic performance and appraise these in light of aggregate supply that would occur when all resources (labor, land, and capital) are used most effectively and to the fullest extent in producing the national output or potential GDP.

Aggregate Supply and Demand

When aggregate expenditures are equal to aggregate output and the country experiences full employment of capital and labor, the economy is functioning optimally. This is naturally what everyone would like to achieve. The following is a simple approach to explain when additional attention is to be directed to obtain or restore the match between aggregate demand and a potential gross national product (GNP).

Equilibrium GNP

In this example, aggregate expenditures (AE) are measured on the Y axis. GNP is indicated on the X axis. AE will obtain a particular GNP in buying the supplies available. If total spending covers all goods produced for sale, there is equilibrium. Then AE = GNP, and AE represents the spending on the components C + I + G at the various levels of total spending. By drawing a 45-degree line, we can represent the points where aggregate expenditures are equal to aggregate output. This condition is shown in figure 11.1.

Figure 11.1: Equilibrium Expenditures and Output

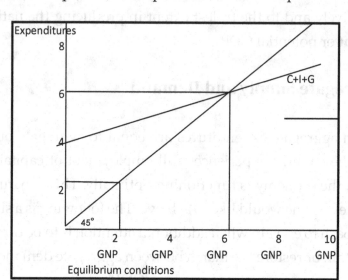

If gross expenditures indicated by the components C + I + G is above the 45-degree line that indicates potential GNP (given the resources used), this is a sign that some kind of intervention is necessary to bring the economy back on a path to equilibrium. At 4 billion GNP, AE is above the 45-degree line. An analysis of the components may for instance show that imports exceed exports. This is further reflected in a high rate of consumption relative to disposable income. There is a chance that prices will soar and cause inflation, so government will introduce a contractionary policy to lower the money supply and so lower spending.

If aggregate expenditures AE (C + I + G) is lower than the 45-degree line as illustrated by the gap occurring after a GNP of 6 billion, the economy seems to be producing more than is demanded. In that case, the government may step in with an expansionary policy, increasing the money supply so that the economy will not contract by itself.

These policies are relevant in that they are introduced to bring stability to the economy, generating an environment in which employment can be secured without affecting the real wages. When and if equilibrium between supply and demand occurs at 6 billion, as shown on the graph at a point on the 45-degree line representing potential GDP, labor and capital are fully and effectively employed.

The social ramifications of excessive unemployment include increasing "underground" activity or even criminal activity in society by those left out to insure some kind of income or "satisfaction." Or, as has become more usual during the last decades of the twentieth century, many leave to find jobs and an income abroad, especially in the Netherlands.

The following simplified table (with only *C* and *I* as aggregate expenditures) shows the equilibrium conditions for a country with a disposable income of which 90 percent is consumed. This is shown as (marginal propensity to consume as explained in a later section below), mpc = .90. Employment is not an issue here.

Table 11.1 Equilibrium DI

mpc =	0.9					
	DI	C	S	I	C+I	DI-(C+I)
1	5900	0	5900	900	900	5000
2	6900	0	6900	900	900	6000
3	7900	0	7900	900	900	7000
4	8900	0	8900	900	900	8000
5	9900	0	9900	900	900	9000
6	10900	0	10900	900	900	10000

The country manages to put an extra 310 million beside the savings in autonomous investments. Keeping everything else unchanged, C + I, which is aggregate expenditure for period one, is smaller than DI, with 310 million. If each year only the amount of savings is invested, there will be no indicative growth. With the additional funds invested and a yearly assumed growth in disposable income as shown in Column 1 above, aggregate expenditures on consumption and investment will be equal to the disposable income after Year 4. This process is shown in figure 11.2 where the C + I line crosses the 45-degree line with GNP potential output a little above 8.9 billion, which actually takes place in Year 5.

Figure 11.2 AE/GNP equilibrium

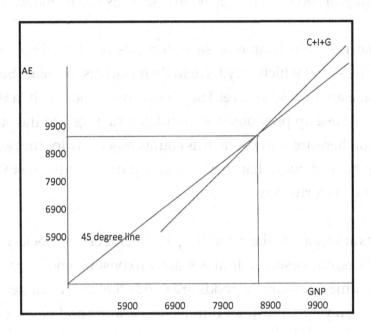

In this example, the AE line is lower than the 45-degree line at a lower GDP and higher than the potential GDP line past the equilibrium point.

In the following section, we attempt to develop some insight as to how the pattern of consumption and increases or decreases in consumption over a period of time affects the performance of the economy.

Consumption and Disposable Income

Consumption is generally one of the largest spending components of the GDP. If the disposable income is consumed completely, there are no savings. It holds that without old savings or foreign savings, no investments can be made.

What people consume or save depends on their disposable income—that which they have in their pockets to spend. Some people are unable to save! They spend more money than they earn or use up previously accumulated savings. On the other hand, there are some—and this counts especially for the rich— who have enough that they can save more than the rest who are not as fortunate.

Consumption is the spending by members of society on services, on consumer durables, and on consumer nondurables. Consumer nondurable goods are goods that are consumed up during a year. Consumer durables, like shirts and pants, cars, and furniture last more than a year.

J. M. Keynes made two assumptions with regard to consumer spending:

1. People make their consumption spending based on their current take-home pay (disposable income).
2. When people get additional income, they do not spend all of it.

The level of consumption is also influenced by the following:

- *present wealth,* the amount of income one can receive from funds available from past profits, inheritances, monetary prizes from a lottery, and so on

- *price level*, the expectations with regard to how inflation or deflation can affect the way people spend their current income
- *future income prospects*, the amount of income one expects to receive from current sources of wealth, from earnings from investments and employment, or from proceeds from pension plans during retirement.

These are important factors weighed by the members of society in spending current income. The decision of how much to consume could be further influenced by government fiscal policy.

Disposable Income

Disposable income (D) refers to the amount of money private individuals have available to them every year to spend. The amount of disposable income in the economy is obtained by subtracting depreciation + taxes from the GNP. More accurately, GNP−(depreciation + taxes)−net corporate savings (excluding distributed profits) + transfer payments of welfare gives the disposable income. Distributed profits refer to payments made to shareholders in a company in the form of dividends.

Disposable income is what remains available to households after they have paid their taxes and received their transfer payments. Table 11.2 illustrates in millions of local monetary units the build-up of disposable income for the Netherlands Antilles in 1996 and 1997.

Table 11.2 Disposable Income

Year	1996	1997
GNP	4,970	5,050
Less:		
Depreciation	525	585
Net National Product	4,445	4,465
Less:		
Taxes and	820	810
Net Corporate savings	600	615
Plus:		
Transfer payments	280	250
Unrequited transfers		
Disposable Income	**3,305**	**3,290**
Table SIDI		

Adapted from the National Accounts of the Netherlands Antilles for the selected years. The information is simplified; not all data is reported.

Disposable income is this sum (Y) that people will divide between consumption spending and net personal saving. The disposable income declined in the second year in table 11.2. This means that the people in the country have less to spend on consumption or less to save. The amount of national savings in the national statistics gives an impression of what is available for investments and capital formation in the domestic economy.

Pattern of Consumption

The propensity to consume is explained by J. M. Keynes as the functional relationship x between Y at a given level of income (in terms of wage units) and the expenditure on consumption (C) at that level of income. The average propensity to consume (APC) is calculated by the equation $APC = C \div Y$, where Y stands for disposable income.

What is not consumed is considered saved. As a consequence, there is also a resulting pattern of savings denoted as the average propensity to save (APS).

The alternative computation is $APS = (Y - C) \div Y$.

An example from the Windward Islands of the Dutch Antilles shows consumption and savings for the household sectors for the 1996 and 1997 years as indicated in table 11.3.

Table 11.3 Savings

	Year 1	Year 2
Disposable income: (D.I).	700	715
Less: Consumption (C)	590	600
Savings	110	115

Adjusted from SISC -CBS_1996-1997 Windward Islands, Netherlands Antilles

The disposable income and consumption, alternatively savings data, is used to estimate the pattern of consumption for, in this case, the Windward Islands for the two consecutive years. The APC for 1996 is found by dividing consumption, C = 590, by disposable income, Y = 700. Consequently, the APC for Year 1 is 590 ÷ 700 or 84.28 percent. This means that people on the island will consume 84.28 percent of each florin of disposable income. In Year 2, the APC is 83.92 percent. In those years, the pattern of saving is indicated by the APS for Year 1 is 110 ÷ 700 = 15.72 percent and APS for Year 2 is equal to 115 ÷ 715 = 16.08 percent.

The small reduction in APC from Year 1 to Year 2 could be a result of the expectations of the future by the households in terms of continued and growing income. The increase in average savings shows that there could be a concern about spending too much. For instance, people may have decided not to travel that second year or spend less on painting the house in order to save for future expenditures.

Marginal propensity to save or consume

Measuring the consumption pattern and savings pattern are useful as instruments to forecast how extra savings or consumption are likely to affect national income in the future. This is achieved by computing the marginal propensity to consume (MPC). The MPC under the given circumstances for the Windward Islands is obtained by dividing the change in consumption from one year to the other year by the change in disposable income from one year to the other. This relationship is also known as the consumption function. If there is consumption when disposable income is zero, this consumption is regarded as autonomous consumption. Otherwise it is induced consumption. The autonomous and induced consumption are illustrated in figure 11.3. The induced consumption is due to changes in disposable income.

Figure 11.3 Consumption function

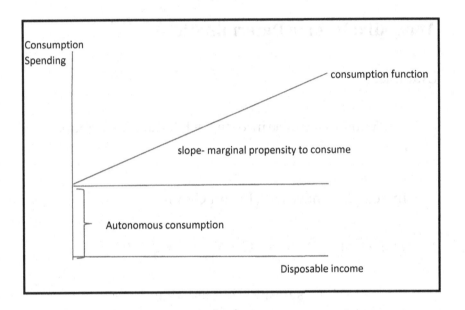

Using the example of the Windward Islands, the change in consumption (see figure 11.3) from Year 1 to Year 2 is 600-590 = 10. The change in disposable income for the period is 715-700 = 15. As a result, the MPC based on these two periods is 10 ÷ 15 = .667 or 66.7 percent. With this information, we can answer the following question: If MPC is 66.7 percent, how much will consumption increase if disposable income increases by, for instance, 10,000 florins? The answer is that consumption will increase by ANG 10,000 × .667 = ANG 6,670.

The MPS (that is, the part of disposable income that is not consumed) is obtained similarly using the savings relationship to disposable income. The MPS is then 5 ÷ 15 = .333 or 33.3 percent. It follows that if income in Year 2 is higher by 10,000 florins, 3,330 florins will be saved.

Appendix: Income Determination

Example:

The Year 1 disposable income Y = 100 and consumption C = 95.

In Year 2, Y moves to 110 and C to 103.

The resulting MPC = $\Delta C \div \Delta Y = 8 \div 10 = 0.8$

MPC is positive but less than 1.

It indicates that some portion of additional income is spent, but not all.

Alternatively,[1] when investment spending increases by ΔI, this affects consumption and income due to the marginal propensity to consume of the funds released by the additional investment spending. If autonomous investment is 100 and b (the marginal propensity to consume) = .8, then

$\Delta Y = bY + \Delta I$

So, $\Delta Y = .8Y + 100$

$\Delta Y(1-.8) = 100$

$\Delta Y = 1 \div (1-.8) \times 100 = 5 \times 100 = 500$

If we consider the situation that $C = a + mpc(Y)$, with a being a level of autonomous consumption that would occur even when income is zero, then if $a = 20$ and $I = 100$ and $b = .8$, then $C = 20 + bY + 100$. Then it follows that

$$Y(1-b) = 20 + 100$$
$$\Delta Y = 1 \div (1-.8) (20+100) = 5 \times 120 = 600.$$

If this holds true, then

$$S = Y\text{-}a\text{-}mpc(Y) \text{ or } S = \text{-}a + (1\text{-}mpc) \times Y.$$

The marginal change in consumption ΔC

$$\frac{\Delta C}{\Delta Y} = (\delta c / \delta y) = MPC$$

If the MPC is higher than unity, dis-saving is taking place, where more than the additional florin in disposable income is consumed. Consequently, no additional income is saved.

---

[1]   See E. J. Chambers, R. Haney Scott, and Roger Smith. *National Income Analysis and Forecasting* (Scott Foresman and Company, 1975).

CHAPTER 12

SAVINGS AND CAPITAL FORMATION

While this chapter discusses the essence of savings, this is done with the understanding that small, miniscule islands do not tend to have an amount of savings on the national level or on an individual level to cater to the needs of the island for the building and maintenance of a physical infrastructure and at the same time redistribute income to the needy. The chapter tries to introduce ideas for a new national thinking on the application of savings to investments and to give some background for identification of ways to use even the scant savings for investment in those areas that can provide growth in conjunction with, or without, additional foreign financial assistance.

Introduction

The subject matter in this chapter regards how savings are obtained, held, and applied toward capital formationusing the existing theoretical base developed by the classical and modern economists, and this is related as much as possible to the apparent realities of the islands. The chapter presents the motives for savings as well as the determinants for investments in order to establish a viable background for supporting innovations.

The motives for saving in small islands do not differ from those generally held for larger countries. Savings are held for precautionary or liquidity reasons, for investment or speculation purposes, or to provide for a future need, like old age or guarding against a rainy day. Savings that go into the old-age pension are mandatory savings. Sometimes people save just out of habit. In the very small islands, savings that can be turned into investments are generally relatively small, and the islanders generally turn to cooperative ways of building and island-specific solutions to survive.

The tables in chapter 6 and chapter 9 give an indication of the distribution of goods and services among the peoples in the islands. It is held widely that those in a country who cannot afford all of the material goods shown will spend their incomes largely on the necessities of life: food, shelter, and clothing. But as income increases, people tend to shift away from cheap foods to more expensive foods. Still, there are limits to the amount of extra money people will spend on food when their income rises. Often the percentage of food expenditure decreases as income increases. It even appears that spending on some goods decreases absolutely with increase in income. Furthermore, expenditures on clothing, recreation, and automobiles increase more than proportionately with increases in disposable income. The island will in general show a pattern of consumption and saving dependent on the general level of income.

Business firms save depending on the retained earnings and depending on how many dividends they pay to shareholders.

Retained earnings are the accumulation of net profits by a firm over a period of time.

"Savings" as used in the national account is a compilation of all savings in society and is the result of subtracting gross consumption from gross disposable income. National savings and national investments are computed by the national bureau of statistics and presented in the national accounts publications of the islands. Table 12.1 shows the gross national disposable income and gross savings by island and island group.

Table 12.1: Gross Savings 2004

Year 2004	Disposable income and savings by island		
	Bonaire	Curaçao	WWI
Gross national disposable income	327	4214	1156
Gross savings	169	847	486

Source: CBS; National Accounts 1997-2004

The disposable income in the table is the amount that is disposable for spending and saving. "Savings" is the amount of disposable income that is not consumed. The data above shows that the largest economy of the Dutch Caribbean had savings of approximately 20 percent of disposable income in 2004, while the Windward Islands and Bonaire show gross savings of 42 percent of disposable income in 2004.

Complex Phenomenon

The savings are held at a variety of sources, and they are held in a variety of ways. An important percentage of domestic savings is also funneled to international markets for investment purposes and is not available in the local economy for investments. It is also true that the islands are often recipients of a flow of foreign savings, which are turned into investments for domestic purposes. These are channeled via development banks or similar organizations, which carry out the administration and control the disbursement of funds.

Domestic savings that in principle can be turned into investments are those of private citizens, government agencies, and firms that hold current accounts and savings accounts with depository institutions like saving banks, commercial banks, and credit unions, or have accounts at a pension fund or with insurance firms. The latter three organizations also use banks for depository purposes. Naturally, there are still some savings that occur by holding currency in a secure place at home, like in a safe, a sock, or a pillowcase, but the size of the savings that are kept this way is quite insignificant nowadays.

Banks hold client savings in current accounts or as passbook savings and in fixed-term deposits. Banks also act as depositories for financial assets like bonds and equities traded by third parties, and may be active in intermediating in the trading process.

Pension funds and insurance companies, the Social Security bank, and the mortgage banks are classified as institutional investors. Deposits received for the payment of insurance premiums or to fund a pension plan are generally invested in fixed financial assets. These organizations belong together with the commercial banks, finance companies, and the central bank to the financial sector of the Dutch islands. The so-called offshore banks operate on the island but their business is with foreign clients.

The central bank imposes regulations like, for instance, a cash-reserve ratio on the deposit banks. This requires the deposit bank, acting as a commercial bank, to keep a certain percentage of its available cash at the central bank. The deposit bank is also responsible for maintaining a capital adequacy ratio as a participant in the Basel agreement.[1] These policies may limit somewhat the amount of funds available for borrowing in the domestic financial markets. Furthermore, due to the small domestic economy and credit and market risks, the governments of the Dutch Caribbean allow that 40 to 50 percent of the investment funds held at the institutional investors are invested abroad. Private citizens and other nonfinancial businesses facing the same domestic market often also deposit a portion of the earnings abroad, creating, as it is not regulated and under the central bank, capital flight.

Brank branching and foreign investments

As each island is relatively small, the savings held at a variety of sources are scattered and often too small to be turned into large productive investments—this despite the fact that foreign savings are regularly injected into an open economy and despite the ability of the banking sector to use the demand deposits on the books in a recurrent way, termed money creation, to provide loans.

Foreign savings are generally directed to specific projects. For major projects on one island where the loan funds are not available, it is within the capacity of commercial banks to finance capital investments on one island through bank branching[2]—channeling funds from one island to another. Obviously, movements from a portion of the deposits between islands will be dependent on the domestic monetary policy, the degree of financial integration among the islands and the bank's policy to diversify its lending.

Real Impact of Foreign Assistance

Foreign financial assistance helps to offset temporary shortcomings in the balance of payments and is used to finance investments in areas where the private sector falls short due to the degree of risks involved. However, at the same time foreign financing of this kind can discourage a more risk taking behavior by the private sector. This could occur, for instance, when the private sector actors, aware of the stream of funds toward the government, rather trade in government bonds than invest in risky ventures with commercial benefit.

Several economists have expressed reservations with regard to the true contribution of foreign financial assistance to value-added. These funds are channeled to projects by the government and, together with the borrowings from government on the local open market, lead to a crowding-out condition regarding business borrowing.

Innovating and Adapting

The little savings available on a very small island are generally not sufficient to induce activities that contribute to economic growth. It takes instead a concerted effort that contains:

- a *private-public partnership approach and direct foreign financing* to turn a portion of the savings into viable investments.
- *A new vision where competitiveness does not depend on the static abundance or scarcity of a factor of production* (cheap labor or cheap raw materials). This is a point raised by Miguel Ceara Hatton and Orlando Reyes, economists from the Dominican Republic who at a conference of the Association of Caribbean Economists in 1993 in Curaçao remarked that "a new vision and strategy through restructuring of the production pattern by means of a technological transformation, optimization of management procedures, and search for market niches in the context of flexible specialization will be central concerns". Furthermore, investments in human resources will be vital to increase in productivity. For this strategy to work, Ceara and Reyes observe that the financial sector should be reformed to increase efficiency in the intermediate term and a long-term

capital market should be developed in the short-run to help finance the restructuring of production patterns.[3] This position is also held by Jose A. Ocampo when he observes that dynamic improvements in productivity come through the process of technological diffusion, learning, adaptation and absorption.[4]

If innovation in the past was based on the use and adaptation of imported technology, mostly from multinationals, now the experience and technological know-how on the islands—often acquired through working with multinationals—is to form a foundation for further development. The identification of these skills to build and support the development of a new sector or industry is equally important as the identification of foreign markets to export to. The development banks and investment banks can assume an additional role in guiding this transformation, and support the introduction of innovative products and services.

Capital Formation

Yearly additions to the stock of capital financed either by domestic savings or by foreign savings, tend to contribute to economic growth and stability. In the small islands, there is sometimes confusion as to who will take on this responsibility. New and unknown ideas are not easily financed by the banking sector, and government is generally not equipped to deal with innovations that have private-sector leanings. The successive governments in the Dutch islands have been actively involved with the private sector over the years, stimulating private sector development by establishing the Free Zone, setting up a tax-holiday scheme to attract foreign investors, introducing guarantees for the Hotel Real Estate Development sector and special legislation for the offshore financial sector. The Private-Public Partnership concept has evolved to a level that it is now common place that private sector and public sector can embark on joint projects that can be financed by third parties.

Net National Product

The national statistic that provides a feeling of how the economy is performing with respect to capital formation is the net national product (NNP). The NNP is the sum of all final products, including net investment, as shown in chapter 6. To determine net investments, the net additions to the stock of buildings, equipment, and inventories are considered. The investments are categorized as those in plant and equipment and those in inventory during a year. *Plant* includes investments in factories, office buildings, shopping malls, and the like. *Equipment* includes machine tools, display cases, tractors, cash registers, computer systems, and office furniture. *Inventory* refers to the addition to inventory (of final goods or raw material) during a year. Accordingly, net investment is equal to gross investment minus depreciation.

An example of gross and net investment for two different periods is provided in Table 12.2.

Table 12.2: Net Investments

	Year 1	Year 2
Gross fixed capital formation	1,360	1,280
Changes in inventory	60	25
Net Acquisitions	20	40
Gross Investments	**1,440**	**1,345**
Depreciation Allowance	(525)	(557)
Net Private Domestic Investments	915	788

Source: CBS N.A.

How much money is invested, as shown with additions to gross fixed capital, will depend on how optimistic the investor is about the future prospects, the interest rates that he has to pay, and the return versus risk circumstances that he or she is facing at the moment. In the case of the Dutch Caribbean, there is a discrepancy between net private domestic investments and savings that is probably due to the amount of foreign assistance flowing into investments. Notice that in chapter 13, the possible effects of investments in capital goods on the economy of a small island are discussed.

Determinants of Investments

There are a number of factors that will stimulate investments in any given year.

1. *Future expected profits.* This indicates clearly the business involvement in the economy. An entrepreneur expecting

profit possibilities from an investment will seek the needed financing to invest in the venture.

2. *The real interest rate.* If the interest rate for financing of capital investments is high, business firms will lower their profit expectations and as such may be reluctant to invest.

3. *Optimism about the future.* Firms and individuals may be optimistic or pessimistic about the future. In 1995-1999, the Structural Adjustment Program was introduced, taking account of the fact that the general outlook with regard to the economy of especially Curaçao was bleak. People were very pessimistic concerning future economic activities and held off investing. Optimism, on the contrary, will generally have as an effect that more investments occur.

4. *The accelerator effect.* The accelerator model assumes that investment is related to changes in expected sales. This idea is implicitly held when we introduced the marginal propensity to save and invest as a way to indicate future increases in GNP or GDP.

5. *The state of the capital stock.* "Capital stock" refers to the investments that are already present and the new purchases of investment goods that are added to the stock. The state of the capital stock is explained by looking at the state of investment in specific industries. The major investments in, for instance, the oil refineries in Curaçao and Aruba were made years ago. That stock of capital has grown quite old, completely depreciated, worn-out, or technically obsolete, and it will need to be replaced. Other examples are the investments in

the Curaçao Dry Dock Company and in the container terminals for berthing and freight-handling facilities. In economics, these replacement investments are aggregated together with investments in new plants, buildings, and equipment as gross fixed capital formation.

Financing

The scarcity of loanable funds is a factor that greatly influences investments in small islands developing states.

- Large-size investments that are considered beyond the carrying capacity of a single bank relative to the size of the domestic economy will not easily find financing.
  - ◊ The nature of loanable funds for capital investments is influenced by the presence of short-term saving deposits and a tendency by banks to favor already chartered territories, like retail and tourism-sector activities. For major capital outlay for investments carrying government guarantees, the local banks form a syndicate.
  - ◊ Non-bank financing alternatives are lacking.
  - ◊ Capital adequacy restraints as prescribed by Basel I and II arrangements for the financial sector also tend to lower the availability of funds for investments.
- Other aspects that influence investments are the size and indivisibility of the proposed capital investment.

Possible investments are discouraged when projects require the importation of capital goods that are too large to achieve proper economies of scale in the local market to compete against imports and to obtain a competitive position in the export market.

• Furthermore, psychological limitations posed by the island borders or another artificial construct can lower the disposition to produce for export, as one cannot "see" beyond the borders.

---

[1] The Basel Committee on Banking Supervision has as its objective to set common standards for banking regulation and improve the stability of the international banking system. In the 1988 accord, the committee defined Tier I and Tier II capital and set minimum standards for the amount of capital banks must hold against credit risks. Tier I capital consists of equity and reserves, Tier II capital consists of revaluations, undeclared profits, soft debt, and general provisions. The sum of Tier I and Tier II has to be equal to 8 percent of the risk-weighted assets of the bank. This indicates the capital adequacy ratio. The Basel I directives were amended in 1996 to hold additional capital against market risks. In 2001, the committee made refinements to the method of calculating the required capital.

[2] Martin Feldstein and Charles Horioka: Domestic Savings and International Capital Flows; NBER Working Paper Series Nr. 310; National Bureau of Economic Research, Cambridge, Mass. 1979.
See also: Sandra Hanson McPherson and Christopher J. Waller: Do local banks matter for the local economy? In search of a regional credit

channel, in Intranational Macroeconomics; Gregory D. Hess and Eric van Wincoop, editors; Camberidge University Press, 2000.

[3] Miguel Ceara Hatton and Rolando Reyes, "Restructuring of Production Patterns, Participation, and Human Development: Core Elements of the New International Competitivenes," in *Roads to Competitiveness, Human Development with Export Growth: The Caribbean Challenge*, ed. by M. F. Hasham (Association of Caribbean Economists, 1995), 43-52.

[4] Jose A. Ocampo, ed., *The Quest for Dynamic Efficiency: Structural Dynamics and Economic Growth in Developing Countries* (Stanford University Press, 2005).

CHAPTER 13
EFFECTS OF INVESTMENTS ON THE GDP

~————•————~

According to the general theory, investments are the lifelines of growth as they have a trickle-down effect on the economy. However, small islands that import physical capital experience this trickle-down effect differently or not at all. The trickle-down process creates a multiplier effect mainly in the exporting country. The effect is over and above the current imbalance due to negative net exports in other sectors.

Introduction

The purpose of this chapter is to discuss short-term effects of investments in the context of a small island or peripheral economy with a small home market and few natural resources and other factors of production. Due to market limitations, much of the capital investments require import of fixed capital and raw material. The import of capital and raw material have balance-of-payments effects while, as observed by George Beckford (chapter 2), the funds used to finance the purchase abroad do not have the expected short-term effect on the domestic economy.

The small-island economy often uses foreign funds to finance large capital investments to develop an infrastructure that can promote growth and development. This chapter attempts to develop some thoughts on how these two aspects of financing and investments affect economic performance on an island. With an economy largely dependent on no-interest grants to finance the development and maintain the infrastructure, the increase in money supply through these means tends to have little apparent short-term effect on the domestic interest rate. The chapter looks accordingly, though briefly, at this interaction between supply and demand of money with investments and how this affects GDP growth.

Effect of Capital Investments

The first step is to determine the effect of a capital investment in the domestic market according to existing thoughts. Next, the effects are looked at if the investment in capital goods occurred abroad. The aggregate investments come out of aggregate savings, and the effect is generally estimated according to the way that the financing of the investment trickles down in the economy.[1] For simplicity, the trickle-down effect through an investment multiplier is considered as similar to the spending multiplier.

The Investment Multiplier

The multiplier starts, in essence, when an initial amount is spent on an investment in physical capital. For instance, someone seeks financing to build a plant to produce tamarind and mango juices for local consumption and export. The funds are used to pay the construction company to build the plant and for purchasing machinery and equipment. The construction company buys the materials needed for construction at the local suppliers and pays the laborers for construction work. One can envisage this process as occurring a second and a third time and so on as the suppliers use part of the funds to pay their employees and pay for the products that they supply to a manufacturer. The employees spend a portion of their income to purchase goods and services that they want. And so it goes on and on. The investment trickles down in the economy.

The trickle-down effect is visible in the economy of the specific island where the investment has taken place. Because of the high content of foreign factors, a portion of the trickle-down effect of the investment occurs on an adjacent island or in a foreign country from which capital goods and consumer goods is imported. Because of the latter aspect, the development of a spending multiplier to record this trickle-down effect should for practical reasons be adjusted to consider foreign leakage. The spending multiplier, without these adjustments, is represented by the following equation:

Spending multiplier: 1/(1 - mpc)

Taken that mpc (marginal propensity to consume) is generally smaller than one, the result of the fraction 1/1 − mpc is greater than one. The change in GNP will also be greater than the original autonomous expenditure. The mpc allows one to assume that the autonomous expenditure will induce additional consumption.

If, as an example, MPC for the Dutch Caribbean (on the average) is 62 percent national income and an autonomous investment is made during the year for 50 million florins, the effect on the GNP will be computed as follows:

$$\Delta GNP = [1/1 - mpc] (\Delta I).$$

So, with an mpc for the islands at 0.62, an increase of 50 million in investments will hypothetically result in

$$\Delta GNP = [1/1 - .62] (50) = 2.6315 \times 50 = 131.6 \text{ million}.$$

This is illustrated in figure 13.1. With the intercept assumed at 10, the economy produces GNP1. When 50 million is invested, this brings about an increase of the national income to GNP2. GNP2 as GNP1 occurs at the equilibrium point between the expenditures with the potential output produced by the economy.

Figure 13.1: Income Determination

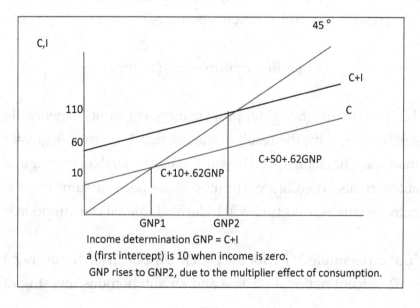

Income determination GNP = C+I
a (first intercept) is 10 when income is zero.
GNP rises to GNP2, due to the multiplier effect of consumption.

If the mpc is 0.90 (meaning that only 10 percent of every additional unit of the local currency in disposable income is saved), the GNP will hypothetically increase by

$$1/1 - .90 \times 50 = 500 \text{ million.}$$

The trickle-down effect because of the consumption pattern in this situation is huge. Unfortunately, the mpc also shows that there will be insufficient funds available in the economy from savings to carry out the investment. It is more probable that the 50 million in investment funds will come from outside, for instance through direct foreign investments or foreign assistance.

Since the multiplier will have an effect on GNP following autonomous expenditures, the government in fact can use this factor to stimulate increased performance of the economy. The autonomous expenditures generally affecting the GNP are autonomous consumption (a), autonomous investments (Io), autonomous government spending, and lump-sum taxes.

Government Fiscal Policy Effect

The effect of a tax on the GNP can be seen in the following equation:

$$GNP = 1/1 - mpc \; [a - mpc(T) + Io + Go].$$

So a combination of expenditures by government and private investors together with a lump sum tax (T) can help the government obtain an intended effect. As the tax has an effect on the economy that less can be consumed, expressed by the marginal propensity to consume in the equation, it will have a lowering effect on the total aggregate increase in GNP.

Balanced budget

An understanding of the effect of the tax is useful, for instance, in the construction of a balanced budget. The equation for GDP is

$$C + I + G - T + X - M.$$

The concept of the balanced budget is that revenue and expenditure are the same. It is important that the effect of the multiplier is considered in the decision process. As is shown in the equation above, the increased investment and the multiplier effect increases the GNP. The effect of the tax is that the trickle-down effect is mitigated.

The following example shows the results of an increase in investment spending equal to an increase in tax revenue. With a marginal propensity to consume of 0.62315789, the government could increase its investments by 50 million, impose a tax that brings in 50 million florins, and obtain a net increase in GNP of 50 million florins.

Increase due to government investment spending:

$$2.6315789 \times 50 = 131.58$$

less increase of tax by 50 million:

$$-.62/1 - .62 \times T = 1.631578 \times 50 = 81.58.$$

Net increase in GNP (in million florins) = 50.00

The tax multiplier used in the computation is [-mpc/1 − mpc] × T].

The end result is a positive growth in GNP of 50 million florins. If the increase in taxes were, for instance, 100 million and the investment expenditures the same as above, then theoretically the end result will be a decline in the GNP growth.

Multiplier of Small Islands

When countries purchase capital equipment abroad, an investment multiplier occurs benefiting the domestic economy as well as a foreign country. Naturally, foreign purchases are made with the intention that they will bring long-term beneficial effects, which include maintenance or growth in the domestic workforce and improvement of the living environment. Furthermore, investments are made with the expectation of lowering the dependency on imports and on lowering continuous export of foreign exchange to buy finished goods, when considering business investments. The truth is that enhancing domestic production ability can also lead to continuous import of raw material and fuels. There are many variables to take into account in determining the benefits and costs of investing. This section focuses on the impact of capital investments from the small island open-economy perspective.

The following table shows grants provided by the European Union (EU) for the period 2009 to 2014 to the various islands that were formerly part of the Netherlands Antilles. The data reflect the socio-economic relevance of the investments.

Table 13.1: European Ninth Development Funds

Islands	Population Served	households Served	Investment (ANG) Total	per capita	Household
Bonaire	4,777	1,594	5,875,625	1,230	3,686
Curacao	1,103	358	6,012,768	5,451	16,795
Saba	1,434	622	3,141,786	2,191	5,051
St Eustatius	2,292	902	12,053,839	5,259	13,363
St Maarten	2,280	858	10,854,732	4,761	12,651
Total	11,886	4,334	37,938,750	3,192	8,754

From: Feasibility Study Urban Infrastructure for Socially Deprived Communities in the Netherlands Antilles. 9th European Development Fund; Single Programming Document; WSP Inc; with cooperation by ASCON Bonaire and PLAN'D2 Curacao; January 2007.   Paul Dean, Editor

The investments made with the grants are mainly for improvements of the physical infrastructure, like roads, water catchments and water supply, street lighting, infrastructure for housing, drainage, and so forth. The Saba, Saint Eustatius, and Sint Maarten investments are for a great part to improve water supply on the islands. These investments are generally carried out under the auspices of the government of each island. The distribution of these specific funds is based on the current circumstances of each island as reflected in a feasibility survey regarding Urban Infrastructure for Socially Deprived Communities in the Netherlands Antilles in 2007. In fact, the total grant is ANG 50 million. About 12 million is spent on consultants, with approximately 30 percent going to locals and 70 percent to expatriate experts.

The Shared Multiplier

The trickle-down effect of the domestic multiplier occurs at the moment that a capital investment is made in capital equipment and during the process of production when factors of production and supplies are used to build inventories. For this exercise, only the impact of the investments in capital goods in the given sector is of interest. Machines, plants, and equipment are often imported and paid for, for 100 percent. While a great part of the multiplier effect occurs abroad, the depreciation occurs domestically. Local costs relate to the transportation, import taxes, and set-up and installation of the fixed asset.

Even locally produced buildings have foreign as well as local production factor content. For simple buildings, this generally amounts to a 70-30 mix. That means that 30 percent of the investment has direct effects abroad. Construction of institutional buildings (offices, schools, hospitals, airports), depending on the complexity, seem to require approximately 50 percent of foreign content in the total investment package.

Furthermore, results from a study involving fourteen companies belonging to the Association of Manufacturing Industries in the Netherlands Antilles (ASINA) in the 1980s showed that 40 percent of raw material used in manufacturing processes for these firms is imported yearly by the combination of companies.

The same study showed that a substantial percentage of other supplies for production purposes and for office use are imported. The combined effects of increase in investment to enhance production and the constant import of raw material as intermediate products and finished products impact the long-term results of the GNP as well, using traditional methods of computation.

There are investments that lead to a continuously high local content (70 percent and higher) of raw material input, as is the case with nonalcoholic beverages and alcoholic beverages that use much locally produced raw material (water). It is the combination of the production processes with either low external and high external content that will eventually produce growth on a sustainable basis.

Returning to our first proposition, the GDP growth resulting from new investments will be curtailed by that portion of the investment that has a direct foreign effect.

The investment multiplier computation is illustrated showing an adjustment α, which is 1 − foreign content, or as an example, 1 - .30 for buildings and plants. The multiplier formula becomes:

$$\Delta GDP = [1/1 - mpc]\ (\Delta I \times [1 - \alpha]).$$

With only a 30 percent external effect, the investment multiplier becomes

$$[1/1 - .62]\ (50) \times (.70),$$

and the increase in GDP only ANG 92 million instead of ANG 136 million. In the case of machinery and equipment that are produced entirely abroad, α = .70 hypothetically. As a consequence, the calculation of real GDP should consider both inflation and the adjustment due to external multiplier from local funds. This result will naturally affect policies that try to create a balanced budget and should be relevant in the determination of economic growth.

Table 13.2 illustrates this using the EDF Financing:

Example Curacao of local effect of Capital assets purchased abroad ANG			A 6,012,768	
Proportion invested	Foreign content	Local content	Foreign Effect	Local Effect
B	C	D	A*B*C	A*B*D
0.60 Pavements and resurfacing roads	0.4	0.6	1,443,064	2,164,596
0.15 Street Lighting	0.8	0.2	721,532	180,383
0.10 Underground facilities for electricity	0.6	0.4	360,766	240,511
0.05 Cabling	0.8	0.2	240,511	60,128
0.10 Physical infrastructure	0.5	0.5	300,638	300,638
1.00			3,066,512	2,946,256

In table 13.2, it is clear that only a portion of the total investment of 6,012,768 indicated by the letter A has a local multiplier effect. Each project is rated according to local content and foreign content, indicated as D and C in the table. To calculate the portion of investment that needs to be considered for the local effect, in principle the percentages of local versus foreign content are multiplied by the specific outlay investment. In table 13.2, the total investment is additionally subdivided according to the proportion of each individual investment in the total physical-improvement-project financing. The local versus foreign content is assumed here on the basis of previous research.[2]

The short-term traditional multiplier effect of these investments is on the portion that relates to the domestic sources and activities. As shown in table 13.2, the local portion on which the multiplier effect is applicable is the product of the total spending times the proportion used for a component (60 percent for pavements and resurfacing of roads) times the local content in capital investment applicable locally.

Using a marginal propensity of 0.62, this would produce a growth of GDP of

ANG 2,946,256 × (1/1 - .62) = 7,753,305.

If this refinement was not considered, then one would expect that the investment of ANG on 6,012,768 would have a different result with the same multiplier. The effect would have been a change in GDP of ANG 15,823073, holding everything else constant.

[*ANG 1 = FLS 1.*]

As a result, expectations with regard to the use of local and foreign funds in stimulating short-term economic growth as expressed by the GDP concept are to be adjusted downward. To achieve an expansion and improvement in GDP, the country should look for alternatives for financing of projects with greater short-term multiplier effects and possibly concentrate on projects that have sustainable long-term multiplier effects due to labor opportunities and consumption. The shifting of the multiplier effect to the foreign country acts almost like a tax burden on the domestic economy, lowering the expected GDP growth, given the known current multiplier and propensity to invest.

Expansion

There is a requirement on any size island economy to take control of the affairs that can contribute to sustainable full employment that permit maintenance of an acceptable standard of living. The lack of sufficient private and public savings will remain an issue with respect to the ability to finance particularly the economic infrastructure. In order to grow to a level where Small Island Developing States (SIDS) become relatively self-supporting, they will depend for a length of time on external capital, especially grants and subsidies. This section is concerned with the effect of using external funds on the economy.

The money supply on the islands is generally defined as narrow money and broad money. Narrow money concerns coins and paper money in circulation, defined as M0. When demand deposits are added as part of the money supply, this new total is termed M1. The money available for use in the economy is broadened with time deposits in the banking system. This expansion of the money supply is termed M2. This M2, in the sense of funds available in the economy for investment and spending, is generally reduced by the long-term deposits and investments of local funds abroad and increased by large deposits through grants and foreign direct investments. This adds up to M3. In the next section, the money supply effects are defined as QM0, QM2 and QM3, only meaning the amount of funds (M3) available at a point in time.

Money, Interest, and Investments

Grants3 are primarily channeled to governments and carry no interest, and as a result they do not directly influence the price of domestic supply and demand of money in the private sector. Subsidies from Europe carry a low interest percentage of between 3 to 4 percent. As with grants, the major recipient is the government, which uses the funds for projects. The grants and subsidies are most often linked to projects that have immediate capital-asset-investment outlay. The private sector bids on the projects but is not involved in the financing. A great portion of these funds are used within a relatively short period of time for the reasons they were acquired, including purchasing physical capital abroad. Grants and subsidies expand the short-term availability of funds for investment, and they are inexpensive additions to domestic investment financing.

International direct investments also add to the domestic investment. These investments often occur based on cost-lowering policies (like tax holidays and economic zones with low taxes) to lower operational costs for investors. The higher-income prospects due to lower taxes make the initial cost of establishment and the capital investment acceptable.

The domestic and foreign funds are sourced to the SIDS by ways of:

Domestic sources

- commercial banks, finance companies, and mortgage banks for term loans and mortgages
- credit unions, personal loans, and limited mortgaging
- institutional investors (pension funds and insurance firms) for mortgages and occasional term loans; interest rates, market determined
- a firm's retained earnings and individual wealth

Foreign sources

- *f*oreign financial assistance channeled to sectors through the government agencies or through development banks; examples are: Small Enterprise Stimulation Netherlands Antilles, funds, AMFO, Stichting Antilliaanse Medfinanciering Organisatie[1], European Development Funds and so forth providing project financing; nonmarket interest rates.
- development banks for term loans focused on sector development; part of the available funds foreign-financed
- foreign direct investments; react on risk/return conditions related to lower tax burden on cost of operation

Sustainability of a given level of domestic financing is contingent on the economic conditions in the SIDS. In the domestic economy, the government can influence investment activity by

---

[1] AMFO is a foundation with the objective of co-financing of NGO projects. The funds are provided by the Ministry of Interior Affairs and Kingdom Relations of the Netherlands.

expanding or contracting the domestic money supply, and by channeling foreign assistance to domestic economic sectors. The need to finance private and public ventures and the supply of funds from the various sources indicate the existence of a *market for money*, much alike the product and factor markets mentioned in chapter six. The interaction of demand and supply of funds for use in the product and factor markets is largely contingent upon the price, generally referred to as rate of interest.

Assume a situation with local demand and supply interacting based on elasticity of demand for and supply of money available in the domestic financial markets. This is indicated as a negative sloping curve for demand and a positive sloping curve for supply.

The explanation is that in theory, if the general price for loans stood at 11 percent, some investments will occur at that rate. If the money supply is expanded, the interest rate is supposed to drop, say to 7 percent. When this happens more people start investing, buying capital assets, constructing buildings, and so forth. Because of the increased demand, the average interest rate rises to 9 percent. People invest a little less now than when the interest rate was at 7 percent.

These actions are an elastic interaction between supply and demand of money in relation to the price. Individuals and firms will be willing to borrow more money when the price of borrowing is lower. This is possible if the economy can add the needed funds as they are being requested.

If this supply/demand interaction as proposed above is not possible, the supply curve will be vertical, expressing the amount of money supplied through the central bank. The money supply curve is vertical when there is no market trading influencing the amount of money supplied. This is the case with international financial assistance funds and funds imported for direct investments. This addition to the money supply does not have a direct interest-rate effect. For simplicity and because of the underlying domestic portion of the money demand and supply, we will accept a money demand curve that is sloping negatively, as it is being affected by domestic interest rates and demand for funds.

In figure 13.2, the supply of broad money M_2 is indicated as stock of money available at an earlier point in time, before any adjustments, and labeled as QM_0. This stock of money next decreases by the amount of flow of funds from institutional investors toward foreign economies. Taken that most financing on the local market is bank financing, the central bank reserve requirements and the capital adequacy requirement also reduce the amount of funds available in the domestic banks for investment. The result is indicated as QM_1. The EU and Dutch financing add a new sum of money to the economy, based on funds requested for projects that hypothetically cannot be financed with local capital. The money supply is now at QM_2, which is the total supply of money. With this expansion in the money supply, there is no downward pressure on domestic interest rates. But the marginal efficiency of investment (MEI) schedule at the right in the figure shifts to the right, increasing investments from $I_0 I_0$ to $I I_1$. Obviously this expansionist mode of financing through foreign funds does not lead to inflationary conditions, since the money supply expands due to nonmarket conditions.

In fact, the market experiences simultaneous investment decisions based on market rates and nonmarket rates. One set of investments occur with financing at 7 percent interest rate. For another set of investments the financing occurs at 3 percent interest rate. There is minimal interaction between these financing markets. As a result the private sector investments occur according to the invest schedule producing I_0 investments. The public sector for the additional foreign assistance funds at 3 percent produce I_1 investment.

Figure 13.2: Domestic and International Funds Investments

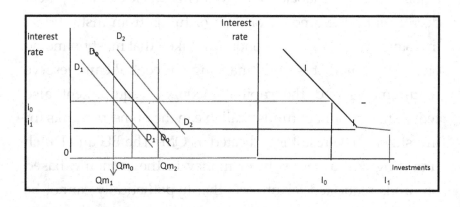

With the external funds, the island can purchase equipment, tools, and plants that it could not afford with domestic savings. The fixed capital can be used to set up or continue a production system that can reduce unemployment and produce for export if the proper economies of scale can be achieved. Naturally, the financing of government investments by external assistance funds that do not enhance productivity can lead to *crowding-in*, while the government participation in the domestic market to maintain stability produces a situation of *crowding-out*, where the first lays heavy requirements on the existing production capacity, for example in construction, and the crowding-out reduces the availability of domestic funds due to increased reluctance of investors to finance more risky projects.

The external assistance, which is primarily directed by the government to selected projects, increases the level of deposits in the banks for a period of time. This and the fact that the enhanced expenditure level also has positive job connotation provides a relative sense of well-being on a receiving island. The portion of deposits that is not used for capital equipment imports becomes part of the domestic money supply and contributes to a surplus of idle fund as long as it is not recycled in a timely way into domestic productive projects.

Remarks

When large investments that require import of physical capital or foreign assistance occur, the addition to GDP needs to be adjusted to take account of the fact that the multiplier effect from the investments is shared with the foreign economy where the purchases are made. As a result, there is a lowering effect to GDP growth in the accounting year. This is certainly a factor to be considered if a balanced budget policy is pursued.

If the investments are financed by grants and subsidies, these funds will be an addition to the money supply—which, however, does not seem to affect the domestic interest rate. This is generally due to the fact that the grants and aid are supplied via the government and do not become a major part of the pool of loanable domestic funds.

Appendix 13.1

Marginal Efficiency of Investments

The negative-sloping investment schedule (I I) shown in figure 13.2 is best explained by the concept of the marginal efficiency of investment (MEI). MEI is the expected rate of return on an investment, or the rate of discount that equates expected net annual revenues to present costs. Investors will invest in a project or capital equipment if the MEI is greater than the cost of capital. Consequently, at a lower cost of capital, one can expect increased investments.

The MEI is portrayed for the entire economy in the form of a schedule of investments that slopes negatively downward, with investments increasing as the rate of interest (cost of capital) decreases.

The zero or soft interest rates for grants and subsidies are negotiated rates that do not seem to have direct impact on general domestic rates. The increased supply is illustrated in the national disposable income statistics and the table showing GDP per sector in the previous chapter, with disposable income greater than the GDP in the given year. Consequently, the country can invest more than its domestic savings would permit without affecting the rate of interest.

Theoretically, if the pace of the demand for money for consumption and investments is higher than the pace with which the money supply can be expanded, the country will face inflationary conditions. This has not been the case in several years where this international assistance phenomenon occurred. It is also noteworthy that the savings leaking to external economies, those from the institutional investors, represent withdrawals from the domestic money supply that in fact seems to be compensated by foreign input.

Appendix 13.2

Shared Multiplier Equilibrium

Equilibrium occurs if total spending matches the output produced in the economy. The proposed equilibrium that also insures full employment occurs at the junction between AE, Aggregate Expenditures and potential GNP.

This is illustrated in figure 13.4 below, which shows a 45-degree line that equates the aggregate expenditures with the GNP. As long as the C + I + G contribution is greater or smaller than GNP, there is a disequilibrium condition. If C + I + G contribute to more than output, firms need to increase production to meet demand. The new investment is to help to reach this condition. The equilibrium position sought is the one where the supply versus demand equilibrium also produces full employment.

Figure 13.3 Effect of Shared Multiplier on GNP

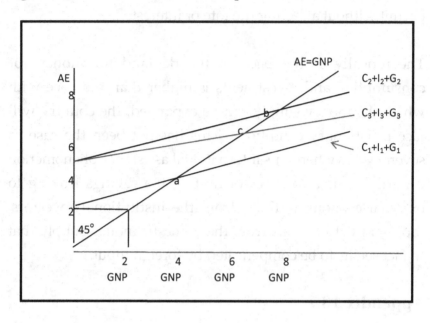

The investment, occurring as an autonomous investment shown on the vertical coordinate, increases the investment returns hypothetically from $C1 + I1 + G1$ to $C2 + I2 + G2$. However, due to the shared multiplier effects, the actual contribution to GNP is smaller than intended. This is shown by the $C3 + I3 + G3$ line that intersects the 45-degree output line at a lower point. These results show why the impact sought from the investments on the macroeconomy can be lower than expected from the multiplier effect for the island. These results with regard to the GNP can also be further influenced by the inflation factor when real GNP is considered. If the local economy had the necessary resources to produce the capital equipment, the equilibrium condition would hold at point b on the graph, given the expenditures on consumption, investments, and government.

1   The autonomous investment by the investing units can be illustrated in a functional form showing that I = I o + mp_i(GNP), where mp_i is the marginal propensity to invest. However, as the same trickle-down effect is expected among consumer categories, the marginal propensity to consume seems a valid surrogate.

2   M. F. Hasham, "Findings Survey for ASINA (Association of Manufacturing Industries of the Netherlands Antilles, 1982), and "Diversification in Industry and Growth in Employment," *Una Cahier* 15 (1985).

3   An expansionary economic policy correlates with increased demand for money for investments. Grants don't have a repayment requirement and are an inexpensive source of financing that helps maintain the domestic interest-rate level unchanged. This is obvious from the tenacity of the mortgage rates and term-loan rates during the period of 1979 to 1995, during which period an average yearly 80 million ANG was received as grants and subsidies from the Netherlands. During this period, the average rate for mortgages in the domestic financial markets stood at between 11 and 13 percent, and for five-year term loans at between 11 and 15 percent in the Leeward Islands, according to the quarterly bulletin of the Bank van de Nederlandse Antillen. This was respectively 12 to 15 percent and 12 to 16 percent in the Windward Islands. The governments also committed to subsidies from the Netherlands that had a repayment condition, with interest rates of only 3 to 4 percent. This was the approximate price of money in that period. The fall in bank interest rates in the Dutch Caribbean after 1995 for transactions in the domestic economy seems to have been influenced by a sharper competitive environment and recessionary conditions, not by the inexpensive cost of grants and subsidies. The zero or soft interest rates for grants and subsidies are negotiated rates that do not seem to have direct impact on general domestic rates.

Chapter 14
Unemployment

~•~

In modern society, the majority of people of working age seek gainful employment to obtain a level of income that helps to achieve a desired standard of living and well-being. This chapter looks at those factors that influence the achievement of full employment in the macroeconomy.

Introduction

Notwithstanding the declaration of human rights by the United Nations in 1948, year in and year out many people who are able and want to work are left out of the workplace. The Universal Declaration of Human rights proclaimed in Article 23 in December 1948 by the General Assembly of the United Nations stated that:

1. Everyone has the right to work, to free choice of employment, to just and favorable conditions of work and protection against unemployment.
2. Everyone, without any discrimination, has the right for equal pay for equal work.

3. Everyone who works has the right to just and favorable remuneration ensuring for himself and his family an existence worthy of human dignity, and supplemented if necessary by other means of social protection.
4. Everyone has the right to form and to join trade unions for the protection of their interests.

Still, the International Labor Organization (ILO) reported that 160 million people were unemployed in 2001, 50 million of them in the industrialized countries. The ILO estimated that 239 million people were unemployed at the end of 2009.

This chapter looks at the problem of employment and unemployment in the context of its influence on aggregate demand and GDP performance. After a brief description of employment and unemployment, the chapter considers the reasons for unemployment and the features determining the unemployment rate as well as the value of using an employment target to indicate the potential GDP. The chapter ends with an overview of unemployment in the region.

Employment, Labor Force, and Participation Rate

Characteristically, when we speak about employment and the labor force, we consider the civilian labor force, specifically the number of people fifteen years or older employed or seeking employment. In some countries, the lowest age is sixteen years. An example of the buildup of a labor force taken from a census several years before the disintegration of the Netherlands Antilles looks as shown on table 14.1:

Table 14.1: Labor Force

Age groups	Employed	Unemployed	Labor Force	Proportion Unemployed
15-19	1,286	967	2,253	0.43
20-24	4,208	1,434	5,642	0.25
25-29	7,528	1,428	8,956	0.16
30-34	10,066	1,490	11,556	0.13
35-39	11,869	1,748	13,617	0.13
40-44	11,067	1,685	12,752	0.13
45-49	9,365	1,343	10,708	0.13
50-54	7,231	930	8,161	0.11
55-59	4,322	525	4,847	0.11
60-64	1,645	204	1,849	0.11
65+	1,095	122	1,217	0.10
Total	69,682	11,876	81,558	0.15

Source: CBS Housing and population census
Netherlands Antilles 2001.

The table, based on Netherlands Antilles data before the breakup, illustrates labor-force characteristics according to age group. A cursory look at the data illustrates that the unemployment rate is 15 percent of the total labor force, ranging from 10 percent in the oldest age group to 43 percent in the youngest. This data is representative for the five islands. Of course, there are differences from district to district on one island and among the islands.

Labor Force Participation Rate

As reported in chapter 1, there is an increase in the labor-force participation rate on the islands, with more females joining the labor force over the years. The participation rate can be calculated for each age group by comparing the labor force for the specific age group to the total population in that age group.

The growth in the labor-force participation rate over the years serves as an indication of how much more attention needs to be given to creation of employment opportunities. For instance, no growth in population and an increase from 40 percent labor participation to 70 percent participation means that per 100 persons, instead of forty members belonging to the labor force now there are seventy people working or looking for jobs. If the population increased, say with 20 percent over a period of time to 120, the labor market has to absorb 84 members of the labor force at a 70 percent labor-participation rate.

The participation rate for the Dutch Caribbean islands, excluding Aruba, at the time of the census in 2001 was 68.7 for those ages fifteen to sixty-four. This participation rate fluctuated from island to island. For Sint Maarten, for instance, this was 81.1 percent and for Curaçao 65.0 percent. Bonaire had a participation rate of 74 percent, Saint Eustatius of 75.3 percent, and Saba of 66.5 percent in the census year. Aruba's population increased from 66,687 in 1991 (census) to 101,484 in 2010 according to census figures for those years.[1]

Table 14.2 Employment and participation rate Aruba

Aruba	1991	2010
Population	66,687	101,484
Population 15+	45,563	81,438
Employed	28,740	46,526
Rate of unemployment	6.10%	10.60%
Participation rate	67.40%	65.10%

In order to maintain the same employment level as before at the same participation rate, economic activities providing new jobs have to maintain the same trend as the increase in population.

Unemployment

Table 14.1 shows that unemployment occurs at every age bracket. Such high incidence for the younger age groups can indicate a mismatch between skill requirements by the suppliers of jobs and lack of the required skills with those seeking jobs. Such a mismatch leaves certain workspaces unfilled and a number of people without work. As mentioned in other chapters, due to these circumstances, the jobs sometimes may be done by foreigners while locals remain without an income source.

The rate of unemployment in the last column of 14.1 is determined as a ratio of those actively seeking a job and not finding employment to all those employed plus those actively seeking jobs, or

$$\frac{\text{All those seeking jobs and not finding jobs}}{\text{All those employed + those actively seeking jobs}} \times 100\%$$

The rate of unemployment provides a base for comparison with past history of unemployment or with unemployment at each age level, or with unemployment in other countries. A persistent high rate of unemployment can furthermore point to underlying difficulties in the economy to employ everyone who wants to work.

Features of Unemployment

Those belonging to the labor force may find themselves unemployed for a short period of time, or alternatively a long period of time during which they do not seem to be able to land a job whatever they try. In fact, some may be out of the workforce so long that they do not even consider looking for a job. Accordingly, those unemployed who continue to look for employment are categorized as *involuntarily* unemployed. Those who have stopped looking but belong to the fifteen to sixty-four age group are categorized as *voluntarily* unemployed. The group that is voluntarily unemployed is not pursuing work, at least not in the formal circuit. They have become discouraged.

The involuntary unemployed are further classified as:

- *Cyclical Unemployed.* This is a feature of unemployment that occurs in the periods that spending on goods and services in the economy is low. When spending increases, unemployment declines.

- *Structural Unemployed.* This feature of unemployment is seen among participants in the labor force who do not have skills that match the need in the job market. This could be due to old skills that have become obsolete, for instance due to new technology or the fact that certain economic sectors or subsectors have become less viable in an economy. According to a group of thinkers structural or hard-core unemployment will disappear with proper tax, spending, and credit policies to correct inadequate demand. For another group, structural employment will persist despite increased spending. For this group, it is important to improve employability by retraining and educating those structurally unemployed. Retraining subsidies will be useful.

- *Frictional Unemployed.* Frictional unemployment exists when individuals are out of a job for a short period of time, perhaps due to movement from one job to another or when looking to become part of the workforce after finishing an educational process.

Accurate data regarding the composition of these categories makes it possible to direct efforts like retraining, schooling, and work programs to improve the possibilities for those falling into each category. There are, furthermore, a number of aspects that can contribute to volatility in employment. Technological changes, as experienced in the petroleum refining industry, can displace labor (by machine) indefinitely. It is not always feasible for displaced workers who remain on the island to find jobs in adjacent industries or industries that manufacture or assemble for the automated plants where they used to work. When firms in a sector represented by a sole or very few companies close down and settle elsewhere, the impact is greater as workers in firms supporting these industries lose their jobs. The circumstances that lead to short-term or long-term unemployment generally trigger the government to step in with corrective actions.

Policies to Reduce Unemployment

J. M. Keynes ties a rise in unemployment to an inadequate level of demand for goods and services. This is due to the fact that productive inputs, labor, capital, and land are fixed in the short run. Influencing the demand—that is, spending on goods and services—will affect the supply of goods and services and bring balance between demand in society and the level of production. This will ultimately restore the employment level, or at least lower unemployment. The interpretation is that there is a natural balance between what is demanded and what is to be supplied. Influencing demand will lead to matching utilization of factors of production. The increase in demand can be obtained by using fiscal and monetary measures.

- *Fiscal measures* are introduced through fiscal policy as decisions by government, generally to collect more revenue through taxes with the intent to alter aggregate spending. Government uses the additional revenue to finance, for instance, the maintenance and construction of roads, parks, harbors, airports, schools, and so forth.

337

This increased spending in the economy expands the production capacity, increasing the demand for labor and other factors of production. The greater results with regard to employment can be expected from economic activities that are labor-intensive.

- *Monetary policies* reflect decisions made by the central bank to influence the money supply with the intention of keeping inflation in check, maintaining sufficient money in circulation to buy local and foreign products and services, and maintaining national financial balance by influencing interest rates.

The central bank works together with the government by issuing bonds and treasury bills. The government bonds are long-term "loans" by government for periods of five to ten years or more. The treasury bills are short-term borrowings, typically for three or six months. The buyer (lender) receives interest on the bond or treasury bill. The government can use the funds to do similar projects as mentioned above, with the purpose of maintaining an adequate aggregate level of spending. Or, if necessary, the government can use the revenue income from taxes or the borrowed money for correction of market failures next to the provision of public goods.

It is possible to infer that the government and the central bank can affect aggregate demand by expanding or contracting the supply of money available in circulation. Among the central-bank policies to affect aggregate demand we find the cash-reserve ratio, which introduces restrictions on bank lending or on general borrowing by retail investors by penalizing banks for increasing loans passed a given limit. Another policy is a *reserve requirement* with a portion of the deposits at a bank held in a non-interest-bearing account at the central bank to manage liquidity by restricting credit and controlling demand for foreign exchange. It is also in the power of the central bank to apply an open-market policy by buying up government bonds or selling government bonds, with the intent of reducing or increasing circulation of funds in the economy.

Acceptable Rate of Unemployment

The utilization of these policies rests on the assumption that there is an unemployment horizon that, if reached, will constitute full employment. By stimulating growth in aggregate demand, an equilibrium condition between aggregate supply and demand can be reached at a point that insures full employment. It does not mean that unemployment will be zero, at this point because there will be some people unemployed due to the business cycle or due to personal, and organizational reasons, or due to changing technology.

In the more developed economies, a 4 percent unemployment level is generally considered as indicating full employment. This apparent natural level of unemployment occurs at a point where there is no upward or downward pressure on wage growth and no upward or downward pressure on inflation.

Lower unemployment rates—let's say 3 percent—are considered to produce high inflation rates, increasing the price level in the country, while higher unemployment rates above 5 percent indicate that aggregate demand is dropping, weakening the economy and bringing about more unemployment.

Potential GDP

In the previous chapters, there was mention of the potential GDP as a GDP level that intrinsically leads to full employment of labor and capital. and others proposed an approach to this potential GDP by utilizing a target unemployment rate to determine a target GDP.

This potential GDP can be achieved by transferring all output to man hours and calculating output based on an average cost per hour. The potential GDP would then be

output per man per hour × size of labor force − natural rate.

Evidently, the output per man-hour is affected by the technology used, the capital stock available, and the skills and experience of the workers. As a consequence, these factors need to be considered in the determination of the rate to be accepted as a realistic target. Potential GDP can be thought of as the best level of production and productivity that can be reached if the available resources are used effectively and efficiently. When the actual GDP differs from the potential GDP in a fiscal year, this difference is referred to as a *GDP gap*.

The GDP gap gives an impression of how much of the inputs are being wasted or not put to work productively enough. Of course efforts are to be exerted to close the gap. The GDP gap is illustrated by the following formula:

$$\frac{potential\ GDP - actual\ GDP}{potential\ GDP} \times 100\% = GDP\ gap$$

The assessment of the gap provides opportunity to support efforts in the economy that result in investments to improve the infrastructure, the level of technology, and the skills necessary to increase productivity and production. This will help in closing the gap. In fact, such efforts can lead to an increase in potential GDP beyond what is proposed.

Targeting Unemployment

Targets for full employment are based on what can be achieved given the local circumstances. Each island in the Dutch Caribbean is technically responsible for the pursuit of full employment, confronting seasonal, cyclical, frictional, and structural unemployment conditions. The distribution of unemployment shown in table 14.1 is skewed toward the youngest age groups. Solutions will necessitate focusing on those factors that contribute to consistent unemployment for this age bracket, including lack of entrepreneurial and job-specific skills on one hand and low diversification in the economy on the other.

Two concepts useful as a guideline in the process of targeting unemployment are the Philips curve concept and the principle known as Okun's law. They highlight the relationship between employment and GDP, with employment changing with changes in GDP. There are doubts about their validity under varying circumstances.

Philips curve

The Phillips curve explains that an increase in national income occurs with increased demand and a higher price level. The increased demand and the higher national income lead to job creation. In figure 14.1, this relationship is illustrated by a fall of unemployment: $.03 + 2t$ falls from U_0 to U_1, producing the Philips curve on the right in the figure.

Figure 14.1: Philips Curve

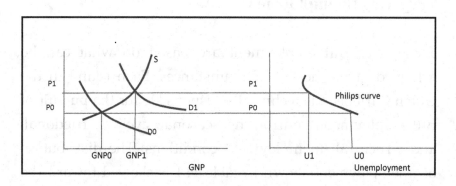

This inverse relationship is not necessarily true in all circumstances of inflation. The world has experienced periods of inflation without real increases in national income and job creation. While the concept provides some insight for analysis and projection, imported inflation remains a major factor in rising prices in the islands, and one has to be cautious and separate domestic from foreign inflation to get a true indication of the causal factors of job creation.

Okun's law

There is also the concept of an inverse relationship between unemployment and national income as presented by Arthur Okun, a relationship that has come to be known as the Okun's law. The relationship can be estimated at each point in time or by establishing a coefficient (the Okun coefficient) that is indicated by the percentage by which GNP changes when unemployment changes by 1 percent. It can be interpreted as follows: if unemployment falls by 1 percent while there is a 2 percent growth in GNP, then a country would strive for a 4 percent growth to lower unemployment by 2 percent.

The inverse relationship using the coefficients is actually between the size of the output or GDP gap and the size of the unemployment gap. The unemployment gap is the difference between the actual rate of unemployment and the natural rate of unemployment. Each island can determine this relationship based on past experiences or on proposed interventions that increase output, altering the coefficient for the economy. The Okun coefficient becomes a handy tool in the determination of the time and effort it will take to close the unemployment gap. The unemployment gap between actual and traditional natural rate of unemployment in some of the islands is often so large that it looks inconceivable for the gap to be closed in a short period of time in order to reach the full employment level.

Determination of Potential GDP

The inverse relationship between unemployment and aggregate demand is obvious in that higher rates of unemployment tend to cause a reduction in aggregate demand. To turn things around, government can stimulate production through fiscal policy, which will bring about growth and lead to lower unemployment. This relationship is expressed as a growth model by Solow, based on a production function:

$$Y = K^a (A,L)^{1-a}.$$

Y represents output, with K being capital investment. L is labor and A the technology factor that increases output by labor. So continuous investments (K) will contribute, given the use of appropriate technology that increases labor productivity and labor output, to economic growth (Y). The Solow growth model[2] presupposes that savings of the country are turned into investments and that the available capital stock is also constantly being depreciated. In the case of a very small island, these savings consist of primarily foreign direct investments and foreign financial assistance. As explained in chapter 13, a portion of the invested funds is shared with the foreign country in terms of the multiplier effect, and as a result the growth impact will be less than expected given the marginal propensity to consume.

A typical policy strategy followed by governments is to stimulate expansion in labor income-generating activities through low-tax provisions to economic activities in growth sectors. The policy acts as a compensatory strategy to an expansionary policy with higher taxes. Note that with an economic expansion to employ more workers, there could be a downside risk in that the new investments and increased economic activities can require manpower in excess of or in lieu of the domestic labor force. Depending on the type of immigrants, this can result in major repatriation of income, meaning that the intended domestic consumption effects on GDP occur elsewhere.

The success of targeting a lower unemployment rate hinges on the introduction of proper incentives and on the availability of the needed skills and the financing of additional investments so that more unemployed are exposed to job opportunities. Short-term success also depends on which type of unemployment is prevalent. The bulk of new entries in the work force will come from the cyclically and frictionally unemployed. Furthermore, work should be done to lower the effect of "institutional barriers that are due to labor laws and practices and could prevent labor markets from operating as efficiently as possible. Of course, individuals may prefer unemployment compensation or welfare payments to jobs that only pay marginally more".[3]

Applying the GDP Gap to Correct Performance

By estimating a GDP gap, decision-makers can appraise the actual performance of the economy in relation to the targeted GDP and seek alternatives to correct a possible underperformance.

Estimating the GDP gap
It is possible to calculate the potential output at a lower level of unemployment. For example, assume that potential output at a target of 8 percent unemployment is 4.8 billion (or 4,870,454,682). The unemployment level was 15 percent in the current year. The potential output is arrived at by multiplying net working hours or alternatively net working days by the average cost per hour, alternatively per day. The cost per day is assumed to be known. If with the increased number of labor days the country still only achieves the output of ANG 4,500,000,000, then the gap is estimated as follows:

$$(4,870,454,682 - 4,500,000,000) \div 4,870,454,652 = 0.07606162$$

This means that the efforts to be made should lead to an increase of 7.61 percent in output compared to the actual GDP before the potential GDP is obtained at the target rate.

Unemployment in a Small Island Economy

A set of factors affect the achievement of employment goals negatively. Factors like indivisibility of the capital asset with related diseconomies of scale, rather fast diminishing-returns conditions, and repeated and rapid introduction of technological innovations have a lowering effect on the input per worker.[4] Additionally, the shortcomings to GDP growth due to the shared multiplier condition require extra investments to achieve an expected growth pattern. Still, sustainable economic growth for a small island is not an illusion. Aruba has had, during a short period of time, an unemployment rate as low as 0.6 percent, which occurred even as the island was experiencing increases in immigrant work population. The achievement of a 0.6 percent unemployment level in Aruba in the early 2000s proves that it is possible to lower unemployment to an acceptable level on a small island.

When there is a semblance of economic growth, an island typically faces a surge in immigrant workers. This growth, if not contained, will affect the ability of the island to maintain a predetermined full-employment level due to limitations in the domestic market and vulnerability to changing economic conditions and adverse physical conditions from natural catastrophes. Downturns tend to have an opposite effect, creating out-migration and a brain drain that weakens the productive base of society. This is different from a large economy where the unemployed can move from one location to another in the same country.

---

[1] Department of Economic Affairs, Commerce, and Industry of Aruba, Labor Market Data, 2013

[2] Charles E. Jones, *Economic Growth* (W. W. Norton, 2002).

[3] Stuart E. Weiner; New Estimates of the Natural Rate of Unemployment; Economic Review—Federal Reserve Bank of Kansas City; 4th Quarter, 1993.

⁴   Indivisibility occurs when companies on a small island order capital equipment in the size that is available from suppliers to use, for instance, to create import substitution. The size of the equipment or plant offers much more production capacity than needed, leading to higher-than-acceptable unit costs. Diseconomies of scale are present when marginal costs increase as a company increases output, *ceteris paribus*. Diminishing returns occur when less and less output is achieved with additional input of labor and capital.

CHAPTER 15

INFLATION

~~•~~

This chapter serves to provide some additional arguments concerning the computation of real GDP as presented in chapter 6.

Introduction

In this chapter, the focus is on the consequences of inflation or, alternatively, deflation on the economic performance of the Small Island Developing States (SIDS). Major questions are whether a small island can manage its economy in such a way that it can insulate itself from inflationary tendencies in countries with which it trades and keep (internal) inflation from soaring as it makes efforts to achieve full employment. Foreign inflation impacts the domestic purchasing power and increases the inflationary effects of domestic fiscal and monetary policies that also have a price-level-increasing effect. That makes it important to be able to monitor indicators of business cycles occurring at home as well in trading partners' countries.

Changes in the price level can have a major effect on the economy. In the late 1970s, the price-level increases were in the double digits, exceeding 10 percent. The governments in the Dutch Caribbean found it necessary to introduce a salary-inflation adjustment using the consumer price index to correct for inflation. A price index is used to tell how the inflation is occurring.

The central bank at the time also introduced a credit-constraining policy as a contraction measure for the economy to counteract the fast increase in money-supply requirements. This was necessary given the budget deficits that the country of the Netherlands Antilles as a whole was experiencing at the time. In an inflationary period, the value of money decreases versus the price of a product. If in 2013 it requires ANG 2.20 to buy a good that cost ANG 1.00 in, say, the year 2009, then the currency is now worth about 45 cents in relation to its value in 2009. The aggregate effect of this type of inflation is visible when there is a general price-level increase affecting most or all of the goods and services purchased by consumers and producers.

Figure 15.1 Aggregate effect of inflation

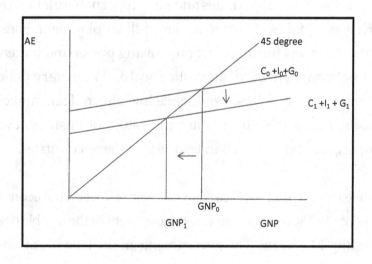

Typically, consumers tend to adjust aggregate consumption (demand) downward when this price-level increase is perceived. When these circumstances are present, the market rate of interest rises due to inflationary conditions, and investment expenditures fall. The exports from the SIDS become more expensive, lowering competitiveness in the international market. This will eventually produce a downward shift in the AE (C + I + G) curve. The smaller the economy, the more pronounced the effects. Looking at only one product, the cattle exports in Saint Eustatius illustrate what can go wrong due to rising prices. The higher cost to feed the cattle on the island prompted increases in prices for beef to the neighboring islands, especially the French Islands. As the surrounding islands could get cheaper product from larger economies, this export practically came to an end.

Inflation

Inflation means a time of generally rising prices for goods and factors of production—for example, rising prices for bread, cars, and wages. Inflation occurs most of the time, but it is recognized as a problem when the rise is widespread and persists at a higher rate, affecting the purchasing power of consumers. The inflation rate in most of the Dutch Caribbean in the first decade of the new millennium has generally been around 2 to 4 percent per year. In the late 1970s and early 1980s, it was at above 10 percent. The inflation rate is measured for a year by subtracting a prior year's price index from this year's price index and dividing this by a prior year's price index. A consumer price index is published monthly by the Central

Bureau of Statistics. The consumer price index measures the cost of a market basket of goods and services, expressed as a percent of its cost in some base year. The statistical yearbook of the Islands of the Dutch Antilles for the year 2000 states that the consumer price index is widely used as an indicator of inflationary trends in the economy and serves as a cost-of-living index.

The price of a basket of goods and services is used to calculate the change in consumer prices and includes food, beverage, tobacco, clothing, footwear, housing, housekeeping, furnishings, health, transport, communication, recreation, and education. The base year is the year that the index is classified as 100. This is generally based on a cost-of-living survey. For instance, cost of living according to the results of a survey held in 1994 grew during the subsequent periods 1996 to 1998 by 3.4 percent, 3.1 percent, and 1.2 percent—meaning that there has been little increase in the cost of living in the years mentioned. This means one less worry with regard to the goals that the government would like to achieve.

Creeping and Galloping Inflation

Sometimes prices begin to creep upward. The latter theoretically happens before an expansion of C + I + G restores the system to full or high employment. Or it happens when there is an apparent excess plant capacity and slack labor market. Sometimes prices rise quickly or literally gallop (increase a millionfold) upward. This could happen when paper money is printed and distributed unchecked. In this period, price increases become the signal for an increase in wages and costs, which again sends prices up still further. This condition is also referred to as hyperinflation.

Michael Salemi, economics professor at the University of North Carolina in Chapel Hill, wrote of hyperinflation in the *Concise Encyclopedia of Economics* that although the threshold is arbitrary, economists generally reserve the term *hyperinflation* to describe episodes where the monthly inflation rate is greater than 50 percent. This can affect production and even the social order. It could even wipe out total wealth of large groups of the population as money becomes worthless. Debtors pursue creditors in order to pay off their debts in valueless money. People start hoarding goods, which only bids prices up even further.

Deflation
When most prices are falling, this is referred to as *deflation*. Under these circumstances, creditors and fixed-income receivers tend to gain at the expense of debtors and profit receivers. If prices fall between the time that a creditor lends money and is repaid, then he gets back more purchasing power than he lent. While the individual would be better off with income from work, the government will find the real burden of its public debt going up relative to tax collections and real national income.

Effect of Inflation

Inflation affects real income. For instance, if the consumer price index (CPI) in 1997 rose from 130 in 1996 to 140 because of inflation, this will have a direct effect on the purchasing power of wages. The wage of someone who is earning ANG 100 per day should now be 140/130 * 100 = 107.69 per day to be able to purchase the same number of goods.

In fact, the real wage per day in terms of 1996 was 100/130 = 76.92. Imagine the person had an increase in wages in 1997 to ANG 120 per day. Then the real daily wage in 1997 is 120/1.40 = ANG 85.71. So there has not been a 20 percent increase in purchasing power but only an increase of 11.4 percent. It is because of this that the government in the Dutch Caribbean decided to introduce a general salaries adjustment in the 1970s.

On the individual level, people may form groups to establish some form of cooperative saving. In the Dutch Antilles, the *Sam* (a local language expression) is used by the group to gather funds to purchase needed goods. The first person in the group will receive the saved amount. In the next round, another person will receive the saved amount until everyone has had his or her turn.

Features of Inflation

Countries can try to deal with the effects of inflation by implementing a system whereby inflation is anticipated. This occurs generally when inflation has been with a society for a long while. Members of the society will then build in an extra allowance in the market interest rate to protect against the expected price increase. It is important when one understands that inflation tends to affect redistribution of income, for instance, from older people to younger people. As an example, insurance that is started at a young age and paid out at age sixty could show shrinking purchasing power.

Unanticipated inflation

When inflation is not anticipated, people often have a hard time adjusting to it. The main effect of the inflation is that it hurts those who have made fixed-term investment—like, for instance, in bonds—and are receiving contracted payments. The purchasing power of the fixed amount of money that one receives erodes in value. On the other hand, those who have to pay contracted amounts at a lower rate will benefit. The nominal amount will not increase, but the value of what one pays is lower than it was previously.

Causes of Inflation

Inflation is generally categorized as being related to excess demand or supply.

- *Demand-pull inflation occurs* when an economy is at full employment and an increase in overall demand pulls up the general price level. The fixed supply of goods cannot be increased. So when buyers bid against each other for the same goods, prices are bound to rise.

- *Cost-push inflation refers to* price increases that can take place anytime. Unions and corporations with great market power push the price level upward even though output has not reached its maximum level. What happens usually is that wage increases grow much faster than productivity. The higher labor cost is normally passed on to the consumer.

- *Supply-side inflation* is often a result of a wage-push that follows union negotiations in one sector and spills over to other sectors, or of a profit-push, for instance where companies decide that they need to restore their profit level after years of downturn by increasing the prices. The world has also experienced supply-side shocks like those due to increase in the price of energy and other commodities.

- *Demand-shift inflation* happens when demand shifts from one product to another through, say, taste changes and forces factor prices up in that industry, including all those in related production fields and from one industry to the other industries, bringing about a general price increase. The price increases in the oil industry in 2005 seem to be a result of a bottleneck occurring in the production of oil-related products like gasoline rather than real or assumed scarcity in petroleum. This is different from the 1970s inflationary increase due to the price increases of the mineral by the oil-producing countries belonging to OPEC.

Keeping Inflation in Check

When inflation is unanticipated, the economy can be seriously affected as firms and consumers lower their spending when confronted by quickly rising costs. Or when the economic situation in a country is characterized by a simultaneous increase in the general price level and stagnation in aggregate economic performance, the country is said to be experiencing *stagflation*. In this situation, characteristically there is a simultaneous occurrence of unemployment and inflation. This is different from what is indicated by the Philips curve in the last chapter and general Keynesian thinking. Countries may try to get out of this predicament by using supply-side strategies like lowering direct taxes, improving the flexibility of the labor and investment market to expand production capabilities and exports.

Some countries that experienced double-digit inflation in the past introduced general index price adjustments, where firms were regularly asked to restate their nonmonetary assets with reference to a market price. Depreciation is restated as well to be able to obtain a realistic picture of the net income of the firm. The CPI is used as reference. The government distributes information on the rate of inflation and the indexation rates monthly. Companies will use these to revalue the fixed assets (including depreciation) on the balance sheet. Salaries, financial assets, and nominal contracts are typically also adjusted in the process. Often firms introduce inflation-adjustment methods in times of rising prices. The Constant Purchasing Power Accounting Method (CPP) is accepted as an international accounting standard for firms to apply during periods of inflation.

Role of the central bank

The central banks, in an effort to maintain stable prices and employment, can control inflation by influencing short-term interest rates. This is centered on the idea that when interest rates are reduced people will spend more and economic growth is stimulated. But if interest rates are increased instead, this will lead to less spending, and so inflation due to a heated economy can be curtailed.

The central bank in targeting inflation further can raise the reserve requirements or carry out open-market operations. When the reserve requirements are raised, the lending capacity of banks is reduced. During open-market operations, the finance department through the central bank sells bonds in the open market and so contracts the circulation of funds in the market. The central bank can also have the local currency appreciate. This was evident in the 1970s when the central bank changed the pegged exchange rate with the US dollar from ANG 1.89 to $1 to ANG 1.79 to $1. The stronger Antillean guilder would also have some effect in reducing inflation.

Core Inflation

Recently, central banks have tended to focus on the components of inflation in the basket that are less volatile on the short run and could provide a better grip for economic/monetary policy. This provides the core inflation rate[1].

The core inflation rate is obtained by adjusting the headline inflation rate, which is based on the total basket of goods and services, taking out the components that are characterized by short-term volatile movements. As a result, core inflation will better indicate the direction of long-term inflation. This enhances the chances of the central bank to implement a policy that is credible and timely and is not affected by temporary fluctuations that may not hold over a longer period of time or cannot be influenced by economic policy. The approach could entail excluding the components characterized by volatile movements or by using a weighted mean of the middle part of the ranked distribution of the CPI component of the price movements. This is referred to as a *trimmed mean*.[2]

Many countries use the *exclusion method* to determine the core inflation rate. The prices of the goods and services considered most volatile are left out. Depending on the country's experiences, the following items may be excluded: fresh food and energy items; changes in indirect taxes and mortgage interest payments; and transportation cost. The exclusion is based on criteria formulated by the central bank in terms of the type and magnitude of the shocks.

Some of the goods that have shown price volatility are gasoline, air transport, fruits, and vegetables. Generally, after core inflation has been determined, the CPI is reweighted for policy purposes. The core inflation rate is a complementary indicator of price movements and will most probably not be published.

Example of determination of core inflation

Table 15.1 shows an example of the composite index for Sint Maarten, Dutch Caribbean. In this section, the data on inflation is illustrated utilizing the data for the island of Sint Maarten. A similar pattern is used on each island. Evidently, it is possible that the weights used for each item differ from island to island. The table shows the inflation data for all components used in deriving the consumer price index for that island. The base year is 1996 and is reflected in the index of 100.

Table 15.1: Composite Index 2001-2005

Sint Maarten, Dutch Caribbean Composite Index	Consumer Price index Numbers 2000-2005						
					February 1996 = 100		
	weight	2000	2001	2002	2003	2004	2005
Components							
Food	1377	105.5	107.7	112.2	113.4	115.2	123.4
Beverages and Tobacco	243	110.2	109.8	112.1	112.3	113.4	113.7
Clothing and footwear	889	101.4	101.6	101.1	101	101.1	99.5
Housing	3053	112	113.3	113.9	118.4	122.8	126.6
Household Furnishing	720	104.3	105.8	106.5	107.4	108.1	111.3
Health Care	235	106.6	106.8	106.7	107.2	106.1	105.1
Transp & Comm	2064	113	113.5	110.5	111.1	114.6	119.2
Recreation and education	894	104.6	106	107.5	107.8	108	108.9
Miscelaneous	725	107.1	107.8	109.8	110.7	111.4	112.7
Total index	10000	108.8	109.7	110.6	111.6	112.9	115.1

CBS- Statistical Yearbook 2005

The table shows inflationary growth for all components from the year 2000 to 2005. Food has a weight of 1,377 of a total of 10,000. Housing, at 3,035, and transportation and communication, at 2,064, carry more weight, meaning that they represent a greater amount of expenditures by the population in the basket of goods and services during the period considered. These weights may change if the spending on each component varies. The changes are due to the use and cost of the item.[3]

Headline and core inflation

The next table shows the subcomponents of the food item in the composite index. It is also used to illustrate the headline inflation rate, which consists of all items in the basket of goods and services utilizing the schedule of *Classification of Individual Consumption according to Purpose* developed by the International Labor Organization, ILO.[4] In this case, only the food component is shown.

Table 15.2: Headline Inflation Rate

Sint Maarten, Dutch Caribbean Sub-components Food	Consumer Price index Numbers 2000-2005 Headline inflation February 1996 = 100						
	weight	2000	2001	2002	2003	2004	2005
Food							
Cereal Products	215.0	105.5	107.5	110.6	110.2	110.5	114.4
Meat and fish	313.0	96.8	99.4	105.4	103.3	105.1	115.9
Fats and cooking oils	34.0	103.7	104.5	101.4	106.1	112.2	127.6
Dairy Products (except butter)	157.0	103.8	103.1	104.5	106.4	109.0	116.1
Potatoes, vegetables and fruits	241.0	117.9	121.3	125.9	132.5	136.8	155.4
Sugar and chocolate	37.0	101.5	105.0	112.1	114.7	117.9	123.2
Prepared food	43.0	101.3	103.5	106.9	107.2	107.3	108.5
Outdoor consumption	248.0	106.1	108.7	116.7	117.3	117.5	119.4
Food n.e.s.	89.0	107.5	109.9	111.3	111.3	113.8	114.8
Total index	**1377.0**	**105.5**	**107.6**	**111.2**	**112.8**	**115.1**	**122.4**

CBS- Statistical Yearbook 2005

The price indices in the subcomponent food table surge from 105.5 in 2000 to 123.4 percent in 2005. The yearly increase can be reason for monetary policy to contain the rate of inflation. A closer examination of the items in the subcomponent food may show volatility in the sense that spikes in price during a year may be short-term and prices fall back to an earlier level. For instance, the potatoes, vegetables, and fruits category in the food subcomponent can be considered too volatile. If so, it is excluded in the determination of the core inflation table. The weight is then distributed proportionally to the other food-subcomponent items. Volatility may be caused by temporary effects from restrictions of exports by a country or other factors that may be of relatively short duration. This is illustrated in table 15.3.

Table 15.3: Example—Core Inflation Rate

Sint Maarten, Dutch Caribbean				803.69			
Sub-components Food	Core- inflation rate	Consumer Price index Numbers 2000-2005			February 1996 = 100		
	weight	2000	2001	2002	2003	2004	2005
Food							
Cereal Products	260.7	105.5	107.5	110.6	110.2	110.5	114.4
Meat and fish	379.4	96.8	99.4	105.4	103.3	105.1	115.9
Fats ansd cooking oils	41.2	103.7	104.5	101.4	106.1	112.2	127.6
Dairy Products (except butter)	190.3	103.8	103.1	104.5	106.4	109.0	116.1
Potatoes, vegetables and fruits	0.0	0.0	0.0	0.0	0.0	0.0	0.0
Sugar and chocolate	44.8	101.5	105.0	112.1	114.7	117.9	123.2
Prepared food	52.1	101.3	103.5	106.9	107.2	107.3	108.5
Outdoor consumption	300.6	106.1	108.7	116.7	117.3	117.5	119.4
Food n.e.s.	107.9	107.5	109.9	111.3	111.3	113.8	114.8
Total index	1377.0	**102.8**	**104.7**	**108.1**	**109.1**	**111.1**	**116.9**

CBS- Statistical Yearbook 2005 Adjusted

As you can see, the data on potatoes, vegetables, and fruit are taken out of the schedules in order to arrive at the core inflation rate. The central bank on the basis of the adjusted inflation rate can design monetary policies that are more realistic in relation to the temporary conditions in the market.

Remarks

Inflation is recognized as a problem when the rise is widespread and persists at a higher rate, affecting the purchasing power of consumers. Options include the following:

- using alternative energy for water desalination and electricity production
- establishing an alternative route to imports favoring less expensive countries
- using the central bank to introduce short-term strategies like interest rates or open-market policies

Appendix

Price Deflator

The value of money has a tendency to change over time due to inflationary or deflationary pressures on price. To maintain a realistic net national product (NNP), economists make use of an index number of prices to measure this year's NNP in terms of a base year. The index number of prices is referred to as the consumer price index or cost-of-living index. The price index is based on the prices in a "market basket" of goods and services. Changes over time in the prices in the market basket are considered to be changes in the cost of living. In a chosen year (as shown in the table 15.4), the cost is given the value of 100.

An example: The market basket consists of bread and soft drinks. In 2002, these items cost ANG 1.80 per loaf of bread and ANG 1.20 per bottle of soft drink. In 2002, people bought 200 loaves of bread and 400 bottles of soft drinks. The market basket totals ANG 840 for the two products. If next year the new market basket for the same product costs ANG 882, then the cost of living has increased by

$$(882 - 840) \div 840 = 5 \text{ percent.}$$

To construct a cost of living index, let the ANG 840 of 2002 represent 100. Then the 2003 rise in cost of living will be represented as

$$882 \div 840 = 1.05 \text{ or } 105.$$

The GDP is calculated originally at market prices and is translated to real prices using the price index and restating the GDP on the basis of the price index in a prior year. If the economy that we looked at had only those two products in the basket, we could use them to deflate the GDP as shown in table 15.4.

Table 15.4 Deflating GDP

Year	GDP	INDEX	DEFLATED	
2012	4,000	100	4,000	
2013	4,500	105	4,286	(4500x100)/105

Consequently, the real GDP is 4.286 billion. What it also tells us is that the purchasing power of the currency has decreased. With 4,500 florins one can only buy 4,286 worth of goods compared to the year 2012. As a result the CPI is used to illustrate changes in the cost of living.

Consumer price index

The CPI could be a simple index number consisting of one set of data over a period of time or a composite with several different sets of data combined. In the case of the composite index, weights are assigned to each item.

Composite Index

The following is an example using the price development for three retail products. The steps to establishing a composite index start with computing a simple index from a base year. In this example, the base year is 2008. The index is set at 100 for the product. Next, the change in prices—partially due to the cost of import and local pricing or cost of production—is recorded and adjusted showing the price sold to the public. The simple index is shown in the three columns on the left for each commodity.

Table 15.5 Composite Index

Year	Argentine Beef	Dutch Cheese	Antilles Chicken	proportion of Consumption 0.4	0.3	0.3	Composite Index
2008	100	100	100	40	30	30	100
2009	115	110	110	46	33	33	112
2010	120	120	115	48	36	34.5	118.5
2011	140	150	120	56	45	36	137

This forms the simple index for each product. Each product is analyzed to find out how it relates to total sales.[2] In the example above, beef makes up 40 percent of total sales, cheese 30 percent, and chicken 30 percent. These are the weights given to the separate products. By multiplying the weights and the indices, one establishes a composite index for the year after adding the results for the three items. The rate of inflation is subsequently determined by comparing the composite index for one period to another.

---

[2] The relationship to total sales are expressed as weights which are generally determined using a weight reference period, a price reference period and an Index reference period, on the basis of an expenditure survey. The index reference period usually is expressed as 100. The weight reference period is important considering that certain consumer items tend to disappear over time and have to be replaced in the calculation of the price index. The price reference concerns the period relevant for price comparisons. This is described in the ILO Consumer price Index Manual: Theory and Practice of 2004.

Rate of inflation based on the composite price index:

(price index – price index t – 1) ÷ price index t – 1,

where t – 1 indicates the previous period. Consequently, the inflation from 2010 to 2011 for these foodstuffs will be the 2011 composite index number less the 2010 index number divided by the 2010 index.

---

[1] RachelHolden; Measuring Core Inflation; The Reserve Bank of New Zealand Bulletin; 2006 and Timothy Cogley ; Core Inflation; Journal of money, Credit and banking; 2006. These two articles provide the reader additional insight concerning the various approaches to measure core inflation.

[2] Ibid 1.

[3] ILO-*Consumer Price Index manual: Theory and Practice* of 2004 provides an excellent overview of the approach to Price index calculations. The goods and services are aggregated with regards to groups, class, sub-class and region using the Classification of Individual Consumption according to Purpose (COICOP) method.

[4] Ibid 3

Chapter 16
Planning for the Future

$$\sim\!\!\bullet\!\!\sim$$

The previous chapters introduced a variety of views on economics and economic development. Improving life in the islands requires sustainable growth. Sustainable growth is not only about economic growth but also about achieving and maintaining a degree of quality of life, security, equal opportunity, and standard of living. Success will be contingent upon the characteristic behavior on the islands with regard to individual public efforts and the current value system. So while planning for the future is a sine qua none, the effect and success of implementation will be contingent on the dominant sociocultural forces. Planning for the future will require the uncovering of available qualitative and quantitative data to model and interpret how decisions made now can influence the future outcomes.

Introduction

The drastic changes in technology of late have brought new challenges to countries everywhere around the globe. The major challenge is to manage the welfare of the nation-state in a global environment with a high degree of informational and technological integration and shortcomings in the degree of financial integration. Furthermore, in the pursuit of development, many countries have allowed the use and misuse of natural resources without considering the consequences on the environment in the long run.

It is becoming clear that not only do countries face the depletion of resources, but they also face the result of long-term pollution, such as greenhouse gases and their effect on the ozone layer and global warming. This seems to lead to climatic change and health threats never experienced before.

Under these circumstances, economic growth will depend on how economic activities and public policies can provide the necessary impulses to turn the economy around if it is stagnating and establish a sound and sustainable base for the country to develop and grow. Finding ways to obtain a sustainable economic growth and development is a critical element in the country's economic management.

Purpose of Economic Planning

The main purpose of economic planning is to establish proper grounds for commitment of funds for steering the economy in a desired level to achieve a level of economic well-being that can sustain an acceptable quality of life for the entire society. Quality of life for the entire population calls for equal opportunities for those participating in the economy and a guarantee for a degree of safety and security.

The lack of equal opportunities is often expressed by economic and social deprivation or social exclusion. A portion of the population has no access to certain social (security) benefits and is excluded from economic benefits. This could have as a result that some members of society will be reluctant to participate fully in the labor force. It could also be one of the causes of a deterioration of physical and personal safety.

These circumstances have seemingly resulted in a steady increase in theft and robbery and drug-related trade over the last thirty years in some of the Dutch Caribbean islands. This growing trend practically created an economic sector based on crime that motivates new businesses and employment with the establishment of security firms, security-equipment dealers, and gated residential-area developments. Successfully combating the crime economy will require an environment that is more accommodating to those socially deprived and excluded, with more meaningful jobs and opportunities for personal growth.

Cooperation to Change

However, to implement a process that reaches these goals, there is a need for cooperation among members of society to break away from existing molds if these structurally impede the achievement of planned growth and development. Some aspects, such as traditional norms, political structure and social culture, and the value system, are elements of society that do not change easily. These factors tend to generally be overlooked, although they may affect successful implementation of a plan.

Sociocultural aspects

The set of norms to which society conforms evolves over time and become a stabilizing factor in the interaction between people and the context that describes the accepted norms. If government, for instance, has an instrumental role in economic progress, the success of attainment of growth and development for the society as a whole is affected by the dominant values exhibited by those in a position to govern, which in fact can be the values held by the general population.

Values as defined by Milton Rokeach and discussed by Kleindorfer et al.[1] represent personal and social preferences for desired end states and appropriate means of attaining these. The preferred end states may include a better life for all living on the island. The mode of conduct, or what Rokeach calls *instrumental values*, may allow different preferences on how to reach this end state.[2] An increase in the requirement for immediate material compensation and display of material wealth could sometimes push back other preferences like honesty, courage, ambition, and courtesy. Certain modes of conduct can display a mix of personal and social preferences that dominate the pursuit of the end state. There are several observations to this regard, mainly concerning the island of Curaçao.

Professor Alejandro Paula, in a breakfast meeting in 1987 in Curaçao, pointed to a particular isolationist attitude that developed during the boom years with Shell and Lago among part of the population "where some fancied themselves superior to those who came to this island to secure themselves a better future. His [that is referring to the Curaçao population] own migration to Cuba, Colombia, Dominican Republic, Surinam, and Venezuela was buried in oblivion."[3] Everybody considers him or herself self-sufficient—that is, able to maintain oneself without aid or cooperation from others.

Another view regards the major motivating factor that drives societal actions. In the beginning of the 1970s, after the upheavals in and around Willemstad of 1969, human-relations and sensitivity-training sessions were held on a wide scale, allowing employees in many firms to participate with the purpose of building a society that was more responsive to its own needs and enhanced the achievement motivation perspective. From surveys by the group[4] that instituted these programs, it was inferred that power was a major motivating factor throughout the Curaçao community as compared to the achievement motive and the need for affection. The outcome of the study did not relate these conditions to an assumed lack of equality of income and opportunities in society. One can, however, surmise that these characteristics, if they are true, are compensated by a drive for political power that in view of lack of other opportunities can be an avenue for supplemental income. These are personal modes of conduct that can become a norm even to the extent that possible ethical ramifications are suppressed.[5]

If these preferences are widespread, they can affect macroeconomic pursuits of the specific island nation, and how and why the economy moves (or does not move) in a certain direction. One may attribute the existence of a variety of political parties and frequent entrance of new political parties to some extent to both factors described above, as one (the individual) sees the party as an avenue to satisfy the need for more material gains and for obtaining some degree of influence, power, and prestige, which may be equated with achievement.

William A. Anderson and Russell R. Dyne also studied the social and political environment in Curaçao in the period after the social unrest of 1969 and observed that

> the nature of Curaçao's political system also set limits to social reform. Politics in Curaçao are highly pragmatic and opportunistic. There is considerable wheeling-and-dealing by political parties, both inside and outside the public political scene, often at the expense of solving problems or making reforms. The emphasis is given to acquiring and maintaining influence. This lack of concern for reform is also reinforced by the personalistic nature of politics in Curaçao. Again it should be mentioned that there is a tendency for voters to react to a politician on the basis of his personal style and what he can do for them in the way of personal favors rather than his performance in office. Partly because of this quality of politics in the Antilles, there has been little sustained impetus for change and reform. New parties have emerged in Curaçao from time to time to challenge

this situation only to find themselves submitting to it and assuming many of the characteristics they had originally sought to reform."[6]

These observations and interpretations of sociocultural aspects are important for reflecting on noneconomic factors that affect public and private organizations. While these several expressions regarding attitudes have been referred to for Curaçao, no research results are available or in my possession to describe and define possible divergent attitudes and dominant motives in the rest of the Dutch Caribbean.

Poverty

The persistence of poverty, using George Beckford's formulation, is based on the openness of the island economies with respect to the more advanced economies as well as with the sociocultural patterns that have developed from the colonial history. These two factors need to be addressed to insure sustainable growth and development that is supported by indigenous efforts. The level of poverty among the populations of the islands illustrates the baseline from which to initiate a process toward satisfying the quality of life requirement.[7]

The level of poverty is reflected by the number of unemployed and the number of families who have an income at or below a subsistence level. The sociocultural pattern exhibits features that inherently regard achievement, ideas, products, and services from the more developed countries as superior to one's own. Characteristically, this can lead to quick dismissal of domestic proposals or production.

Freedom of choice and social opportunities

The poverty and sociocultural patterns mentioned above as well as other external factors (see chapter 13 on investments) hinder wider participation of the population in entrepreneuring. However, Amartya Sen[8] (1999) maintains that the success of the country is measured in accordance with what the people can do and what opportunities are available to meet one's own needs. His point is that people should be free to act on opportunities, and he categorizes the principal ends of development as follows:

- political freedom, which is the right of people to determine who should govern and by what principles
- facilities for economic opportunities for all people to utilize economic resources for the purpose of consumption, production, and exchange
- social opportunities including arrangements for education and health care social
- interaction based on trust and transparency

These freedoms would imply that each island is to examine the socioeconomic environment for shortcomings in the areas above and put policies in place to clear the road to success.

Planning and the New Economy

The tool of macroeconomic planning is useful as guidance toward obtaining economic growth and economic development that can expand opportunities to generate more employment-creating activities. Planning can include the eventuality that more individuals in society obtain access to capital that can be applied toward economic endeavors. The applicability and sophistication of a plan is contingent on the level of development achieved by the country and on the extent of freedom of enterprise.

Planning helps in determining whether controls should be set *a priori* or after the fact. Planning also presupposes an ability to recognize the factors limiting the pursuit of economic gains resulting from man-induced externalities on the natural environment. The negative externalities are shown by deforestation, land degradation through continuous urbanization and overbuilding, and waste and toxic chemicals polluting the air, land, and water.

This creates loss of biodiversity and the erosion of coastal areas. This awareness generally leads to conflicts with regard to land use for agriculture, urbanization, tourism, and maintenance of biodiversity. It appears that it is to a great extent the man-induced externalities that are the cause of climate change that threatens coral reefs and marine resources and the rising level of the sea.

Strategic economic planning

In modern days, the economic plan is generally a subset of an overall or grand strategy that determines a long-term view of where the country wants to be at some point in the future. This grand strategy can require implementation of one or more policies that have direct consequences on the behavior of members of society. Strategic economic and societal planning becomes necessary with the multiple changes in the global environment, which also provide for new opportunities.

If the attitudes and sociocultural aspects described above persist, economic planning can be a futile exercise. If those characteristics are prevalent and dominate, the island will typically introduce important changes (requiring major investments) only as a reaction to major impacting conditions in the environment and after the fact, or after enormous social pressure, unless the changes are brought from the outside. Chances are that such an economy faces constant financial and unemployment pressure and therefore is in constant crisis.

Strategic societal economic planning will instead allow the determination of the strengths and weaknesses of the domestic economic system as well as opportunities and threats from the domestic and international environment that need to be dealt with. Wide-scale participation as proposed by Amartya Sen earlier in this chapter will be contingent on the introduction of adequate policy instruments to safeguard fair trade and competitiveness and to stimulate dissemination of research findings about strategic options. These inputs will support the upgrading in terms of entrepreneurship as proposed in earlier chapters and help in perceiving strategic opportunities. It is in this environment that the domestic population will display greater acceptance for domestic innovative behavior.

Modeling growth

The effects of the policies in the paragraph above and policy measures like minimum wages to improve the standard of living for the low-income population or increased taxes to expand national health-insurance coverage of a larger portion of the population are generally gauged by way of economic models. These macromodels of the entire economy are used to guide economic efforts and long-term plans and help in expanding the understanding of how the economy functions. As a result, they help to examine policies taken by the government (ex-post) and can be useful to forecast the impact of policy scenarios. They are also useful to develop what-if scenarios.

There is an increasing focus on growth models, and these take account of as many aspects as possible to get a more realistic view of the impact of development by incorporating, among other things, social, environmental, fiscal, and monetary variables. The purpose of the macroeconomic exercise, according to William Arthur Lewis, is

> to help to ensure that the Plan is internally self-consistent; that the resource requirements of the proposed increases in private consumption, public services and investment do not add up to more than is available; that the expected increases in

output of individual sectors are consistent with
the expected increases in inputs; that demand and
supply will balance . . . ; that imports will not grow
faster than exports; that the expected rate of growth
will be consistent with available skilled capital and
manpower; and so on.[9]

Current macromodels generally consist of several basic parts—
including, for instance, the fiscal sector, the household sector,
the monetary sector, and the external (tourism/offshore) sector.
The macromodel concerns both economic aspects and social
factors while it allows for influences on the environment or
influences from the environment, like global warming.

Models can be based on econometric techniques using time
series, regression analysis, and other highly mathematical
methodologies, or on arithmetic techniques using spreadsheets
and databases. Some models have an accounting structure that
generally seeks equilibrium, or are of an optimization nature
with the intent to determine the optimum outcome with the
variables used.

Predictive Ability of Plans

The macromodel generally makes use of a combination of
functional models that have a predictive ability. The production
and consumption functions as well as more complex models
like the Harrod-Domar economic model and the input-output
model are used as building blocks of the macromodel.

The highly detailed models also take into account microeconomic preferences, the effects of current technology, interest rates, tax rates, reserve requirements, purchases, and other related variables. The following paragraphs provide some insight into three general economic behavioral equations that are integrated in the models used in the islands, followed by a short description of the models used in the Dutch Caribbean.

Production function

A production function (see its use for economic growth in chapter 15) describes the output that results from the combination of inputs that are presumably in a constant ratio with each other. An example is the situation in a micro-island, as shown by the data in table 16.1. An investment of 100 thousand dollars and 100 labor units produces 100 thousand units of a good. The investment is shown at the bottom of the table. Production is shown in the second column. As more labor (see first column) is used with the same injection of capital, there is an increase in units produced; however, beyond 200 units of labor, the number of units produced with the investment of 100 dollars starts falling.

Table 16.1 Labor input

Labor units	Units Output1	Units Output 2
100	100	150
200	200	220
300	260	280
400	300	320
500	340	360
600	360	400
	100	200
	Invest 1	Invest 2

Figure 16.1 Production Function

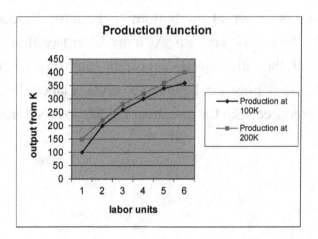

The data in the table indicate that increasing the amount of labor leads to diminishing returns. This is because of the small market that does not allow economies of scale. Figure 16.1 shows graphically that the increases in output taper off with additional workers. The Harrod-Domar economic model referred to in chapter 2 and the Solow growth model in chapter 14 are models based on the production function. This is expressed as the production function $Y = F(K,L)$. Y represents output or GDP, while inputs of K (capital) and L (labor) influence Y. F indicates the level of technology as an exogenous factor influencing the relationship between K and L. Capital and labor in the Harrod-Domar model are in a constant ratio with each other. Consequently, the model explains that when K is raised, L will increase to maintain the ratio, and these together impact the GDP.

The input-output model

Another model used in macroeconomic modeling is the input-output model by Wassiliv Leontief. This model provides insight with regard to interindustry transactions that is useful for estimating the impact of growth in these industries on the entire economy. With the input-output model, one establishes how much is bought and sold between the sectors of an economy. This model helps to compute the intersector activities. For instance, in the case of an island like Saba, if a fisherman buys wood from a store, the input-output model registers a transaction between the retail sector and the agriculture/fishery sector. This approach also provides insight as to the longer circulation of invested funds in the island economy before a portion is sent abroad to purchase goods and services. As a general equilibrium model, it depicts the interrelationships between different industries. Table 16.2 shows another example—the relationship between water production (desalination), beverage production, electricity production, and transport sectors.

Table 16.2 Input-Output Table

	Water	beverages	electricity	transport
water	0.3	0.4	0.1	0.1
beverages	0.1	0.1	0.1	0.1
electricity	0.3	0.2	0.3	0.2
transport	0.1	0.1	0.3	0.3
labor	0.2	0.2	0.2	0.3
Total	1	1	1	1

This table shows four sectors: water desalination, beverage production, electricity generation and transportation. To produce one unit of water (see Column 1), the water-producing (desalination) industry needs to spend 30 cents in water, 30 cents in electricity, 20 cents in transport, and 20 cents in labor. Similarly, to produce one unit of beverages, 40 cents goes to buy water from the desalination plant, 10 cents is used in its own operations, 20 cents goes to electricity, 10 cents to transport, and 20 cents to labor. The beverage industry is not necessarily considered a basic industry. However, the table still illustrates that if demand for locally produced beverage changes—say from one unit to two units—this will have a direct effect on production and supply of water, electricity, labor, and transport.

For simplicity, we focus only on the two first columns and rows of the water and beverage sectors. We take as example the columns on water production and beverage production. Assume that the total demand for beverages (B) is 100 million units and for water (W) 500 million units. This reflects 100 million units of water that comes from the desalination plant and is alternatively converted into juices, sodas, and beer by the beverage industry, along with other ingredients.

We can use the input-output model to determine just for these two products, water and beverage, how much water and beverage has to be produced by the two sectors in order to satisfy first the internal demand of the sectors and second the external demand by consumers. The model asks for a simultaneous equation. Using for simplicity the data water and electricity cost in table 16.2 for the sectors water and beverages, a two-by-two matrix can provide some insight as to the effect of one sector on the other:

$$W = 0.3w + 0.4e + 500.$$
$$B = 0.3w + 0.2e + 100$$
$$W = \text{water}; B = \text{beverage}.$$

The data on water is found in row 1 at the top of table 16.2 in columns Water and Beverages. The one on electricity is found in the third row.

The variables in the equation tell us that in the sector water 30 cents of water is needed for production of water and 40 cents of electricity. With regards to the beverage sector this is 30 cents for water and 20 cents for electricity. The external demand for water is 500 florins. The external demand for beverages is 100. To meet internal and external demand for these two products, the sectors will have to produce 1001 florins worth of water and 499 florins worth of electricity, applying the input-output analysis with the two-by-two matrixes.[10]

Example calculation 2x2 matrix water and beverage production

In this example we chose water and electricity cost
for the sector water desalination and the sector beverages
for which we establish the determinant and the inverse A^{-1}.
The outcome provides us with insight as to what effect a change
in demand can have from one sector to another.
We subtract the 2x2 matrix from the Identity

$$I = \begin{bmatrix} 1 & 0 \\ 0 & 1 \end{bmatrix} \quad \text{Identity matrix}$$

$$\begin{array}{c} & w & e \\ w & [\,0.3 & 0.4\,] \\ e & [\,0.3 & 0.2\,] \end{array} \quad \text{2x2 matrix}$$

we are left with:

$$\begin{bmatrix} 0.7 & -0.4 \\ -0.3 & 0.8 \end{bmatrix}$$

The determinant is found by multiplying diagonally
0.7x .8 = .56 and -0.3 x -0.4 = 0.12. The result is .44
or 1/0.44
The inverse is found by multiplying the determinant by the
two by two matrix after swapping the upper left factor with the lower
right factor and changing the sign of the other two factors.
This provides the following result

$$\begin{array}{cc} & & & & w & e \\ 1/0.44 & \begin{bmatrix} 0.8 & 0.4 \\ 0.3 & 0.7 \end{bmatrix} & & \begin{bmatrix} 1.82 & 0.91 \\ 0.68 & 1.59 \end{bmatrix} \end{array}$$

Demand for water 500 liter =   500 x 1.82 _ 100X .91 = 910 +91 = 100:
Demand for electricity =   500 x .68 + 100 x 1.59 = 340 + 159 = 49ς

If due to decreased demand for beverages the amount of water and electricity
demanded by the beverage industry decreases, say to 80, this can have a
simultaneous decrease in the demand for water and electricity. As a result
demand for water may increase to 400. In that case, and holding everything else
constant , now the overall demand for water and electricity affect the economy

If one or more of the beverage companies in the beverage industry close their operations locally and equivalent beverages are imported, this will affect both *W* and *B* with regard to input and output of water in the production processes. In this case, demand for beverages does not change but supply of water from the desalination plant will fall drastically. If these two industries are major employers, chances are that the change will lead to massive unemployment as the provision of beverages shifts to the wholesale/retail sector, which is not greatly affected by this change. Further impact is felt in energy production and on transportation in the manufacturing sector due to the lower domestic production of beverage and water, and this will have an indirect impact on service sectors. As a result more than one sector is impacted. Additionally, the increased importing of beverages will require foreign exchange to settle transactions on finished products. The concomitant decrease in the import of raw materials for beverage production will generally not be of such a degree that it offsets the effect of the increased imports of final goods.

The input-output model allows a fast review of the impact of domestic and external economic cycles on the various interrelated industries. The vulnerability due to outside forces requires a constant detailed view of the economy and where it can be heading. Just as an existing industry can be failing, one unique foreign investment can be of such magnitude that it creates employment over and above the current requirements for labor. This is referred to as the *incidence of causation.*

Modeling is done to achieve a view of how the expansion or contraction in productive activities maintain a balance between aggregate supply and demand and produces a shift outward (or inward) in the production possibilities curve that generates employment. It becomes a what-if game that can even include possible variations in the pegged exchange rate to see how this could obtain a real wage reduction to achieve the targeted employment level. Or it could include the redirection of the local savings deployed abroad in foreign securities to enhance output in, say, agricultural activities.

Macromodels in the Dutch Caribbean

The models used by the departments of economic affairs in the islands consist essentially of two parts. One is a macroeconomic module that is supported by a data set considering transactions between sectors; national income and spending; production; wages; import/export; government income; price level (changes); and monetary variables. This module is in turn supported by microeconomic modules, such as a block that explains developments in the export sector of the country. This block includes such variables as the value of exports, price of exports, and investments by the export sector. Another block is made up of a micromodule concerning climate-related issues. Yet another part regards the effects on economic performance due to behavior of the consumer, labor unions, and business as a response to cues in the environment like government measures or policies, changes in world trade, changes in investments by households or business that affect export, or a possible closing of the oil refinery and introduction of more cost-efficient energy production alternatives.

The Sint Maarten macromodel and the Curaçao (Curalyse) model provide an opportunity for evaluating on one hand the existing competency and on the other the economic benefits regarding efforts to change macroeconomic policies, looking at the national accounts, monetary and financial aspects, and labor market effects. The system is built on the micro macro method using a spreadsheet for modeling the economy of the islands. Currently, such models are being contemplated for other Caribbean islands like Saint Kitts and Grenada. The micromodels include detailed modules that provide key indicators with regard to cruise and stayover tourism, purchasing-power effects, income, and social-aspect-related outcomes.

---

[1] Paul R. Kleindorfer, Howard C. Kunreuther, and Paul J. H. Schoemaker, *Decision Sciences: An Integrated Perspective* (Cambridge University Press, 1993).

[2] Paul R. Kleindorfer, Howard C. Kunreuther and Paul J.H. Schoemaker; Decision Sciences, An Integration Perspective; Cambridge UniversityPress, 1993 pp 36-37

[3] Dr. A.F. Paula; Understanding the Whole. Key-note speech delivered on the occasion of a prayer breakfast organized by ASINA, July 26th, 1987

[4] Dr. Harry Lasker and Dr. Victor Pinedo were instrumental in establishing an organization, Fundashon Humanas, in the years following the 1969 upheaval in Willemstad to train management and personnel in a wide array of firms with an intent to bring about societal change toward greater achievement orientation. The ideas of achievement motivation as well as power motivation and affiliation motivation are concepts introduced by David McClelland in his book *The Achievement Motive* (1953). Lasker and Pinedo interviewed thousands of people on the island of Curaçao and obviously found that the power motive and affiliation motive were more dominant traits of the Curaçao population. According to McClelland, when individuals are achievement-motivated, they are more productive and valuable to their organization. When achievement motivates an entire society, the society thrives economically. Affiliation-and power-motivated countries fail. This is found in the publication *Tsunami: Building Organizations Capable of Prospering in Tidal Waves* (iUniverse, 2004).

[5] A politician who enriches himself or herself during his or her tenure is sometimes held to have worked intelligently. In this case, a specific (unethical) mode of conduct is (tacitly) preferred over an ethical one to obtain power and wealth, and perhaps to insure achievement of some national goal.

[6] William A. Anderson and Russel R. Dyne, *Social Movements, Violence, and Change* (Ohio State University Press, 1975), 121.

[7] The subsistence level for a family of four was estimated in 1997 at ANG 1,100 for the Dutch Caribbean islands, including Aruba. The 2001 census held in the Dutch Caribbean, now excluding Aruba, shows that 38 percent of the population age fifteen and above in Curaçao

has an income of ANG 1,000 or less, and for Sint Maarten this is 21 percent. The situation in Sint Maarten is much different from that in the Leeward Islands. In Sint Maarten and also in Saba and Saint Eustatius, the predominant currency used for financial transactions is the US dollar. Before the breakdown of the political union, most salaries in these territories were in Netherlands Antilles florins, but the spending required US dollars. Note that since October 2010, the US dollar is legal tender in the special municipalities of Saba, Saint Eustatius, and Bonaire.

[8]   Amartya Sen; Development as Freedom; Anchor Books, 1999.

[9]   William Arthur Lewis, *Development Planning: the Essentials of Economic Policy* (New York: Harper and Row Publishers, 1966), p 147.

[10]   The application requires solving a two-by-two matrix equation:

Epilogue

જ∾ઙ

The Shifting Microeconomic Base

The economic history of the Dutch Caribbean is one of continuous change with respect to the basic industry. While in the past it was the conquerors, the colonial powers, and the multinationals that determined the pace of change, now pressure for change comes from actions or inactions within the domestic economy, which are increasingly influenced by events in the most remote corners of the globe.

Reforms in the global marketplace, like the introduction of the European directives concerning tax havens and earlier withdrawal of the United States from the double-taxation treaty, affected the offshore financial sector in the Caribbean region negatively at a time when the multinationals operating the oil refineries were withdrawing in Curaçao and Aruba. Consequently, domestic well-being and maintenance of a standard of living depend on island-level economic management. Furthermore, the increasing degree of integration in economic blocs in the global community, the effects of disruptive strategic decisions abroad, and disruptive new advances in technology attacked the foundations of the local basic industries and set new challenges that could best be responded to by increasing the information base and the knowledge base in the domestic society, in an effort to enhance the flexibility to adapt.

The study of economics prepares members of society to develop an overall insight as to the possibilities of achieving growth in income and in quality of life for oneself and for the population. There are several ways to measure progress. The expenditure approach and income approach used to determine the gross domestic product (GDP) and GNI give an indication of economic performance. These measures can be further refined to determine the impact on the environment. The human-development index adds progress in housing and education to the progress in income and so provides an overall picture of growth of the human factor.

Given the frequent shifts in leading sectors with visible retrenchment and geographical relocation by companies that have cohabited the islands for decades, maintenance of economic performance and growth will depend on the ability of cooperation between economic sectors and the public sector to propose and determine development objectives that can contribute to policies that strengthen the chances of successful participation of firms in an industry. Nicholas Braham pointed out that the (then) Netherlands Antilles prospered by adopting laws and regulations to support the offshore finance industry. It is this flexibility on the part of the government and cooperation between the private sector and the government that made sure that the offshore sector thrived.[1]

The increase in regional economic blocs consisting of free-trade agreements and custom unions brings a new challenge for economic survival. Furthermore, the European Union influences the creation of economic partnership agreements (EPAs) in such a way that certain benefits that accrued only to overseas countries and territories (OCTs) are being eroded.

These challenges and the gradually increasing pressure for economic development from within require more understanding of the domestic economic and sociocultural environment and their effects on economic growth.

The islands face complex issues, and a complex internal and external environment. As a consequence other important economic factors than those covered in this publication need to be reviewed. We have opted to leave for a follow-up publication such issues as poverty, government, money, banking, international trade, and corresponding growth management.

A major message included in this writing regards special attention to skilling and educating of the workforce to meet the needs of the domestic market. These needs include developing exportable products and services and enhancing the opportunities for financing of investments from both indirect and direct local and external sources. The fact that for small islands, required import of fixed capital creates a less-than-expected multiplier effect calls for compensatory creativity and innovation to stimulate growth in exports of goods. Only in this way can the standard of living be safeguarded.

---

1   Nicolas Braham, "Cooperative Laissez Faire," in *Free Enterprise in Curaçao*, eds. M. F. Hasham and D. Dare (Curaçao Chamber of Commerce and the University of the Netherlands Antilles, 1992).

References List

꙳ꙮꙐ

Adelman, Irma and Erik Thorbecke,; The theory and Design of economic development; John Hopkins Press, 1966. p. 47. with reference to Arhtur Lewis.

Aiyer, Sri-Ram, Maarten J. Ellis, Christofer G. Smeets: Netherlands Antilles Fiscal Commission; Removing Obstacles to Growth and and restoring Jobs in Curacao: Issues, Strategic Agenda, and Implementation" Final Report. June 2007.

Altig, David, Terry Fitzgerald, and Peter Rupert: "Okun's Law Revisited: Should We Worry about Low Unemployment?" Economic Commentary (Cleveland) (1997): 1+.

Altman, E.I.; I.Walter; Contemporary Studies in Economic and Financial Analysis, Volume 35 (1982) JAI Press INC.

Araujo, Carlos Hamilton. "The Role of Potential Output Growth in Monetary Policymaking in Brazil." Federal. Reserve Bank of St. Louis Review 91.4 (2009): 383+.

Arhtur, Owen; Economic Policy Option in the twenty–first century: In Contending with Destiny; the Caribbean in the 21st Century; Kenneth Hall and Denis Benn, editors.

Bell, G.; Jan Kees Martijn: IMF Papers: Recent Developments, Selected Issues, and Statistical Appendix, April 2001,);

Browning, E.K and J.M. Browning: Public Finance and the Price system; 4th edition; Prentice Hall International. 1994.

Bruntland Commission; Toward sustainable Development: in Our Common future; Norton 1987. Excerpted by Stephen Wheeler and Timoth Beatly: The Sustainable Urban Development; Reader; Routledge; 2004.

Campagna, Anthony S.: Macroeconomics Theory and Policy; Houghton Mifflin Boston

Cardot, Carlos Felice; Curazao Hispanico (Antagonismo Flamenco Español); Biblioteca de la Academia Nacional de la Historia; Caracas 1973.

Carnes; W. Stansbury; Stephen D. Slifer: The Atlas of Economic Indicators: Harper Business

Casler, Stephen D;:Introduction to Economics, Harpers College outline; 1992; HarperCollins publishers.

Chander, L.V; S.M. Goldfeld: The Economics of Money and Banking (1977) Library of Congress Cataloging in Publication Data.

Clayton; G.E.: Economics principles and practices; Glencoe/ McGraw-Hill; 1999

Cline, W. R.: Potential Effects of Income Redistribution on Economic Growth, Latin American Cases (1972) Praeger Publishers, Inc.

Cohen, B.J. Balance of Payments Policies. Penguin Modern Economics, 1974.

Comenencia, Paul; Free enterprise in a limiting environment; In Free Enterprise in Curacao; M.F. Hasham and Drs. D.Dare, editors; joint publication of the Curacao chamber of Commerce and the University of the Netherlands Antilles. 1992

Committee on the Debt Predicament of 2003: Op weg naar gezonde Overheidsfinancien, Politieke Daadkracht, Visie, eigen Verantwoordelijkheid en de Wil elkander bij te Staan, Rapport Commissie Schuldenproblematiek 25 juli 2003–

Commonwealth secretariat; Small States: A review of literature and major development problems; Paper presented at Symposium on small states: Problems and Opportunities in a world of rapid change; St Kitts, 1991

Contessi, Silvio.: "An Application of Conventional Sovereign Debt Sustainability Analysis to the Current Debt Crises." Federal Reserve Bank of St. Louis Review 94.3 (2012): 197+.

Curacao Chamber of Commerce; Curacao's economy in brief. August 19, 2005

Daal, Wendly and Francisco Nadal De Simone; International Monetary Fund; Kingdom of the Netherlands; Netherlands

Antilles; Selected issues and Statistical Appendix; February 2006. Includes; Recent Economic Developments and a Tale of two groups of Caribbean Economies.

Dai, Feng, Jing Xu Liu, and Song Tao Wu. "The Impact of Endogenous Investment on Economic Growth: An Analysis on Advance-Retreat Course Theory." International Journal of Management 27.2 (2010): 342+.

Deane, P.; The evolution of economic ideas (1978) University Press, Cambridge.

Deshommes, Fritz; Vie Chère et Politique Économique en Haiti; 1992

Diaz Santana, Miriam; Competitiveness, Education and Training; in Roads to Competitiveness; Editor: M.F. Hasham; Association of Caribbean Economists; University of the Netherlands Antilles,1995

Dillard, Dudley. The Economics of John Maynard Keynes: The Theory of a Monetary Economy. New York: Prentice-Hall, 1948.

Elliot, John: Comparative Economic Systems; NJ; Prentice Hall, 1973.

Elu, Juliet. "The Journey So Far: The Effect of Structural Adjustment Programme (SAP),

Europe Information; The European Community and the Overseas Countries and Territories; Commission of the European Communities; Directorate –General of Information, Communication, Culture; DE 76; Brussels, October 1993

Farrell, T; D. Worrell; Caribbbean Monetary Integration (1994) Caribbean Information Systems & Services Ltd. (CISS)

Fransica, E.T.; Toezicht op het Antilliaanse Bank-en Kredietwezen; Rechtsgrondslagen; Doctoraal Scriptie 1985, University of the Netherlands Antilles; and P.B. 1979 No. 329

Friedman, Milton. "John Maynard Keynes." Economic Quarterly—Federal Reserve Bank of Richmond 83.2 (1997): 1+.

Fromm, G.; P.Taubman; Public Economic Theory and Policy (1973) Collier-Macmillan Publisher, Fundamental issues; ISBN; 99914 2 019 3

Gill, Henry S.; Defining a Caribbean position on NAFTA; in Roads to Competitiveness; edited by M.F. Hasham; Association of Caribbean Economists; Univ. Neth. Antilles; 1995/1997.

Ginsberg, Anthony S. Tax Havens; New York institute of Finance; Simon and Schuster; 1991

Girvan, Norman and George Beckford editors: Development In Suspense; Selected papers and proceedings of the First Conference of Caribbean Economists; Publisher:Friedrich Ebert

Stiftung in collaboration with the Association of Caribbean Economists; 1989.

Girvan, Norman; El Gran Caribe; John Sealy Memorial Lecture Trinidad, 2001

Gonzalez, Alfonso, and Jim Norwine, eds. The New Third World. 2nd ed. Boulder, CO: Westview, 1998.

Goodman, J.B.; Monetary Sovereignty, The Politics of Central Banking in Western Europe (1992) Cornell University Press.

Goslinga, Cornelis, Ch. Curacao as a slave-trading center during the war of the Spanish succession (1702-1714); In: Nieuwe West-Indische Gids; No. ½;52ste jaargang, November 1977; Publisher: Stichting Nieuwe Westindische Gids Utrecht

Hagen, Jeanette, Offshore Banking Centers: the case of Curacao, April 1990, PhD dissertation;

Hallwood, C. Paul; Ronald MacDonald; International Money and Finance; Blackwell Publishers; First published 1986;Second edition 1994; Reprinted 1995

Hasham, M.F in—UISDC 9th EDF Netherlands Antilles report by WSP Ltd. Paul Dean Editor, 2007.

Hasham, M.F. and Dennis Dare; editors: Free Enterprise In Curacao; Joint publication of the Curacao Chamber of Commerce and the University of the Netherlands Antilles. 1992.

Hasham, M.F.; Financial Markets and Financial Development in the Netherlands Antilles; Unpublished manuscript.1990

Havermans, Mr dr. A.J.E Havermans, drs GAG Martes, RA and Chr. A Peterson, RA; commissie van Advies over het Solidariteitsfonds (eerste advise); Naar een nieuwe financiele verhouding; November 2000.

Helleimer, Eric. "Reregulation and Fragmentation in International Financial Governance." Global Governance 15.1 (2009): 16+.

Hoekman, Bernard M., and Michel M. Kostecki. The Political Economy of the World Trading System: The WTO and Beyond. 2nd ed. Oxford: Oxford UP, 2001.

Hoff, Karla and Joseph E. Stiglitz; Modern Economic Theory and Development

Holt, Richard P. F., and Steven Pressman, eds. A New Guide to Post Keynesian Economics. London: Routledge, 2001. .

Homans, George C., and Charles P. Curtis, Jr. An Introduction to Pareto: His Sociology. New York: Alfred A. Knopf, 1934. .

Howard, Michael. Public Finance in Small Open Economies: The Caribbean Experience. Westport, CT: Praeger, 1992.

Kamer van Koophandel en NIJVERHEID Curacao: Ombuiging Fiscaal Regime: meer dan een noodzaak! 2001.

Kennes, Walter. Small Developing Countries and Global Markets: Competing in the Big League. Basingstoke, England: Macmillan, 2000.

Keynes, John Maynard; The General Theory of Employment, Interest and Money. Publishers: First Harvest; Harcourt; 1964. Originally published 1953.

Kleindorfer, Paul, H.C. Kunreuther, P.J.H. Schoemaker; Decision Sciences; An integrative Approach; Cambridge University Press; 1993.

Knotek, Edward S., II. "How Useful Is Okun's Law?" Economic Review (Kansas City, MO) 92.4 (2007): 73+.

Kroszner, Randall S. "Enhancing Sovereign Debt Restructuring." The Cato Journal 23.1 (2003): 79+.

Lall, Sanjaya; Industrial Policy: A theoretical and Empirical Exposition; In Industrial Policy and Caribbean Development; Dennis Pantin, editor. 1995.

Leibenstein, Harvey; Economic Backwardness and Economic Growth; Studies in the Theories of Economic Development; John Wiley and Sons, 1967.

Levitt, K; The George Beckford Papers (2000) Canoe Press, University of the West Indies.

Lewis; V.A.: Size Self-Determination and International Relations: THE CARIBBEAN (1976) Publications Editor, I.S.E.R.

Lipsey R.G; An introduction to positive economics; 1963; Weidefeld and Nicholson

Lister, Marjorie. The European Union and the South: Relations with Developing Countries. London: Routledge, 1997.

Marshall; Alfred: Principles of Economics; London Macmillan & CO LTD 1956 Eight edition

Mayer, M.: The Fed; The Inside Story of How the World's Most Powerful Financial Institution Drives the Markets (2001); Published by Plume, a member of Penquin Putnam Inc.

Mayer, Martin; the FED; "the inside story of how the World's most powerful financial Institution drives the markets. Cornell University Press, NY 1992.

McKinnon, Ronald; Money and Capital in Economic Development

McLure, Michael: Pareto, Economics and Society: The Mechanical Analogy. London: Routledge, 2001.

McNamara, R.S.; the Assault on World Poverty (1975) the Johns Hopkins University Press.

Mehrling, Perry G.1, and Roger J. Sandilands, eds. Money and Growth: Selected Papers of Allyn Abbott Young. London: Routledge, 1999.

Melcher A.J.: Structure and Processes of Organizations. A systems approach—published by Prentice Hall. 1976.

Mennis, Edmund A., How the Economy works; an Investor's Guide to tracking the Economy; New York Institute of Finance; 2nd edition, 1999.

Mhango B. H Economic development and structural adjustment; Phd. Dissertation University of Surinam, 1984.

Montiel, Peter; Macroeconomics in Emerging Markets; Cambridge University Press; 2003

Musgrave, R. A.; Fiscal Systems (1969) Yale University Press.

Nesadurai, Helen E. S. Globalisation, Domestic Politics, and Regionalism: The ASEAN Free Trade Area.London: Routledge, 2003.

Netherlands Antilles; Memorandum of Economic Policies; September 15, 2000

Ocampo, Jose Antonio; the quest for dynamic efficiency: strucutural Dynamics and Economic growth in Developing Countries;: in "Beyond reforms; structural dynamics and macroeconomic vulnerabilities" J.A. Ocampo, editor; Stanford university Press; 2005

O'Connell, John, Laurence Harte, and Dermot Ruane. "Quantification of Output Growth and Value-Added Captured by the Irish Food Processing Sector." Irish Journal of Management 25.1 (2004): 68+.

Ottosen, Garry K., and Douglas N. Thompson. Reducing Unemployment: A Case for Government Deregulation. Westport, CT: Praeger, 1996. .

Owyang, Michael T., and Tatevik Sekhposyan. "Okun's Law over the Business Cycle: Was the Great Recession All That Different?" Federal Reserve Bank of St. Louis Review 94.5: (2012): 399+.

Palma, Jose Gabriel; Four sources of "De-Industrialization" and a new concept of the "Dutch Disease" in: Beyond Reforms; Structural Dynamics and macroeconomic vulnerability; Jose Antonio Ocampo editor; Stanford University Press, 2005; Economic commission of Latin America and the Caribbean.

Pantin D, The Caribbean in a World of Economic Blocs; In Memory of George Beckford; Social and economic studies; Vol.41, no.3, September 1992

Pantin, Dennis; Industrial Policies in the Caribbean in a time of Liberalization, globalization and Regional Blocs; in Industrial Policy and Caribbean Development; Dennis Pantin Editor;

1995; Publishers: University of the West Indies:– Department of Economics, Trinidad and Tobago, and Consortium of Graduate School, Jamaica.

Pardo, A. and Elisabeth Mann Borgese, 1980, "Marine resources, ocean management and international development strategy for the 1980's and beyond", Malta, International Ocean Institute (mimeo),

Parsan, Elizabeth; The International Transport Problems of Small States; 1991

Philippe Hein; Croom Helm Ltd. 1985; ISBN 0-7099-0862-8 pp 40-69.

Quigley, J.M.; Perspectives on local public finance and public policy (1987) Jai press Inc.

Reisman, George. "The Value of "Final Products" Counts Only Itself: Today's Gross Product Is Net Product." The American Journal of Economics and Sociology 63.3 (2007): 609+.

Rich, David Z. The Economic Theory of Growth and Development. Westport, CT: Praeger, 1994.

Rokeach, Milton; The Nature of Human Value, N.Y. University Press; 1973.

Root, F.R.; International Trade and Investment (1978) South-Western Publishing Co.

Plan'D2, Institute of Development and Design: Ruimtelijke Ontwikkelingsplan Aruba produced by in 1983/84 for the Government of Aruba.

Rupert, Linda M.; Contraband Trade and the shaping of Colonial Societies in Curacao and Tierra Firme. November 2006.

Sachs, J.D.: The End of Poverty (2005) United States of America; The Penguin Press.

Schumpeter, Joseph A.: Ten Great Economists, From Marx to Keynes; George Allen and Unwin

Sengupta, Jati K. New Growth Theory: An Applied Perspective. Northampton, MA: Edward Elgar, 1998.

Siliro C.; An application of conventional sovereign debt sustainability; Analysis of the current debt crisis. Federal Reserve Bank of St Louis Review 2012;

Simmonson Jr. Harry; The Brazilean Experience; in Management under Inflation; The Economist Intelligence Unit Limited; Spence House;1975.

Govt. Netherlands; Slotverklaring van de Miniconferentie over de toekomstige staatkundige positie van Bonaire, Sint Eustatius en Saba; 10 en 11 oktober 2006; Den Haag

Snowdon, Brian, and Howard R. Vane, eds.: Reflections on the Development of Modern Macroeconomics. Cheltenham, England: Edward Elgar, 1999.

Sorokos, F.A. The Main development issues relating to Cyprus in the context of the changing world environment; St. Kitts,1999

Sowell, Thomas; Economic Facts and Fallacies; Basic books, 2006. p7-30.

Lalta, Stanley and Mary Freckelton, editors: Caribbean Economic Development; the first generation. Ian Randle publishers. 1993

Stiglitz, Joseph E.; Globalization and its Discontent; W.W. Norton and Company, 2002.

Stretton, Hugh. Economics, a New Introduction. Sydney, N.S.W.: UNSW, 1999.

Suss, E.C, Oral H. Williams and Chandima Mendis; Caribbean Offshore Financial Centers; Past, Present and Possibilities for the Future. IMF Working paper WP/02/88. May 2002.

The World Bank; Latin America and the Caribbean Region. Elements of a Strategy for Economic Recovery and Sustainable Growth. April 2001.

Thomas-Hope, Elizabeth; The role of the Environment in Caribbean Economic Development; Integration and Trade;

in Integration and Trade; a publication of the Inter-American ent Bank, Integration and Regional program Department, and the Institute for the Integration of Latin America and the Caribbean, Volume 5—September December 2001.

Tromp, E.D. Dr.; 175 years of Central Banking in the Netherlands Antilles; Preserving price and financial stability; SWP Publishers; 2003.

Van der Tang, G.T. and S.E. Korthuis,, Special section on the Netherlands Antilles in: Constitutions of Dependencies and Special Sovereignties, A. Blaustein and E. Blaustein, editors, Oceana Publications, 1984

Wace, N., "Exploitation of some of the advantages of remoteness and isolation in the economic development of Pacific islands" in Shand pp 87-118. 1980

Wachtel, Paul; Macro-Economics: From Theory to Practice; NY McGraw-Hill, 1989

Wheeler, S. and T. Beatley; The Sustainable Urban Development Reader, editors. (Routledge 2004). .

Whyte, Melinda; De Offshore Sector op Curacao: Niet alleen een begrip in zee; doctoraal scriptie, Sociologisch Instituut, Nijmegen, 1985; unpublished thesis.

Wignaraja, Ganeshan, ed. Competitiveness Strategy in Developing Countries: A Manual for Policy Analysis. London: Routledge, 2002. Questia. Web. 28 Dec. 2013.

Williams, M. The Pre and Post Seattle WTO Trade Regime: Status of the debate and challenges facing developing countries. Study prepared for ACE/CPDC; 2000.

Wood; Ethel; Stephen C. Sansone; American Government; Great Source

Worrell, Delisle. Small Island Economies: Structure and Performance in the English-Speaking Caribbean since 1970. New York: Praeger, 1987.

Zank, Neal S., John A. Mathieson, Frank T. Nieder, Kathleen D. Vickland, and Ronald J. Ivey. Reforming Financial Systems: Policy Change and Privatization. New York: Greenwood, 1991.